Not All Beer and Bezencenet

Yet More Adventures in Pursuit of Wild Fish

JON BEER

RIVERSIDE STUFF

Other fishing books by Jon Beer

GONE FISHING

THE TROUT AND I

First published in Great Britain 2012 by Riverside Stuff

A catalogue record for this book is available from the British Library.

ISBN 978-0-9571716-0-2

Designed by Max Fielding and Otter Valley Books

Printed and bound in Great Britain by Information Press, Eynsham.

Contents

Introduction

It's pronounced *buzz-ON-sun-ay*, but it's easier to call him by his first name: Philip.

Philip and wife, Jenny, run a clothing company in the Cotswold village of Duns Tew. We met twenty years ago when I went to buy my small daughter a pair of dungarees. We've fished and played snooker on and off ever since. Philip turns up in a lot of my stories in *Trout and Salmon* because flexible working hours and Jenny's generous indulgence allow him to join me on fishing trips to the remoter bits of Britain and beyond. But I fish with lots of other folk - which is why this book is *Not All Beer and Bezencenet*.

I met Vaughan nearly 30 years ago when he came to deliver a tankful of surplus grayling to the River Cherwell. They'd come from the exquisite waters of the River Coln where a misguided management didn't want its precious trout mixing with the riff-raff. We'd learn to call this "ethnic cleansing" in the years to come. Vaughan was a fisheries officer with the National Rivers Authority (in the days before the Environment Agency). He'd electro-fished the grayling from the Coln and needed somewhere to put them. I lived beside the Cherwell and fancied a bit of fly-fishing on my doorstep. And so it came about. The grayling are no longer outside my back door. They buggered off upstream when a new weir below my house raised the water level and slowed the flow. They still thrive in the faster water a mile up the valley. But on the River Coln, where once grayling were so plentiful they were regarded as vermin, they have all but disappeared. I bet the blokes there would like a few back.

Bill and Jeff have turned up in these pages before. They are traditional char fishermen, fishing for these beautiful fish of the cold, deep lakes with a bewildering rig involving sixteen-foot bamboo poles, two-pound lead weights and an array of hand-made lures swimming a hundred feet down. They'd been invited to troll this little lot for the char of Lough Melvin in Ireland. I'd gone out to meet them, taking Alice, my four-year-old, with me. No char were caught - but Alice caught a nine-pound salmon. The photograph showed this curly-haired tot beside her fish, of much the same size, hanging from a char-pole. It did not show a rather tight-lipped Jeff and Bill holding the pole. That was twenty years ago. They've taken me out on Coniston Water several times since then. There is a serene magic about this fishing: every part of the rig is hand-made. It fascinates me. After the last outing on the lake I vowed to make my own char rig over the winter. A few weeks later a small parcel arrived in the post. It was a notebook filled with Bill's hand-written instructions and hand-drawn illustrations, detailing the making of a traditional char rig: it's a treasured possession.

I've described my first meeting with Gordon in the first of these stories. We've fished together many times since then and I've chronicled the bizarre goings-on that inevitably punctuate these trips: there must be something in the air of Shetland. They'll be included in some future volume – Gordon's stories could have a book all to themselves. This is a man who rode his horse into a council chamber to make some point about fox-hunting: I forget what. The time may come when I'm able to recount the saga of the Lost Flock of Fetlar – a story for which the world is not yet prepared.

And then there is Sandy. He appears but rarely in my stories for we rarely fish together. But, in truth, he is a part of all of them. Sandy became the editor of Trout and Salmon in 1986 and his support and abuse, both generously given, inevitably shaped my writing through the years. My spelling got a lot better, for a start. Sandy has a gimlet eye for error and every month he'd delight in announcing that he'd saved me, once again, from public ridicule. In pleasant contrast to editors of other publications I've written for, Sandy would phone to discuss any changes or cuts he thought necessary, either to improve the thing or to avoid litigation. He was usually right. We didn't always agree - as you'll see in chapters 11 & 12 - but in this book, I've got my own way. These stories are pretty much as they were originally sent to *Trout and Salmon* or the *Daily Telegraph*. Any mistakes are thus my own – and Sandy is going to have much joy in circling them with his little pencil. I look forward to the phone call.

Many of the stories are followed by a passage in italics. These bits were not part of the original. They could be up-to-date information about the places I fished, in case you have a fancy to do something similar. They might be bits that I had no room to include the first time. Or they could be about things that have happened in the years since.

The photos on the cover were all taken at the time and place of the stories inside. There's one of Philip and one of me. All the others are not Beer and Bezencenet.

Jon Beer, Cropredy, January 2012

This book is dedicated
with all my heart
to Judi

1

Man's Dog Ate My Trousers

I was having a cup of tea. I had just arrived at the hotel and Gordon had sat me down in a comfy chair and Marjorie had brought me a pot of tea and Teal the dog was snuffling around my ankles in the way they do to be friendly or if you've trodden in something interesting. I was settling into Herrislea House rather nicely.

Herrislea House is not a fishermen's hotel, not in the racks-of-rods-in-the-hall-and-a-selection-of-the-local-flies-for-sale-at-the-desk sort of way. It has no waters for the exclusive use of guests. Also, there were a couple of blokes playing chess in the bar. They don't allow that sort of thing in a fishing hotel: fishermen aren't that brainy and it unsettles them.

But on the other hand, there were signs that someone around here was committing fishing on a fairly regular basis. There was a hefty sprinkling of old fishing magazines on the tables and in the sitting room, on the shelf beside the fireplace, there was a large Holy Bible. And next to that was Hugh Falkus's *Sea Trout Fishing*. Fair enough.

Gordon came over to see if the dog was bothering me but I was quite flattered by all the attention the dog was giving me. We got to talking of the fishing round and about – Gordon and I, that is: the dog was too absorbed in my ankles – and it turned out that

Gordon was suffering serious withdrawal symptoms. Running a hotel, it seems, is a time-consuming business and, like everyone else on the islands, Gordon and Marjorie have several other jobs as well. Amongst other things they have two crofts, breeding cattle and sheep. They were lambing at the moment, taking turns to stay with the ewes through the night. So what with one thing and another Gordon had not been fishing for some time.

And nor had the dog. I had been absently patting his head as he nuzzled around my ankle. Now I looked down at him. The bloody dog had chewed a fair-sized hole in the leg of my trousers. Gordon saw it, too. He said the dog did that when he hadn't had enough exercise. I thought it might be a good idea to get Gordon and Teal out fishing as soon as possible: I only had one spare pair of trousers with me.

So the next morning, as soon as breakfast had been poured into the other guests, the three of us set off. It was sunny with just wisps of cloud in a huge sky and the gentlest of breezes. It was not raining. It was not blowing a gale. It was all rather extraordinary. It was, after all, Shetland. Did I mention I was on Shetland?

I love islands - especially islands with trout lochs and Shetland is the mother-lode of these trouty islands. Even Mainland is an island and there are trout lochs everywhere: we passed a couple of fine examples, Tingwall and Asta lochs, as soon as we left the hotel. Gordon had to feed the cattle before we could start and the cattle were three islands away, at the croft where Marjorie was born, on the island of East Burra. Bridges now link Mainland to Tronda, to West Burra - and thence to East Burra. With the cattle fed we headed for the first loch just a short distance away across the peat moor.

Houss Loch is typical of a hundred Shetland Lochs. It lies in a shallow depression of moorland, unrelieved by trees of any sort. Low wire fences, mercifully free of barbed wire, are the only features that stand above the grass and heather. Everywhere squelches just a bit. The loch itself is shallow for the most part and it can be disconcerting on the larger lochs to see blokes wading a hundred yards or so from shore. The waters can be very rich – there are bands of limestone throughout the islands - and the fertile, shallow water can weed up as the season goes on. But there are deeps as well and some sudden drop-offs and gooey bits so you wade on almost every Shetland loch but you wade with caution – or someone who knows the water.

Gordon got the first fish of the day, a nice fish of twelve inches. The first fish is always a nice fish: it shows the thing still works. Part of the magic of fishing on Shetland is the huge variation in the fish. At any time you could catch something extraordinary. Later that week a fish of 5lb 7oz was caught – not, alas, by me. There are no big rivers on Shetland. The coastline is so convoluted that nowhere is more than a mile or so from the sea and most lochs trickle down to the tide through a tiny burn and are fed from water seeping out of the peat. Sometimes the spawning in the burn is good and there will be a lot of small fish. Sometimes it is bad, producing just a few big fish. Then there are the sea trout which can surge up through the thinnest of burns to populate a loch. And then there is the Shetland Anglers' Association which goes about like the Caped Crusader, righting wrongs and stocking waters. So you just never know.

But we knew about Houss Loch on East Burra because we had a fish. We drove to the next loch with Teal the dog bounding across the peat beside the road, working off spare trouser-eating energy. The sun was higher now and the breeze had all but petered out. Gordon said he couldn't believe it. Not in early May: it just doesn't happen. We crossed the bridge to West Burra and the little hamlet of Grunnasound. Here, just beyond the garden fences lay another shallow bowl of a loch. It was flat calm. I asked Gordon if it was possible to find a fish in a flat calm under a cloudless sky. He said he didn't know: the weather had never been that way before.

It can be done. Just as I was beginning to lose hope there was a long, slow draw on the line as a fish took the fly in the depths. It was a better fish of fifteen inches with a buttery belly and bold spots that leaked down into the tail. Even the little adipose fin got into the act with spots of the deepest red. It was noon and already we had caught fish on two islands.

That was not my first Shetland trout. That had been yesterday on the island of Bressay. Bressay lies a short ferry ride from Lerwick, the capital of Shetland. I was with Alec Miller, the secretary of the Shetland Anglers' Association. Two years ago, in the Western Isles, Philip and I had made an attempt at the World Lochisle Record. A *Lochisle* is simply an island off the coast with a population of trout – usually in a loch. Catch a trout on that island and you have bagged a *Lochisle*. In five wet and windy days in June, Philip and I bagged a total of eleven lochisles, a record - if only because we were the first fishermen foolish enough to try it. I had phoned Alec Miller to ask about the fishing on the Shetland Islands and explained my curious inclination to fish on as many islands as possible. Alec had taken the thing up with a will: he offered to pick me up from Sumburgh Airport on the southern tip of Mainland and drive me to the hotel – via a couple of islands - and to fish along the way.

So we'd done that. The first fish had come from Setter Loch on Bressay, another water of broad margins where Alec found fish for us feeding in a bay of bright sand. With a lochisle bagged within a couple hours of arriving on Shetland, we caught the ferry back to Mainland and headed north and west to the island of Muckle Roe that hangs like a testicle beneath the belly of North Mainland. We had tried Kilka Water - the Laird's Loch - and the little Orwick Water without seeing a rise or feeling a tug. The evening wore on without a fish and the sun sank as it does even here at 60°N. There was one final chance on Town Loch, which lies about as far from any town as a water can get. The tarmac petered out at the southern tip of Muckle Roe: Town Loch lies at the northern tip, at the end of a twisting track gouged into a moonscape of rotted granite and peat bog – which I promptly managed to fall into, flat on my face, under the excitement of Alec hooking the first fish from Muckle Roe. It was a very small fish and a very boggy bog. All in all, I'd been ready for Marjorie's pot of tea.

Back on West Burra, under a blazing sun, it was time to move on. We had bagged two lochisles that morning. For the afternoon Gordon had planned something a little different. Gordon has led a variegated life, as most islanders do, especially growing up in the Wild West days of "Klondiking". For some years he ran a sea-taxi service, ferrying people and stuff through all weathers out to the Russian factory ships that lay off Shetland. He still has one of the craft he used. We were going to try bagging the small uninhabited island of Oxna.

I had imagined a white clinker-built boat with a comforting diesel whose *puk-puk-puk-puk-puk* would echo across the voe as we rounded the headland. Gordon's boat isn't really like that. It is an Avon Searider with a 90-horse-power Suzuki engine that had us skimming the sea out of Scalloway, weaving between the rocky islets of Papa and creaming into Oxna bay in less than ten minutes.

Look: we did not catch a fish on Oxna. I am not sorry because the little loch on Oxna is, I believe, the most beautiful spot I have ever fished and now I shall have to go back. I don't know what it was about the place. It could have been the day - sunshine helps - or the loch itself, its water the colour of malt whisky in a rocky bowl. Or the birds teeming overhead. Birds teem everywhere on Shetland. I have never heard a place like it. Within an hour or so you will hear every noise a bird can make and one or two you would swear they cannot. They were doing all that on Oxna that afternoon. But when I think back to the few days I spent in the islands it is Oxna and its little house by the bay that I picture.

From Oxna we skimmed across to Hildasay. Here we actually saw a fish that bent Gordon's rod for a few tantalising seconds before disappearing back into the rocky depths.

We were not to be defeated. That evening we sped to the other side of Shetland to catch another ferry to another island. Alec's wife was giving a talk in the village hall of Symbister on Whalsay that evening. Alec had offered to drive her there and Gordon and I had offered to come along for the ride. Lochisling is, after all, a team effort. And while the good ladies of Whalsay were learning about herbal remedies and alternative therapies, Alec and Gordon and I were off to the remarkably-named hamlet of Sodom and the Loch of Huxter. Where, in the last rays of the sun, we scored the third lochisle of a memorable day.

It was brighter than ever the next morning. I don't know how it could get any brighter: it just did. This time it was Gordon's wife Marjorie who provided our excuse to go island hopping. One of her jobs is to monitor the Meals-on-Wheels services throughout the islands. It seemed like an excellent time to monitor those on Unst, the farthest north of Shetland's islands. We caught the first ferry to Yell and drove the length of the island to Gutcher where the ferry leaves for Unst. Beside the jetty in Gutcher a narrow shingle bar separates a small loch from the sea. We could see the ferry crabbing through the tide rips from Unst. It would arrive in ten minutes. A fish rose in the edge of the ripple from a faint breeze off the sea. In seconds I had the telescopic dapping rod set up and it took no time to sail a fly out towards the rise. Anon, a fish leapt at the fly but a fluke of the breeze wafted the thing from the surface and the fish missed. By the time the ferry was making its way into the jetty Gordon was ready to cast. Teal looked on. The few cars rolled off the ferry and we kept fishing. As the waiting cars drove down the ramp Gordon had a tug and then, in rapid succession, a fish, a photograph, and a quick dash across the road to the ferry as its door were shutting. First Lochisle of the day.

We caught trout on Unst, in fact we caught several. They were not large, but the one I shall remember longest was perhaps the smallest. On Unst there is a long, dramatic loch, the Loch of Cliff. It is the most northerly loch on the island and that makes it the most northerly loch of the Shetland Islands - and so the most northerly loch in Britain. But we did not catch a fish in the Loch of Cliff. Under a third, unbelievable day of remorseless sunshine the fish shrank away from the shallows and hid. Gordon took to snoozling in the sun, something of a novelty on Shetland. But the little burn that drains the loch to the sea flows north. In a pool along that little burn I spotted a trout. And so I caught that trout – the most northerly little trout in the British Isles.

It was Friday evening in Lerwick, the night before the Shetland Trout Festival, a week-long bonanza of furious fishing and competitions to be taken just as seriously as you fancy. On that Friday they have a bit of a *do* in the cosy upstairs bar of the Shetland Angling Association club rooms. I am not sure the Shetland Anglers should have a bar in their clubhouse. It is irresponsible. Like leaving a sharp knife in the hands of an infant. They could do themselves some harm. Not to mention any visitors from England who are of a delicate disposition. The bar of the Shetland Anglers' clubhouse should carry a government health warning. It was a good do though. And at some point in the middle of it all I found myself agreeing that it would be a fine and noble notion to go fishing at dawn, to bag one last Lochisle before my morning flight back home.

And so we did. Four hours later, on Grass Water, just beyond the village of Twatt, Gordon and I bagged Mainland.

Almost all of Shetland's 300 or so lochs are controlled by the Shetland Anglers' Association – annual subscription £25. Visit www.shetlandtrout.co.uk for details and a wealth of useful information. A new guide to "Trout Fishing in Shetland" is available (£2) through the website.

The association once produced a superb guide to "Angling in Shetland" (£9.95) 76 pages with colour illustrations, flies, and 106 maps. It was indispensable. There is talk of a new edition some time soon. Until then, beg or borrow a copy of the old one.

I've stayed and fished with Gordon and Marjorie many times since that first visit. Amongst many other ventures they still run Herrislea House Hotel. Tel: 01595 840 208 or visit www.herrisleahouse.co.uk

Eight Lochisles in 72 hours is still my best yet.

2

Ripon Yarns

*L*ife. Tricky business all round. But perhaps the trickiest bit, the stickiest gobbet in the jam pot of life, is the naming of a house. It is easy enough to name the thing: it is very, very hard to name the thing without making a prat of oneself. It is strange: it doesn't matter how pretentious the name is as long as you inherited it from the previous owner. "This Other Eden" at the top of Red Lion Street in our village is quite a jolly name - but it is not something you could name a house in cold blood, not without blushing. My friend Paul built a new house and named it "Windlecroft" and the next person who lives there will, I'm sure, think it a charming, cosy name and not the least bit ootsy.

Much the same applies to fishing tackle shops. There are three main approaches to the naming of tackle shops. There is the plain. This is the safest. Farlows of Pall Mall; Crudgingtons; Veals; Veniards; Ducker & Sons - and so on. All fine names, all sounding, for some reason, like high-class butchers or bespoke bootmakers. In fact Ducker & Sons of Oxford *are* bespoke bootmakers but they sell fishing tackle as well: a curious combination but far from unique. I know two other tackle-and-shoe shops. Where was I?

The second approach to the naming of tackle shops is the "cutesy". These are often an item of tackle - The Rod Box; The Bait Tin; The Creel - or some other angling reference: The Compleat

Angler; Castaway; Catch 22. In its most virulent and egregious form you will find an 'n' in the shop name: Rod'n'line; Hook, Line'n'Sinker - you know the sort of thing.

The third approach is the grandiose. This may not have been the intention - but it is the effect - of naming a tackle shop the somewhere-or-other Angling Centre. The "Banbury Angling Centre" conjures visions of pushing a trolley down neon-lit aisles stretching into the distance, flanked by shelves stacked high with a bewildering kaleidoscope of exotic fishing tackle, towards a bank of service tills. The Banbury Angling Centre is at 76a East Street. East Street is in Grimsbury, a residential suburb of Banbury. The ground floor of number 76a houses "Double-J Aquatics". The Banbury Angling centre is up the stairs at the back of this shop.

So I wasn't expecting much from The Ripon Angling Centre, 64 North Street, Ripon. But I was mistaken. True, it has no neon-lit aisles but it is a well stocked shop and, more important, behind the counter is a knowledgable flyfisherman in Colin Mackay. He asked us what we wanted and we said we had come to fish the River Laver. Ripon is a pleasant Yorkshire city on the banks of the River Ure which is a fine and famous river for trout and grayling and a good enough reason for building a city. And if you look on a map you can see the River Laver winding east from the moors above Pateley Bridge, down to Ripon and the Ure. But it had better be a big map for the Laver is not a large river. Mr Mackay pointed this out to us. It was small, he said. We said we liked small. And overgrown. Overgrown was OK too. It was never stocked, he said. And I said that we were looking for wild fishing. The fish were small as well, he said. I said we weren't expecting monsters. In that case, he said, you will enjoy fishing on the Laver. And we did.

The Ripon Piscatorial Association has some five miles of the Laver (pronounced like the stuff that come out of volcanos). We got to the river at Galphay Mill Bridge. It was a dark day of heavy grey cloud. Above the bridge much of the course of the river is through woods. Below the bridge the southern bank is a high wooded slope: the northern bank is tree-lined but flanked by open fields. We set off downstream, peering between the hazels and alders, looking for deeper runs in the thin water that trickled over the gravel bed. The Laver was everything Mr Mackay had promised. It was certainly small and overgrown but it had promise. It was certainly not over-fished. This is the magic of fishing a small, unregarded stream for the first time: around each bend, below each little run there could be a special spot, a favourable hole where a trout has lurked undisturbed for years. If you fish a river regularly you will find the better water, the pools where the fish feed, where trout are usually to be found. It is fun when you find them and catch fish. As you get to know the river better you will catch more fish but inevitably that thrill of discovery diminishes: you know the place; you know that the best lie is three bends down and the tasty bit of water that looks so good above the second pool holds nothing. On a small, overgrown and overlooked stream every pool, every corner could be the place where the finest fattest fish is waiting.

Of course, usually it isn't. That doesn't matter: it could be. Also the finest fattest fish on the little stream might be only a few ounces. That doesn't matter either. And so we explored downstream.

Sometimes, with some boys, there comes a time in their teens when the face changes; it becomes a man's face. It is not just the beard, it is the whole face. It is hard to say what has changed: it was a boy's face, now it is a man's. And so it is with trout streams. Some just gradually get bigger, others change suddenly from a stream with the occasional fish into a real trout river. On the Laver it happens at Ellington Banks. Here a small but lively brook tumbles into the Laver at a large pool with a deep, undercut bank. It is as good a spot to become a real trout river as one could wish.

11

And trout were rising along the channel where the brook struck the bank. Soon enough Father had one. A nice little trout of three or four ounces. There were bigger fish in that pool, lurking in the enticing eddy and protected by the trailing strands of bramble but we couldn't tempt them.

From that pool down, every run looked as though it might hold fish - and some did. By lunch time we had caught fish up to half a pound, a good fish for that stream, and we had explored the Laver for the mile or so down to the farm at Birkby Nab.

The river is a little more open hereabouts, with nibbled pasture going down to the water in places. We had stopped for a bite of lunch. Lunch places need the most careful consideration. The place must be within sight of some good-looking water, somewhere where something might happen. This must not be too close or there is a temptation to get up and cast as soon as a fish rises. On the other hand it must not be on a stretch where nothing is happening or there is the temptation to wander off and look for something round the next bend. We were parked a few yards above a swifter run that bounced into a nice little pool. We could see anything that started in the pool but we could not cast to it from where we were. The water in front of us was thin, trotting swiftly over a bottom of bright gravel. A couple of tiddlers were flipping at the edge of the main current under a hawthorn bush. Tiny rises but so small I could not see the fish against the bottom. You know how it is: I flipped a line down the run to watch the small parr drown the fly. The fly disappeared in a tiny flip. I retrieved the line and suddenly it tightened: there was astonishment on either end. The fish that came to the net out of that shallow riffle was fifteen inches long.

Lunch was a rather quiet affair after that. We were both thinking back to tiny rises in thin water we had ignored on our way down the river. It was also a quickish lunch. The steady rises in that nice little pool below us looked suddenly heavier than when we had first sat down.

We weren't to be disappointed. In the distance of a few hundred yards below the farm we had four fish around a pound. I was staggered. Now, a pound trout may not seem a lot in these days of stillwaters and stocked rivers. But I have gone a season on little streams like the Laver and not seen a fish of one pound. And one of these four fish was a grayling, another surprise in such a small water.

The sky had remained uniformly dull and grey and now, in the late May afternoon, a thin drizzle began to fall. The rises became more sporadic and we thought about working our way back up the river. Above the junction pool the river was quiet and then we spotted one of those small, twiddly rises we had taken for the feeding of a tiny trout. Father eased into the tunnel of trees and cast up to the miniature run. The fly disappeared and father was connected - to a tiny trout. Real life is not always the stuff of fishing stories.

*   *   *

It had been a good day and it had a curious parallel the next morning. We had spent the night in a campsite in Wensleydale. The Ure hereabouts was desperately low, moving feebly between the dry rocks in midstream. Drought is understandable in the long, hot days of summer. It is profoundly irritating in a grey day of strong wind and drizzle. We headed south through Widdale to cross the fells and look for more water. Across the watershed is the headwater of the River Ribble which chuckled down the fellside. It did not look too shrunken. By Horton-in-Ribblesdale the amount of water in the river looked much the same - but its bed had doubled in width and it was beginning to look a little sad. At Settle it was a three-act tragedy. I had always wanted to fish the Ribble. The river had a fine reputation and the fish must be somewhere even in a drought. We found the Royal Oak Hotel in the middle of the town where we got our day tickets and some sorely needed advice. The advice was to talk to Derek Soames, the club bailiff for the Settle Anglers' Association water.

We found Derek at work: he is a railway signalman. I have always wanted to look inside a signal box. I was prepared to be disappointed, to find all those magnificent, manly levers and brass dials replaced by grey buttons and winking LEDs. I needn't have worried. They were all there: the levers, the dials, the cosy coal stove, even a dog curled on a cushion and a copy of T&S on the chair. It was a damned sight more inviting than the river. The Ribble itself flows behind the signal box where Derek can keep an eye on it. He gave us advice on the favourite flies for the water, a traditional north country team of Snipe & Purple, Partridge & Orange, Partridge & Yellow fished down and across although today there was little enough water to move the flies.

It was to be a difficult day. It was cold and the wind was gusting hard, ruffling the thin water. We took the occasional fish but these were the small tiddlers that persist in feeding when anything old enough to have any sense has given up and retreated under a stone to wait for water. An occasional drizzle was just enough to wet the assault course of rounded stones exposed by the low water and make life difficult. I think you have the picture. We had parked the car down a small lane that ended in a courtyard of houses down by the river. It could have been the original set for Coronation Street but surrounded by the beautiful valley of the Ribble. From here there is a footbridge suspended over the river, just below a weir. We had called it a day and were trudging back over this footbridge when we stopped to look at the pool below the weir. A little water was sliding over the face, the most part at the right-hand side by a small fish-pass from where the main current, such as it was, flowed. We stood on the bridge above this current. A tiny trout twiddled in the tail of the current.

A rise of any sort was something of a novelty on that day. I absently flicked a fly into the current and a twiddle drowned the fly. We chatted and I flicked again and this time when the fly disappeared the line followed. I was joined to a fish and it was not a tiny fish. I was in something of a predicament, stuck up on the footbridge some way above the water. I couldn't walk off the bridge and down to the pool without getting the line in a tangle of branches washed down in happier, wetter times. I pushed the rod into father's hands and ran off the bridge with the net. Down on the stones of the shrunken pool I held the net while father manoeuvred it from above. It was not a huge fish; twelve inches, perhaps twelve ounces. But it was a proper trout. There were other fish twiddling in the current and below the face of the weir so we both stood in the pool below and cast small dark dry flies and lo! another fish. And another. And then a fourth. All twelve inches long. And then it dawned on us that we had found the spot where the Settle Angling Association had stocked their trout that year. With little or no rain following the spring stocking these fish had had little inclination to leave the depth of the weir pool for the thinner waters downstream.

Don't get me wrong. These were splendid trout: fine fat fellows with beautiful markings and perfect fins and they fought like any wild trout, like the fish we had caught the day before on the Laver. And had we caught just one I would have had no idea that this was not a wild fish. I would have been chuffed to little mint balls. But we had caught four and now I was sure that they had been stocked. I cannot, for the life of me, see why this should make the slightest bit of difference to my enjoyment: the fish are indistinguishable from wild fish. It just does.

It shouldn't make any difference whether "Windlecroft" was named three centuries ago or last year. It just does.

Paul still lives at Windlecroft. The Ripon Piscatorial Association still has several miles on the River Laver, excluding a short stretch held by the Army. It also has a six miles, mostly double bank, of the Ure at Ripon. This is streamy, trout and grayling water in its upper half, above Bridge Hewick, Day tickets are now £6 and cover both waters. Details at www.ripon-piscatorial.co.uk

The Ripon Angling Centre, alas, is no longer extant.

Settle Anglers' Association decided to stop selling day-tickets in 2009. Was it something I said?

3

Making Things With Egg Boxes

*I*n 423 AD Simeon the Syrian took to living on a pillar. It was a modest pillar, six foot high, but Simeon was still a young man and upwardly mobile: over the next six years he moved to successively higher pillars until, in 429, he ended up on top of a 60-foot item. Here he remained for the next, and last, thirty years of his life. He never descended: his food and post were pulled up in a basket on a rope. It does not do to dwell on the other practicalities of living on top of a 60-foot pillar. That's about all I know about St Simeon Stylites, the patron saint of rising trout.

I made that last bit up. I don't know what St Simeon is the patron saint of. But the only other bloke I know to spend several years of his life on top of a tower was studying feeding trout. Robert Bachman did not stick to one tower: he had six, all sited on the banks of Spruce Creek in Pennsylvania. Each day, from dawn to dusk, Bachman would sit in one or other of these towers in turn, watching the wild trout in the stream through polarising binoculars. Before long he could recognise each fish by the unique pattern of spots below its dorsal fin. He mapped the pools beneath the towers, identifying 96 foraging sites (feeding lies) in one pool beneath one pair of towers. *"Once each hour, each brown trout in the observation area was located and identified . . . Between these inventories each brown trout was observed in turn for 15*

17

minutes. . . By this system the distribution of brown trout was mapped 10 times a day and each individual was closely studied (on the average) every two days". Thus Mr Bachman spent ten hours a day staring at fish. In the close observations he recorded everything from the height of each food item in the water to encounters with other trout. He measured everything from the rate of tail beats to distances moved by each fish. And he did this in all months of the year for three years. It beggars belief.

The results of Bachman's prodigious scientific research form a fascinating insight into trout behaviour and an education for anyone who likes bunging flies at fish in running water – which I do. And if enough of such fishing folk care to write in and badger the management I will describe them (the results – not the management) in some future edition. For the moment I have other fish to fry.

The trouty world is all of a doo-dah these days about the Environment Agency's National Trout and Grayling Fisheries Strategy. The subject that has most contorted the angler's underwear is the proposal to phase out the stocking of farmed and fertile brown trout in rivers with a resident population of wild brown trout. The Agency is anxious to protect what little remains of the wild trout's genetic integrity. And quite right too. But there is another, unexpected problem with stocking farmed fish, fertile or otherwise, and it has nothing to do with genetics.

On 23 August Robert Bachman was sitting on his tower beside a pool on Spruce Creek. He had been watching the resident brown trout going serenely about their business for two years. He was accompanied by another trained trout observer because on that day 200 brown trout from a local hatchery were to be released into the river. Within 20 minutes there was pandemonium in the pool, with wild and hatchery fish facing up and chasing each other all over the place. Sometimes the wild fish won these encounters, sometimes the hatchery fish, either way there were fish ricocheting around the pool like pinballs. Things settled a little in the weeks that followed but the hatchery trout never behaved as the wild fish had done. They ate less and they expended more energy feeding. They moved more, rattling round a much larger home range and all this brought them into conflict with other fish and these conflicts went on much longer than those between wild fish. The stockies were, all in all, a pain in the pants. They had severe behavioural problems: these were delinquent trout.

The causes are not hard to divine. Trout are fairly solitary creatures. Where some fish like nothing better than a million mates around them, the trout prefers to keep himself to himself. He starts life like that, alone and secluded in a crevice in the gravel of the redd. Most farmed trout are hatched in trays: with no enclosing nursery of chunky gravel to nestle into, the little creatures spend much of their limited resources flipping in an effort to stay upright. This is no sort of start in life. Trout were not designed for the hurly-burly of communal living in the melee of the hatchery. They do not adapt to stress: they just go quietly barking.

The hatchery trout in Spruce Creek did not thrive. Of the 179 farmed fish stocked in the pool, only two were seen again the next spring. They were spotted just once, thin and moving continuously. Another two hundred fish were stocked that second season. Eighteen months later, at the end of the study, the creek was electrofished. None of the 400 stocked fish was found. It has long been know that stocked fish do not fare as well as wild trout: Bachman's meticulous observations showed us why. They also demonstrated the disruptive impact these stocked fish can have on the resident trout.

In a perfect world all streams would come with acres of silt-free spawning gravels. Come autumn, gangs of enthusiastic trout would be at it like knives, shuddering away like the last night of a summer pop festival and filling the redds with the fruit of their loins before rolling over for a fag. The eggs would hatch deep in the gravel, the sun would shine all day long and everything would be oojah-cum-spiff.

Life is not like that. Gravels become compacted and clogged with silt and abstraction and low flows just make matters worse. Some of the richest waters can struggle to produce a new generation each season, the trout grow scarce and the sport disappears. In more feudal times a keeper might spend long weeks with a rake, loosening the gravels and cleaning the redds but he had to stop scratching when the fish begin to spawn and the eggs could still become choked under the blanket of silt from a chocolate spate.

In the 1980s, the Thames division of the NRA began experimenting with spawning weirs built into the river bed. These were magnificent edifices and *le dernier mot* in luxury trout knocking-shops. The weir is built across the width of the river and pierced at the bottom by several thirty foot lengths of 3-inch plastic pipe with small holes drilled along their length. The upstream end of each pipe, above the weir, is covered with large stones and a layer of fine gravel to filter the water entering the pipe. Downstream of the weir, the lengths of perforated pipe are buried beneath the spawning gravel which stretch for twenty feet or so below the weir. The head of water behind the weir forces the water through the filter, into the buried pipes and then up through the spawning gravel. This is a pregnant trout's idea of hog heaven.

Spawning weirs like this have been very successful on the Thames tributaries. You can measure just how hard your trout are working for you and to what purpose by freeze coring samples of the gravel to count the number of eggs and measure their fertility. The trout fry emerge from the gravel naturally, with fins and psyche intact. But spawning weirs have their limitations. They are pretty pricey and they are, after all, just enhancing the natural spawning of the stream: you can't stock the water with a spawning weir.

Why not? The Americans tried it first. They took a spawning weir, standard model, as above, and put it in a concrete box. I don't know why they put it in a box. Sticking handles on a box and labelling it "portable" isn't going to alter the fact that the thing is twenty feet long, six feet tall, weighs many tons and has all the architectural charm of a brick privy - a whole terrace of brick privies. The principle remained the same as the conventional spawning weir: filtered water was pushed upwards through an artificial redd. This time the redd was constructed of fifteen layers of astroturf, each seeded with fertilised salmon eggs and covered with two inches of gravel. The sides of the box were insulated to stop cold winds chilling or freezing the water flowing through the spawning box. Eighty five percent of those eggs hatched: each cubic metre of the artificial redd produced nearly half a million fry. The thing worked.

So did H1. H1 was the first chronometer built by John Harrison in pursuit of the longitude prize. To win, the chronometer had to be carried aboard a ship from London to the West Indies without losing more than two minutes. It would have had to be a big ship: H1 is enormous. You will find it squatting inside a vast glass case in the Royal Observatory Greenwich. Alongside, in another case, is Harrison's second prototype, H2. It is even bigger. H3 is much the same. He finished H4 in 1759, 29 years after he had begun work on H1. Take a look at H4. It is exquisite. Little bigger than a pocket watch, it is easy to miss it after the enormous engineering edifices of Harrison's earlier clocks. But it was this lovely little H4 and its copies that eventually won the longitude prize.

Much the same length of time has passed since the first appearance of those huge concrete "upwelling incubation boxes" in North America. Last week I went to look at the latest development in the genre, the H4 of incubation boxes. It was sitting in a stream near Woodstock – Oxon, that is, not upstate New York.

I met Vaughan by the bridge over the little River Glyme. You may well have cast over these waters: a mile downstream the river flows through the park of Blenheim Palace, sometime host of the Game Fair. Vaughan Lewis is a fisheries biologist who worked for the NRA on some of those earlier spawning weirs. Nowadays he is a fisheries consultant. He is also a keen fisherman and member of the Cotswold Fly Fishers, a club with waters on the Windrush and Coln and several Cotwold streams - including the little River Glyme as it runs through the Blenheim Estate.

The Glyme is a fine little stream of clear water with a tinge of grey that these Cotswold streams can carry in winter. There are crayfish in the Glyme, the big American signal crays which may be a scourge to the nymphs and larvae but have the advantage of turning them into a meaty meal for a large trout. And there are some very large trout in the River Glyme. Large trout are not always the sign of a river in the pink. It can mean that the food is being shared between fewer mouths than it might. And so it was with the Glyme. Injudicious dredging in the past had removed much of its spawning gravels and those that remained had compacted. The Cotswold Fly Fishers have begun an enhancement scheme to restore the spawning redds: meantime they plan to stock the river.

The less appealing characteristics of farmed stockies, the fin damage, the poorer survival rates and the tendency to buzz off, are a result of their upbringing, not of their genetics. The children of farmed stockies that have managed to spawn in a river are indistinguishable – in form and behaviour – from the wild fish of that stream. Hatching eggs in an in-stream incubator is the next best thing to stocking a river with wild fish.

We ambled upstream along the Glyme. It was the first outing

for Vaughan's terrier puppy, Midge (named for something small and irritating) who picked her way through the frosted grasses of the meadow. We reached the Glyme where the stream broadened into a shallow ford. Sitting in the water against the far bank, tucked in beneath an overhanging briar, was a black box. It looked like the sort of thing you might find holding cold water in your loft. If so it was leaking badly: streams of water were trickling from three holes near the top of the box. The whole thing would fit in the boot of your car. We waded the stream and Vaughan lifted the lid.

It did not look very technical. H1 had it well beat for springs and wheels and things going in and out. Inside, it was full of gravel beneath an inch of water which was overflowing through the holes in the side. All a trout egg asks to hatch is gravel with clean, oxygenated water passing up through it. It is not a lot to ask. Some natural redds do this and some don't. The spawning weir does it by piping the water beneath the gravel. Vaughan's little black number does it by siphoning the water from a short distance upstream, far enough to give a head of water to push the stuff up through the gravel in the box. I could see it now. The box stood up to its armpits in the stream and a fat flexible hose led off upstream beneath the surface with a filter at the far end. Gravity does all the work, feeding water into a screened chamber in the bottom of the box and then up through the gravel. And passing 20,000 trout eggs on the way.

They are hatching as I write. Deep in the gravel they are resting and growing, each in its own private crevice. When their yolk sacks have been absorbed they will start to wriggle their way upwards. By the time you read this some will have made it. They are drawn to the light coming through the holes in the side of the box where the water overflows and the trickling water will carry them out into the River Glyme, first in twos and threes and then in their hundreds and thousands later this month.

23

Now they are on their own to make their way in the world. They should make it: they have been given the best start in life a trout can get.

But life, alas, is rarely perfect. Egg-boxes too have their problems for little troutlings. One of these problems is bigger trout who rapidly learn to take up position just below the box – where they receive a steady supply of young trout fry falling from heaven. They can't believe their luck.

4

Boys from the Deep Stuff

I always used to get an Airfix kit for Christmas. It was meant to keep me quiet over the festive season. I would float high above family strife on a cloud of solvent-based plastic cement, tongue poking from one corner of my mouth, picking small pieces of undercarriage from the surrounding soft furnishing. By New Year's Eve I would have reached the row-of-holes-with-a-hot-needle-down-the-fuselage-to-simulate-machine-gun-attack stage. I favoured this battle-torn look for my models to account for the minor discrepancies in the number of bits in the undercarriage.

Airfix modellers in those days, like everything else in this world, were divided into two sorts. There were those that went for the smooth, sleek designs of the Jaguar E-type, the Vulcan bomber and ships like the QEII. And there were those who preferred the old-fashioned intricacies of the Model-T Ford, the Sopwith Camel or the Golden Hind. It was more than just value-for-money – although there were so many more bits on cars with running boards and spare-wheels and a starting handle. (How anyone could make a model of a Vulcan V-wing bomber last past Boxing Day is a mystery to me: two wings and a couple of transfers and the thing's finished). But it was more than that: I loved the intricate, logical chaos of bi-planes struts or the rigging of a three-masted ship. I still do.

In time, I graduated to balsa-and-tissue gliders of prodigious wingspan that could last well into February but I was susceptible to the heartache at the end of each maiden - and only - flight. And so, at last, I discovered fishing tackle. Every December I would order all the delicious bits and bobs that go towards constructing a fishing rod. I would put out some fairly specific hints of the sort of things I would like to see under the tree. And I would spend the Christmas hols in a haze of old movies, cork rings, cold ham and pickle and whipping thread.

And so it has gone on, intermittently, ever since. But this year I may have gone a step too far. I have embarked on the 1:80 scale, fully-authentic-in-every-detail-Cutty-Sark-under-sail of fishing tackle. This Christmas I am making myself a traditional Lakeland char rig.

The idea began, I suppose, on the last Sunday in September. The day had dawned calm and grey but a light breeze had whispered in from the northern end of the lake, enough to take the polish of the surface. A dawn like this can go either way: the clouds can lower themselves onto the fells, darkening until the weight of water is too much to hold aloft and the sky bleeds all over the landscape. Or not. That Sunday the breeze jostled the clouds and a low sun broke through the pack-ice of grey sky to sweep the hills on the western shore. We were pulling steadily for the eastern side of the lake when, behind us, the flanks of the Old Man of Coniston began to glow in the morning sun.

So you have a fair idea where we were.

It was many years since I'd been on Coniston Water. It was here I first set eyes on an arctic char, raised from the depths on traditional char tackle. I was a younger man then, a virulent fly-fisher and rather sniffy about what was, after all, trolling for a smallish trout. My first char and that day on Coniston were revelations: I discovered that any form of fishing can have its own magic. And since that day I have jigged, netted, trapped and trotted my way down several leafy little B-roads off the main highway of fly-fishing. And I've enjoyed every wayward minute. Last September I returned to Coniston and its char.

The first fish came as we pulled along the eastern shore beyond Beck Leven Foot where the bottom plummets away beyond 100 feet. It's hard to say who catches a char: it's a team effort. Bill was at the oars, pulling with the breeze, when the port pole dipped, tinkling the bell at its end. The bamboo pole spreads the line sixteen feet out to that side of the boat but a "lazy line", hung from the back of the boat, allows Jeff to pull the main line in to the boat and start hauling the thing up. This is the exciting bit in char fishing. You can feel life somewhere down the line. Just how much life it is hard to say: there's two pounds of lead at the end of the thing which can take a lot of the zip out of a fish. After ten feet or so the first of the back-lines comes into view. This is joined to the main line by a hand-made "shackle" – which isn't really a shackle but, as no-one has ever got round to writing a comprehensive vocabulary of char-rig parts, char fishermen grab an ordinary word and bash it into place like a jigsaw puzzle piece that nearly fits.

I do not know if all men's shackles are alike: I do not like to pry. Jeff and Bill's shackles are curiously cunning, allowing the back-line to rotate freely around the main line, something it needs to do if a large trout decides to throw its weight around. The shackle also incorporates a ring at the upper end. This is dropped over a peg on the boat's gunwale, suspending the mainline while the back-line is brought aboard.

The back-line is an eighteen-foot leader at the end of which is a "bait" – which isn't really a bait but a small hand-made spinner. At the end of the bait there was nothing at all so Jeff dropped the shiny little bait into the first of eight little wooden pots fixed to the gunwale. Jeff hauled up another ten feet of mainline to arrive at the next shackle. And so on.

27

There was something flashing in the water behind the boat as the seventh shackle came on board. Jeff reached for the large landing net as he drew the char towards the boat. I know about this landing net. On my first visit, years ago, I had scoffed at using it on a fish of 10 ounces – the usual sort of Coniston char. So I brought the little fish in by hand and it fell off the hook into the countless coils of braid and monofilament lying on the seat beside me. And there it thrashed about a bit – not a lot - but quite enough to be going on with. From then on I used the net. And so does Jeff. He reached into the net and brought out a Coniston char. I don't know if you've seen "Lord of the Rings". Beneath his shirt the tiresome hobbit, Frodo, wears a vest wrought of "mithril", a shining, supple, magical chain-mail. Arctic char wear something similar as befits the most beautiful of all salmonids.

By this time the bloke at the oars will be tiring of trying to row straight with one side of tackle out of the water. Time to reverse the procedure, swinging out each back-line and bait in turn until the whole shebang is cutting a swathe thirty-odd-feet wide and twice that deep and trailing sixteen tiny, winking spinners through the depths of Coniston.

These spinners – the "baits" – are hand-made too. Small slivers of brass, copper and silver are cut, twisted and polished to twinkle through the water. I picture them cruising through the dim depths like a shoal of little fish. This is curious because, of all the thousands of char that Jeff Carroll and Bill Gibson have caught in the quarter of a century since they began fishing together on Coniston, they have found only one char with a fish in its stomach. Coniston char feed almost exclusively on plankton and small larvae.

It was my turn to row. There was plenty of time to look around as we fished on down the eastern shore, past Brantwood, once the home of the Victorian art critic, John Ruskin. Other folk had taken to the water. A rash of white sails had broken out against the trees across the lake. A flotilla of small sailing dinghies was pushing before the wind, making for the rocks and islands where Arthur Ransome had played as a child and where he later set the adventures in "Swallows and Amazons".

Ransome knew all about adventure when he wrote his children's stories. He had been the Manchester Guardian's correspondent in revolutionary Russia, travelling back and forth between the Red and White armies, befriending the Bolshevik leaders, Lenin and Trotsky, and rather more than befriending Trotsky's secretary, Evgenia Petrovna, whom he brought back to Britain and married. They settled in the Lake District. Ransome had been a keen fisherman for some years and soon after coming to Coniston he began his *Rod and Line* fishing column in the Guardian. His collection of angling pieces under this title has always been one of my favourite fishing books. I can tell you some interesting things about John Ruskin too: this exquisite art critic had gleaned his ideals of female beauty from classical statues. When he married and got a look at the real thing he was aghast. He had not been prepared for pubic hair: he thought his beautiful young bride was deformed. The marriage was never consummated. I thought you might like to know that. You can have just too much art.

Ruskin's was not the only marriage to end unfortunately hereabouts. In 1976 Mrs Carol Park went to bed suffering from a headache. She vanished that night. She turned up again twenty-one years later, still in her night-dress, but parcelled in plastic and weighted down in 80 feet of water. A local diver found her body in more or less the spot where we caught our second char that morning. I was shivering: after a promising start the day had turned a bit chilly.

Other fishermen were out on the lake now. There are char in several waters of the Lake District, some Welsh llyns and dozens of Scottish lochs but the traditional char tackle is seldom seen away from Coniston Water and Windermere. Did other waters once sport fleets of such contraptions? Or had they evolved something even more unwieldy? And yet, for all its 2lb leads, 80lb line and 18-foot bamboo poles, there is something essentially elegant in the curve of those poles, swept down and back by the tow of the tackle under way. For me it has the same arcane appeal as a full-rigged sailing ship. Come to think of it, with its intricate arrangement of lines, stays and shackles, a char rig in full flight bears an uncanny resemblance to the Cutty Sark – only upside down.

That elegance was all the more striking in the char boat which was creeping towards us as I unhooked our third fish.

Jim Blaney supports Newcastle United Football Club. You can tell that across the width of a medium-sized lake. Jim Blaney fishes in a black-and-white Newcastle cap. Also, he has painted his char rig, poles and all, in the same stripes of black and white. The effect is startling.

Nice idea, though. I might use it on my char rig. I've always supported Harlequins RUFC.

POTTED CHAR

The traditional rig was once used to catch char commercially. Large numbers were taken, "potted" and shipped to the cities. Potted char was a breakfast delicacy, eaten on toast along with the kidneys, scrambled eggs, sausages and so forth essential for the Victorian sporting gent to start his day. Locally potted char can still be found in shops and hotels in the Lake District. If you wish to pot your own try this recipe:

4 char (or trout),

½ tsp grated nutmeg,

salt, black pepper,

8 oz butter.

Fillet the fish and season each fillet on both sides with salt, pepper and nutmeg. Leave overnight in the fridge. Wipe each fillet and season again with a little more salt. Melt 2oz butter in an oven-proof dish. Sandwich the fillets together and put them into the dish. Cover with the rest of the butter and cover the dish with a lid or foil. Cook in an oven at 150°C for about 90 mins.

Drain off (and retain) the butter, Allow the fillets to cool and then remove the skin. Arrange the delicate fillets in a shallow dish without breaking them (using care and prayer). Clarify the butter in which the fish were cooked and pour over fillets. Keep for 2 days before eating. This will keep for weeks in the fridge.

CHAR FISHING IN THE LAKE DISTRICT

Char can be found in eight (and a bit) waters in England, all in the Lake District. These are: Buttermere, Coniston Water, Crummock Water, Ennerdale Water, Haweswater, Thirlmere, Wast Water and Windermere. The "bit" is a small population in Goat Water, high on the flank of Coniston Old Man. Alas, boats-and-fishing, the two requirements for the traditional char rig, are not allowed on Ennerdale, Haweswater and Wast Water. And getting a boat to Goat Water doesn't bear thinking about.

Char fishing season is the same as brown trout, 15 March- 30 Sept – except on Coniston where it runs from 1 May – 31 October.

5

Heads and Tales of the Valleys

When anglers go back to places they visited in their childhood you can expect a lot of stuff about the old arched bridge that carried the doctor in his pony-and-trap, now replaced by a concrete cantilever supporting the new by-pass. Or sparkling memories of a regular blizzard of mayflies that the diminutive author-to-be struggled through, wiping small splattered corpses off his rimless National Health specs in his path to the riverbank - where now there is but a sporadic hatch of midge of a June evening. This isn't one of those stories: I spent most of my school holidays during the 1950s in the valley of the River Taff in South Wales. They were grey days, as I recall. It was always raining, not hard, but rather pacing itself for maximum duration. The Taff between Pontypridd and Merthyr Tydfil was an unlovely thing, coal-grey and dusty, constrained by corrugated iron and iridescent with pollutants. It wasn't something you'd be eager to dip your tackle in.

Time passed. A quarter of a century or so. I had been fishing the Usk and took a day off to climb the Brecon Beacons. On the southern flank of the summit, Pen y Fan, a tiny crystal stream trickles between boggy banks, forming a miniature pool here and there. I was carrying a tiny rod and passed that happy day in early autumn foozling one small, perfect trout out of each pool.

The river trickled into a small, high reservoir and on again down the slopes of the Beacons, through a second, shrinking reservoir to disappear into a dark line of forestry.

Back home, I traced the course of that stream on the map. It was the Taf. It had lost one "f" in the journey upstream from Pontypridd but it was the same river, right enough. The Taff could stand another look.

My starting point looked unpromising enough: "Cefn Coed Fishing Tackle" looked, for all the world, closed down. Let's face it, if the litter laws of this land were strictly enforced it *would* be closed down - but that would be a great loss, for the shop is a little gem, dispensing advice, tackle, tea and tickets for the Merthyr Tydfil AA water.

Merthyr Tydfil stands at the head of the Taff valley, where the coal measures that made Glamorgan what it is give way to the old red sandstone massif of the Brecon Beacons that climb up behind the town. Between the sandstone and the coal there is a band of limestone. I love limestone. Limestone dissolves in the dilute acid of natural rainfall (and the less dilute acid of industrial rainfall) to form cavities and caves which can collapse into deep steep-sided gorges. I love gorges. When the rest of the countryside is basking in sunshine a gorge gives cooling shade, a little world with a climate all of its own. There are corners and crannies in deep shade where fish can be found feeding at any time. And tumbled rocks to form deep pools and sparkling runs and falls. There is variety.

Incredibly, there is just such a gorge in the heart of Merthyr Tydfil. A few yards down from Cefn Coed Fishing Tackle the A470 crosses a bridge on its way down to the town centre through the urban sprawl. Scramble down the side of that bridge and you are in a different world of bosky light on rippling water. In a few yards you are between two streams, one of them disconcertingly flowing out of sight above your head. It is an ancient culvert carrying water from upstream, now and then spilling though cracks forced open by invading tree roots and splashing down on to the shady path that follows the Taf Fechan (the Small Taff) up through its gorge.

It was a baking afternoon but down there in the cool there were fish rising. Up in the shop I'd met Gavin Jehu, a fly-tyer and expert on this upper water. He uses small dry-flies; a Griffiths's Gnat, a Grey Duster and the Little Awl, a small Usk dry-fly. He said the fish would not be easy. He was not wrong.

Frankly, this season I have been glad to see any fish rising at all: a rise to my fly is an unlooked-for bonus. I got plenty of those but, infuriatingly, I could not get them to stick on the end. From time to time a small trout would take pity on me and consent to lead me round a pool before being put back - but I got the impression it was his idea more than mine.

There are spots in this beautiful gorge where the sides crowd the stream into a deep inaccessible pool where large fish can be seen finning in the depths. There is one such where the rock hangs over the water so that three fishermen could stand one above the other on different ledges to fish. Wasp grubs are the best way to search out the beasts that hide deep under these ledges.

In other places the sides widen to form a small, hilly meadow dotted with hawthorns, where families were picnicking on that Sunday afternoon. A fish was rising within the twisted sanctuary of an uprooted climbing frame, silhouetted against a sunken traffic cone. A red-faced man in corduroy breeches and trailing an empty dog-leash asked if I'd seen his hound.

The sides steepen again and there is a temptation to follow the river from the path, dropping down to fish obvious pools. I made that mistake yesterday on my first visit. The fish in the obvious pools have seen a lot of flies. Now I was taking the scenic route along the rocks down in the water where, in the runs and corners between the pools, there were tiny rises whipped away by the current, invisible to the man who sticks to the path. I did better with those fish: they have a naivety that suits my style of fly-fishing.

There are miles of this magical fishing up through the winding gorge to Pontsticill Reservoir. I hooked no monsters on the way. Large fish are taken - but not by me that day. It seemed a lot further walking back: this is always the sign of an absorbing piece of fishing. From time to time I stopped for a second crack at pools where I had raised fish after fish and had missed them all. As I crouched beside a rock changing flies, a large hairy face peered forlornly down at me. It was a lost hound.

The Taf Fawr (the Big Taff), which joins the Taf Fechan in Merthyr, tumbles down from the western flank of Pen y Fan, sharing its headwaters with another stream whose name does not spring to mind when the talk gets round to crystal streams of trout and sewin - the Neath. More so than the Taff, the Neath flows over coal measures for most of its lower reaches and has suffered despoliation as a consequence. Nowadays, driving up the Vale of Neath in the unvarying sunshine of this summer, it is hard to remember what the valley looked like from the window of Aunt Rene's Austin Ruby in the '50s. Now there are occasional glimpses of a bright stream through the bushes with forested hillsides high on either side. And then the great grimy hulk of the Rheola aluminium works with its rusting gantries slung over the road brings a sharp reminder of the recent industrial past.

But even in those dark satanic days the river was far from fishless. The Rheola works mark the downstream boundary of the Glynneath and District AA, founded in 1950. Forty years later one of the founder members, Harry Lewis, took a walk with me up the water he had fished all his life. His father, Ernie Lewis, had kept a fishing diary of weather and water, fish and flies throughout his life. Some of the flies Harry showed me in his bulging fly-wallet were Ernie's creations that have become trusted standards on the

Neath.

Like its neighbour the Taff, the River Neath starts life on old red sandstone before crossing a broad band of limestone at the head of the Vale of Neath. On its principal tributary, the Mellte, the river plunges underground (in the way that rivers do in limestone country) before emerging again in a large pool that is the beginning of the club water. There are spectacular waterfalls on this piece of the Mellte, with deep pools of crystal water. On hot afternoons you can be sharing your fishing with families splashing and swimming in these spectacular basins.

On that morning in late May there were swarms of spinners dancing in the gaps between the river and the thickly wooded sides of the gorge. On rocks that stud the thin stream were the discarded cases of enormous stoneflies. Overhead fluttered something remarkably similar to a large mayfly but with a yellow tinge to its wings: I have rarely seen a river less hospitable to the silt-burrowing nymphs of a Mayfly - and, besides, these things had two tails. Back at the car, Goddard's *Waterside Guide* solved the problem: the things were large green duns, and there followed the depressing confirmation that they are of little use to the fisherman as the dun is rarely seen by the trout: unlike almost all upwinged flies the large, flat, stone-clinging nymphs crawl out of the water to emerge on stones - which solved the business of the large "stonefly" cases.

Curiously, the anglers of Glynneath rarely fish dry flies. curiously, because eight miles away on the Taff the dry-fly is supreme. The difference, I think, lies downstream. Between Merthyr and the sea there are numerous weirs that effectively prevent any migratory fish getting to the town and beyond (despite the seeding of salmon parr for the past four or five years). The Neath has always had a run of sewin, despite the obstacle of a large weir at Aberdulais, and it is the sewin that have shaped the fishing techniques of Glynneath even when brown trout are the quarry.

There were no sewin in the shrunken river on that blistering day in May. Harry was showing me the water between Pontneddfechan and Glynneath where he fished when the sewin were running. The river is broader here below the confluence of the Nedd (Neath) and the Mellte and flows between meadows fringed with alder and hawthorn. A small dimple in the neck of a shallow pool made both of us stop and watch. A second dimple. Harry encouraged me to have a try for it in the way older and wiser anglers do when they know that there is bugger all hope in the thin, bright water: it keeps the youngsters in their place.

It was the dry fly that fooled that fish: he just wasn't used to them. When he glided into the net a few moments later, his eye bore a look of weary contempt at such unsporting deception. That fish measured 15 inches and I was delighted. If anything, I would say that Harry Lewis was even more so, generously delighted that his beloved river had been on its best behaviour for a visitor.

We caught more fish that day, down on the lower reaches of the water where the shallow weirs of the flood defences form long shallow pools on a broad river, perfect for an evening of sewin fishing with a flood of water from the hills. Over a final cup of tea in Harry's kitchen we agreed that he would give me a ring at the first flush of rain that would bring the sewin running up the river.

There was a night of heavy rain at the end of July. I waited for a call but nothing came.

And then I heard. Harry Lewis had died.

As I write twenty-two years on, the tackle shop in Cefn Coed is still miraculously open and largely unchanged. It is now called Merthyr Angling Centre (and see chapter 2, Ripon Yarns) but, alas, I hear it may be closed by the time you get to read this.

Also, I'm very suspicious of that diagnosis of a Large Green Dun on the Afon Mellte. Far more likely, I fancy, would be the Large Brook Dun. The yellowish tinge to the wings is a dead give-away and besides, it was hatching at the right time of year. Nowadays I often come across the large brook dun on the small stony streams of Wales. Their stone-clinging nymphs emerge in much the same way as those of the large green dun - and the trout seem to ignore them much the same.

The Taff and the Merthyr Tydfil Angling Association go from strength to strength. You can get details of their waters on the Taff, Usk and various small streams and stillwaters on their splendid website at www.mtaa.co.uk. Day tickets are £10.

Glynneath and District Angling Association have a website at www.fishingglynneath.co.uk. Bits of it work – but not the fishing map. Day tickets are £10 from Dave Pittman, Daves Stylist's (sic), Heathfield Avenue, Glynneath and from the Old White Horse Inn, Pontneddfechan. Tel: 01639 721 219

6

Alpine Events

There were gnomes, a whole gang of them, beside the road. They were not your common-or-garden gnomes. They were bigger for a start. And their red cheeks were not so much jolly as bibulous: these gnomes were pissed and not for the first time. The one on the end had his trousers down, mooning at passing motorists, and one in the middle was giving them the finger. They were quite the most threatening, sinister bunch of artificial elfin folk I had ever seen.

They were hanging around in front of a shop. It was, as far as I could see, a shop selling nothing but gnomes. It was the last shop in Italy. For miles there had been nothing but forest as the road twisted up through the mountains: ahead was the flat-roofed office and stripey-pole-with-a-big-round-thing-on-the-end of a frontier crossing. I was about to cross into Slovenia.

Or Slovakia. I am never quite sure which is which. I have read my fair share of Len Deighton so I knew what to expect at the border crossing: hard-faced men tapping bits of my car for hidden compartments and examining my passport for the wrong sort of ink. Not a bit of it. The smiling bloke waved a lorry through and then the car in front of me. So I held up my passport and with a light heart drove across into Slovenia (or possibly Slovakia) which was when the bloke shouted at me and made me reverse back behind the line while he studied my passport and showed it to another bloke for a while. They looked like they were waiting for the phone call from police headquarters: it didn't come so they gave my passport back. I was in.

I had come in to Slovenia through the back door, an Alpine pass in the north-east corner of Italy, just a mile or so from the border with Austria. I was tooling along a broad valley of Alpine meadows with towering sierras to the north and south and a perfect snow-clad peak against the blue sky ahead.

Slovenian place-names start off swimmingly and just when you think you have the measure of them they bung a "J" in the middle and beads of sweat break out on your forehead: *Podljubelj* – see what I mean? There is another sort. They are short and disconcertingly English - like *Log*. The enigmatic *Lip Bled* turned out to be a timber merchant in the town of Bled.

Bled is an elegant spa town from the days when the dyspeptic gentry of Europe came to Lake Bled to take healing waters and breath Alpine air. Nowadays it bustles with hotels and holiday-makers. A mile beyond Lake Bled something big and a bright and blue was flickering through the trees. It was the river I had come to fish, the Sava.

The Sava Bohinjka (there is another one – the Sava Dolinka) is a bit of a tart, flirting with the road up the valley - now on this side, now on that, a flash of leg as it sweeps beneath a bridge and dives away through the woods. I love it when they act that way. The river swings across the valley floor through little farming villages where new-mown hay was drying in the June sunshine. Alpine guest-houses appeared on either side of the road and between them a stunning lake led away between steep-sided mountains towards the west and the lowering sun. I had arrived at Bohinjsko Jezero – Lake Bohinj.

I have been reading about the limestone rivers of Slovenia,

their crystal waters and beautiful trout, for half a lifetime. Negley Farson, in his classic *Going Fishing*, lived for two impoverished years in this little hamlet of Ribčev Laz at the end of the lake. He described the fishing hereabouts as *"the finest consistent trout fishing I have ever had"* and Negley had fished a bit. That morning I had been on holiday in northern Italy and, seeing that Slovenia was just next door (*Slovakia*, it turns out, is miles away), I had made a dash for it. Here I was.

A handsome, double-arch bridge spans the river where the Sava sweeps away from lake. I stood on the bridge before a sight to set the soul soaring, a spectacular stretch of lake ringed by dramatic mountains reflecting their glory in the mirrored surface. I did what any fishermen would do. I ignored all that glory: I leaned over the bridge and peered down into the water, looking for fish. There they were. There is a special sort of fish that lives in front of this sort of bridge. They are big and obvious and constantly on the move, swooping up to grab stuff from the surface. They are placed at these strategic points to interest the tourists and get a fisherman's juices going. They work really well.

The Hotel Jezero stands by the lake at one end of the bridge. The *motif* on the wall of the hotel is a large fish with a scattering of light spots. It is an arctic char, which shows that the Hotel Jezero has its heart in the right place. I got a room overlooking the lake and waited for the next morning and Vojko.

Vojko is a fisherman. We had met in England many years ago. He had described the country, its rivers and its dry fly fishing and I promised to visit the next year. Or definitely the year after. But what with one thing and another that had been ten years ago: I hoped he hadn't stayed in waiting for me.

Next morning Vojko was in the hotel lobby. He had not changed in ten years: a jolly man with a great Balkan bush of a moustache. He was not so very jolly that morning. The snow I had so admired on the mountain tops was a late and heavy fall that had swelled and chilled the rivers. We would wait until the afternoon had warmed things a little. I had waited half a lifetime to fish these waters: I was quite unreasonably miffed to miss another morning. But I didn't have to. We would fish Lake Bohinj for its arctic char.

So we went to find Boris. If you want to fish hereabouts first you find Boris. Boris runs the Tourist Information Office in the village. He will tell you where you can hire one of the elegant rowing boats on the lake: they belong to Boris. He will also provide the tackle. Boris also issues the fishing licences for the lake and the river. And he runs a comfortable guesthouse. Boris is really all you need to know.

It was a beautiful morning without a breath of wind. The sound of Alpine cow-bells echoed across the water as the early morning mist shrouding the lake began to shred under the sun. Char fishing in June is delightfully simple. Boris, Vojko and I rowed a little way onto the lake, nothing strenuous, and dropped anchor in thirty feet or so. Each had a small, light spinning rod with single weight and a hook. Boris produced a small pot. Inside were the juiciest, plumpest grubs I had ever seen. They were *Lipo čru* – I have no idea what that is in English or if we have them in England. If we do, it is hard to see how any English fish could resist them. They looked yummy. We each attached a single grub and parked the thing a foot or so up from the bottom. And them we waited. Char fishing in Bohinjsko Jezero in June is remarkably akin to sunbathing.

We chatted of this and that and jiggled the bait from time to time when we felt we ought to be doing something. One of the little rods would nod and Boris or Vojko or I would wind in a dashing little char. The arctic char is the most beautiful of the salmonids. Later in the season it will have a belly of strident vermilion and a back of steel-grey sprinkled with pale spots, but in June these are just suggested in a subtle darkening above with a roseate tinge below. They were not big, six ounces or so, although some of many pounds do turn up in the depths. The daily licence allows you six of these lovelies and holiday-makers take a leisurely morning to catch them and the afternoon to cook and eat and sleep them off. I can think of worse ways to make a holiday.

But we had other fish to fry. It was noon and getting hot out on the lake. It was time to take to the river.

It snows a bit round these parts. The mountains around Lake Bohinj rise over 9000 feet so they are entitled to a fair amount of snow. Snow isn't something English fishermen think about much: it doesn't impinge round our way. It does here. In April and May the rivers are cold. It takes a while for the spring sunshine to reach into the deep valleys and when it does it just melts the snow and makes them bigger and colder. The fish stay deep. By the end of May the snow has gone from all but the highest slopes, the rivers settle to summer level and warm, the flies move about a bit and the fish follow them to the surface. By June the legendary dry fly fishing has begun.

It was June but the unseasonal snow storms up in the mountains had knocked all that on the head and hung like a great Sword of Whatisname over the river. I wasn't sure what to hope for: a cold snap would keep the snow where it was but do nothing to warm the river. Hot sunshine would warm the river: it would also melt the snow and flush freezing water down from the mountains to cool it again. And rain would be worse. What we had was sunshine and as Vojko and I drove down the river we could see waterfalls of meltwater plunging down from the high side of the valley.

The Sava Bohinjka was a magnificent sight. Even swollen with meltwater the pale limestone shingle shone through the shallows and shaded into the transparent blue-green depths of a limestone river. In summer the river would fall and slow, the light reflecting from the pale gravels revealing every detail of the bottom and –

for those who know what they are looking for – the splendid fish of the Sava.

I couldn't see a thing. I eased my way into the margins of the Sava and gingerly made my way out into the current. It was a big river and it was fairly sweeping along. I asked Vojko if I should try a dry fly. He said *"why not?"* in the sort of way that told me he didn't think I had a hope in hell. He was right.

I stuck forlornly at the dry fly for a while before changing down the gears through wet fly to heavy nymph. I touched nothing and nothing touched me.

"We could try a streamer," Vojko said. There seemed to be a touch of distaste about the way he said it. I'm not sure Vojko approved of streamers. It sounded like something that might work but you wouldn't want your mother to hear about it. He was at pains to tell me that "a friend of mine" recommended a fly for this sort of water. He opened a box and showed me. I could see what he meant: we both flinched as he brought it out into the light. It was huge and green and hairy. It had a long rubber tail with a flange at the back to make it wag in the current – or perhaps there were batteries hidden inside the thing. It was, I suppose, a sort of monstrous Waggy but bigger than any Waggy I had ever seen on Rutland Water or anywhere else. The body was dark olive with a palmered hackle and a broad gold rib. And there was something with a fair amount of heft under that lot.

Vojko waded upstream and manoeuvred this beast down the length of the run I had been searching. I was rather relieved to find it fared no better than the dries and wets. Below us the river deepened and began a long bend round to the right. The deep channel on the outside of this bend was on our bank, hard under the bushes that lined the river. Vojko began to search this channel, lobbing the beast towards midstream and letting the current bring it back into the channel beneath the bushes. By inching out a little more line after each roll cast he searched down the channel.

Suddenly – nothing delicate was going to happen to this fly – the rod tip dipped and Vojko was into a fish.

The fish had hit the fly hard in the full press of the fast channel directly downstream. It tore line off the reel and it was several minutes before Vojko could fight the fish back up past the bushes and into a small bay out of the main current. Both of them were feeling it by this time. The fish was a fine, fit rainbow trout of around 1½ lbs. Vojko is a gent. He stood aside and gave me his spot at the head of the channel. I got the fly out there somehow and worked out line as Vojko had done. The fly drifted down the stream and began to swing in beside the bushes. There was thump at the end of the line. Whatever on earth that fly was imitating, the trout were lining up to get it. I did not get that trout in. I just wasn't prepared for the savage strength of those dashing fish in the clean, fast waters of the Sava Bohinjka.

I got the hang of the thing in the end. That afternoon we fished our way round that long bend, creeping down through the bushes to cast out across the current. When a boil in the current smoothed a window in the surface I began to spot sleek grey shapes hanging above the pale river bottom. As the monstrous fly swung across the deeper channel a shape would detach, swooping up to make contact. Vojko had found the effective fly and through the afternoon we had refined the presentation: it was a bit like matching-the-hatch but it made you wrists ache more.

That evening we celebrated a splendid day over a meal with Boris – did I tell you Boris has a bar and restaurant along with all the other stuff?

That night it rained. It was still lashing down when we all met the next morning. The river was up and I had to be back in Italy for a meal that evening. And so I left Vojko and Boris, promising – again - that I would be back next year for the dry fly fishing.

But this time I will.

A couple of years ago, while fishing in France, I finally discovered what manner of beast was the grub, Lipo čru. It is the larva of the Greater Wax Moth, a parasite of honey bees with the mellifluous Latin name, *Galleria mellonella*. I bred a batch of these in an old sweetie jar in the airing cupboard and tried them trotting for grayling on the River Severn with singular lack of success. That story will turn up in another book, no doubt.

Historically, fishing in Slovenia has always been extremely well-regulated (see Negley Farson's 1930's account in "Going Fishing"). This has resulted in excellent, but fairly expensive, fly-fishing. 2011 licences are:- Lake Bohinj DT: €25, Sava Bohinjka River (18Km) DT: €42 (catch and release) or € 60 (3-fish limit) using a single fly and barbless hooks. All are available from the Tourist Office by the lake. For more details visit www.bohinj.si/en/Fishing

Boris's guesthouse is the Penzion Rožič. You'll find details at www.pensionrozic-bohinj.com

"Going Fishing" by Negley Farson is a classic of fishing travels in the 1920s and 30s. The last chapter describes fishing Bohinj.

7

Gothic Ghost Story

I was a child of the sixties. We children of the sixties were not hidebound by convention. We each did our own thing. We were proud of that. Of course, there were a limited number of these things: it was just a bit depressing to discover that my thing was much the same thing as every other child of the sixties.

We bought the same LPs: we were just learning to call them albums. Everyone seemed to have a copy of "Candles in the Rain" by Melanie. I don't ever remember listening to this and I have no idea what it sounds like but we all had it. Quite a few blokes I know still have.

We all had the same Aubrey Beardsley prints on our walls. We favoured the risqué prints of women with big chins cavorting with enormous phalluses. I think we hoped it might get visitors of the appropriate sex thinking along the right lines and ignoring the unwashed coffee cups.

And we all had the same books on our bookshelves. We had "Self Sufficiency" by John and Sally Seymour and some of us went and bought pigs and kept them in the garden and ate them. I did. It was a strange time. We all had "Lord of the Rings": many people were more familiar with the geography of Middle Earth than the place they lived. And most of us owned the great fat Gothic novels of Mervyn Peake: "Titus Groane" and

"Gormenghast".

I never quite got round to reading Gormenghast. Which makes it all the more surprising, then, that "Gormenghast" was the name that came to me as we turned off the A66 on a sunny day last June.

"Crackenthorpe Hall" sounds, if anything, slightly more Gothic and doom-laden than "Castle Gormenghast". There were rooks crying portentously in the dark trees that loomed over the gravelled drive as we crunched to a halt - but that might have been my imagination. Crackenthorpe Hall looks every bit as Gothic as it sounds. I had come here to meet David Balfour, the owner of Crackenthorpe. He appeared around the corner of the ancient building. I'm not sure what I was expecting from the Master of Crackenthorpe: a hunchback, at the very least. But David looked quite normal. He approached the car. He didn't lurch and drag one foot across the gravel of the drive. It was a bit of a let-down really. He didn't even drool. But then David is a newcomer as they reckon things in these parts. The Machell family owned the place for 600 years or so until the line was snuffed out on the first day of the Battle of the Somme.

Of course, a place like Crackenthorpe gathers a few ghosts along the way. One, the wife of Lancelot Machell, was so put out by the terms of his will that she appeared before each generation, presaging the death of the head of the family. Which must have been a little unnerving.

A second ghost, the servant girl Peg Sneddle, was not so picky about who she appeared to. She put the wind up folk so indiscriminately that the family had her exhumed from consecrated ground and reburied beneath a large granite boulder in the middle of the river.

Which was what I had come to see. The river, that is, not the tombstone of some stroppy maid. Crackenthorpe Hall lies beside the lovely River Eden in Cumbria.

Crackenthorpe sits two miles downstream of Appleby in the heart of the troutiest reaches of the Eden. Here the river swings in extravagant meanders, steeply tree-shaded on the outsides of the bends with sheep-nibbled pastures enclosed on the opposite banks. The path to the river leads past the King's garden, named for a gardener who lived and worked at Crackenthorpe for a short time in the fifteenth century. He was not a gardener by profession: before the Battle of Hexham in 1464 he had been Henry VI. Crackenthorpe is that sort of a place.

Beyond the woods and the old pump house, the path crosses the parkland to the river. The Crackenthorpe water is divided into two beats. The boundary is an old weir where the water tumbles around a small island. Above the weir, on the Chapel Wood beat, the waters of the Eden are held back in a long deep pool stretching upstream and beyond the bend. The Crackenthorpe bank is heavily wooded and the only option is to wade the centre of the river, casting under the low branches. These long, still pools of the Eden are the home of large trout that do not stir from the cool depths through the long hot days of summer. But at night, when the last glimmer of light has left the sky, these wise old fish cruise the surface for the fluttering of the sedges and moths of sultry summer nights. This is Eden's celebrated Bustard fishing that can enliven the darkest nights of July and August. So it was something of a shame that this was mid-June, ten o'clock in the morning and shaping up for a scorcher. The long flat above the weir was still and dead.

On the lip of the weir a few small fry were dimpling in that last bulge of smooth water. These little fish are put there for folk like me who like to cast at a rising fish. They are quite safe. They ride the pressure wave in front of the lip. Here the water is shallow and smooth so that the leader stands out like a streak of lightening in the sunlight. Also the water is accelerating so that a leader cast from downstream must land in the faster water of the weir, ripping the fly across each fish and scaring the thing spitless. So you cast from above. But, as the water above the fish is accelerating, the fly lands in water travelling faster than the leader and drags across the fish, scaring the little thing spitless again. Either way, fish-spit is going to be in short supply. Also fish. There are two things you can do. You can cast a wobbly leader so that it takes time for the drag to straighten it out. This is the usual suggestion. This may delay the moment of spit-loss enough for the fish to grab but you will only get the one chance. There is one more thing to try. If the water is accelerating smoothly along the length of the weir, you can stand in the water above the weir, a foot or so further from the lip than the little fish. You cast across, parallel to the lip so that all the line is travelling at the same speed. As the accelerating fly nears the fish you move your arm and the rod downstream to keep everything travelling at the same speed. It helps if you have changed the leader to a gossamer thread: these are small fish in shallow water and easily spooked. If everything goes to plan the little fly will disappear in a dimple. It is embarrassing if, at this moment, you discover that the little fish is not a little fish at all but something rather more serious, something intent on returning to the cool depths of the deep pool upstream.

I swore a bit, replaced the remnants of the gossamer leader with something a little more manly and tied on another fly.

Downstream from the weir the river carves its rumbustious way around the island. A small stream, Colby Beck, enters below the island and the deep pool at the confluence looks full of promise, particularly as I happened to know that a good fish had come from this pool the day before. I had spent the previous night at Temple Sowerby House, a sumptuously comfortable hotel in the nearby village of that name. The hotel can arrange fishing on the waters of Crackenthorpe Hall and the day before it had done just that for another guest, Fred Dixon, and in the waters of the

Colby Beck pool he had latched on to a good fish. I know all this because he was back trying to repeat the trick as I passed in the growing heat.

It was getting hotter. The chest waders that had seemed such a grand idea for the deep waters of the Chapel Wood beat were getting a bit icky in the rocky shallows of the Park beat. Here the river swings half-circle in a prodigious bend and the long sedate glides of the Eden break up into something a little livelier. And it was here, amongst the rocky runs that I had my first Crackenthorpe trout, a handsome little fish of twelve inches.

It was one of those days. I had taken a trout or two and missed some others as I worked my way down through the riffles of the Park beat. Under a large boulder at the bottom of the beat lay the bones of Peg Sneddle. In the heat of that afternoon I quite envied her. I sat beside her with my legs in the water and mused.

There is more than a touch of romance and the high Gothic about the River Eden. A dozen miles below Crackenthorpe the river curves around a sandstone crag, rearing out of the wood along its banks. The sheer sides of the crag are pierced by arched windows and a couple of doorways, entrances to a labyrinth of chambers. These are Lacy's Caves, a Gothic folly hollowed into the crag by a Colonel Lacy in the 18th Century. He employed a picturesque hermit to complete the romantic tableau.

There are stranger carvings a few miles further downstream, in the Eden Gorge near Armathwaite. On the sandstone cliffs, invisible from the bank, a series of enigmatic heads gaze out across the water. In a hidden nook, high above these these heads is an inscription chiselled into the rock. The letters are Old English in style: so is the spelling. Some of the letters are carved back to front. They read:

OH THE FISHER'S GENTLE LIFE
HAPPIEST IS OF ANY
VOID OF PLEASUR FULL OF STRIFE

AND BELOVD BY MANY
OTHER JOYS ARE BUT TOYS
AND TO BE LAMENTED
ONLY THIS A PLEASURE IS

A Greek inscription follows and a date: 1855.

The lines are from Walton's "Compleat Angler" but an ironic spirit has switched the words of the third line: the original reads: *Full of pleasure, void of strife.*

These hidden carvings were the work of an extraordinary Eden character who left his mark on other parts of the river. Eight miles further downstream, at the foot of the cliff below St Contantine's Cells in Wetheral Woods, more lines begin: "To meet the Atlantic's boundless time, see old Ituna's waters glide..." Ituna is the Roman name for the river. This inscription, though, is signed: YESNUOM SUMLEILVG – the Latin name, written backwards, of William Mounsey, the "Jew of Carlisle".

William Mounsey was not Jewish. He had joined the army in 1825 and served nearly 20 years, mostly in the Middle East. He was a scholar with a gift for languages and became fluent in Greek, Latin, Persian and Welsh. While serving in the Middle East he had become fascinated by Jewish religion, culture and history. On his return to England, Captain Mounsey became a solicitor in the family firm but his fascination had left its mark: he adopted the clothes, the lifestyle, even the characteristic beard, of traditional Jewish fashion. He became well-known in the borders as "The Jew of Carlisle".

The other great love of his life was the River Eden. He lived at Rockcliffe where the Eden joins the Solway Firth and in 1850 he made a lone pilgrimage, walking every inch of its banks from the sea to its source high up on Black Fell Moss below Wild Boar Fell. There, twenty miles upstream of Crackenthorpe, he erected a monument to his achievement. The column of local limestone was covered in yet more enigmatic carvings from this lover of the arcane and mysterious. A Latin inscription describes the fulfilment of his vow to the "Genius and nymphs of the Eden". The Greek inscription is more obscure and mysterious, beginning "Seek the river of the soul – whence it springs..." There were also Cabalistic symbols that would have been all the rage in the Year of Peace and Love. Prominent on the column was the Star of David that gave the monument its local name of the "Jew" stone.

It might have been the heat, or maybe William Mounsey had put me in a funny Gormenghasty sort of a mood: I turned around from the river to see a figure who had stepped from the stories of Tolkein. The living embodiment of Tom Bombadil was striding towards me across the meadows of Crackenthorpe. It was a lean figure with grey hair swept back in an heroic manner. He wore strange apparel, clad in an intricate harness of leather and buckles and strung about with an assortment of canvas and wicker baskets. He looked like he might be selling moles. Or tallow. I'm not entirely certain what tallow is but he looked like he might have some about his person. A broad-brimmed hat hung from around his neck and he carried a fishing rod, a whipped-cane weapon of mellowed honey furnished with a silk line. You just don't see figures like that round our way.

Terry Cousins is a legendary fisherman round these parts. I had heard him spoken of with awe the first time I had fished the River Eamont many years ago. I had seen his writings in magazines and books. And now I met him beside the magical waters of the River Eden.

We talked for a while, as fishermen do, of waters we had both fished. Then we talked of waters we might fish: he could show me Cumbrian waters where I might find my favourite quarry, the arctic char. I wouldn't have been a bit surprised if he'd told me where I could find the One Ring to Rule Them All. We talked of the heat and lamented the low river as fishermen will and then we went our separate ways to fish the Eden for the fag-end of the day.

I began to work my way back up the rocky riffles that I though held the only hope of oxygen and action through that warm evening. Terry went downstream to the very end of the Park beat, to a deep, quiet corner that I had dismissed at a first glance. And when we met again as the sun was sinking I had nothing more to show and Terry had a beautiful honey-gold creature of fifteen inches.

It had been a strange day, all in all.

It got stranger. Most of the stories in this book are reproduced as they first appeared. But not this one. It has been judiciously shorn of a couple of lines. They recorded that at Crackenthorpe that day I had been vouchsafed a recipe for surreptitiously poisoning cats. So I had - and it had only added to the Gothic aura of the place. I'd omitted to mention that I'd received this recipe from the photographer who'd come to the place with me. On reading the piece in Trout and Salmon, the owner of Crackenthorpe felt there was an implication that he had been the source of this recipe. He felt it damaged his reputation: he intended to sue. The magazine printed a grovelling apology on my behalf.

The bizarre story of the Eden carvings can be found in a small but fascinating book - William Mounsey and the "Jew" Stone, by Charlie Emett, (£3.60), published by W.R. Mitchell. This gem can be found for sale on the internet if you're lucky.

8

Doing the Pools

What is this country coming to? We were burgled the other day. I am not sure when exactly. It must have been some time in the trout closed season: sometime between October and last week, thieves must have broken in and made off with the big red plastic tub I take on a fishing trip. I've got a list of the contents ready for the police: one camping stove and saucepans, two Kelly Kettles (one large, one small), two tin mugs, one float tube, two flippers and a tent. Also some assorted cutlery, a small jar of coffee with lumpy bits and a crusty bottle of HP sauce.

And it is not the first time this has happened. Some years ago I went out to the garage one morning and found the doors wide open and the car gone. It was a terrible moment. I phoned the police. A little while later two policemen arrived and I showed them the empty garage and they spent a little time out there looking for clues. Then we sat down and they asked a lot of questions and I wrote out a statement: it is a lengthy business getting burgled. I was unsettled for the rest of the day. And then there was the shopping: without a car I couldn't get to the supermarket. By the next day we were running out of stuff so I walked down the towpath to the village shop. There was my car, parked in front of the shop.

It was a mystery. Perhaps the felon had suffered a crisis of conscience, a sudden revelation of faith on the road to Banbury, doubled back and parked the car in front of the village shop. Or – and thinking about it later I do remember something of the sort – I might have called in at the shop on my way back from town and walked home along the towpath, forgetting that I gone there in the car. The police, when I told them, seemed to be leaning toward the second explanation.

So I haven't as yet reported the Great Red Plastic Box Robbery which put a bit of a crimp into the trip to the Teifi Pools.

The Teifi Pools are a long way from anywhere other than Pontryhdfendigaid. And, as Pontryhdfendigaid is a long way from anywhere other than the Tiefi Pools, this doesn't help much. Both of them lie on the western slopes of the Cambrian Mountains in mid-Wales so you have to go through the side gate and round to the back door to get there.

I was picking up Philip on the way. Philip lives in Duns Tew. I have this thingummy on my computer. You type in where you want to start and finish and it thinks about it, weighs up this and that and tells you the best route and a couple of alternatives to allow for the gypsy in your soul. As chance would have it, Duns Tew lies close to the A44 in Oxfordshire and the Teifi Pools lie the same distance off the A44 in Ceredigion. So the A44 looked like a good bet. I asked the computer what it thought. This route thingummy treats me rather as Jeeves treats Bertie Wooster. It would not countenance the A44. I tried to suggest the thing by giving places I wanted to visit along the A44. I might have been suggesting a coloured shirt and soft collar with a dinner jacket. It squirmed a bit and remained adamant. The A44 would not do. It favoured a route via Shrewsbury or, if I insisted, I could get there through Tewkesbury and a place called Redmarley d'Abitot - which I think it was making up. You have to be firm with thingummies, however omniscient and high-handed they carry on: you have to know when to use the old iron-fist-in-the-velvet-glove routine. So we ignored the thingummy and took the A44. I had a reason for preferring this route: it looked fairly straight across the map. I had been getting a fearful knocking from the offside drive-shaft on any right turn. I was looking for a route to the Teifi Pools that avoided turning right.

Four noisy hours later, in the hamlet of Ffair-Rhos on the B4343, we turned at a little finger post pointing to Teifi Lakes. The small lane climbed up away from civilisation at a steady rate until the last house on the left, a long bungalow beside the road, where a sheep dog lunged at the tyres in the way they do. A sign by the cottage offered fishing tickets for sale. We got out of the car. The dog circled us and began the lift, rounding us up and driving us towards the cottage door. We went in and the door swung closed behind us – ten points for a perfect pen.

Beyond the house the road kept on climbing towards the top of the world until, around a shoulder of the hill the whole of the Teifi valley was spread out before us towards the south-west and the sea.

It's an extraordinary place up here where the Teifi trickles out of the hills. The landscape is strangely reminiscent of other Welsh valleys to the south where the spoil of the industrial age has been dumped as hummocky slag-heaps along the heads of the valleys. Much the same had happened here long before when the glaciers that had been spawned in heights of the Cambrian Mountains for a million years melted, dumping the spoil of rock and rubbish they had gouged from the land in passing. Water gathered in the dips and hollows between the crags and moraines to form small lakes, overspilling down the valley as the infant River Teifi.

The small lane twists in a most romantic fashion over, round and between the crags, giving tantalising glimpses of water around each turn. It was the first time I had seen all this. It was not the first time I had been to the Teifi Pools: the other time I was here the place was shrouded in a deep blanket of mist. The fishing had been a trifle haphazard. You walked until your feet got wet and then cast forward into thick white stuff and hoped you were over water. Today was quite different. Today was clear and dry. It was the middle of March and the start of a new trout season.

It is hard, at the beginning of a new trout season, to pass a bit of water without trying it. So we didn't. We stopped at the first of those waters winking between the crags. There are six little lakes up here in the hills: two big ones, one medium size and three smaller ones. This was one of the smaller ones and it doesn't rate a name on my map.

We grabbed stuff from the back of the car, put on all the clothes we could find and jounced down the turf towards the water. It is always a good idea to go fishing with a friend for the first outing of the season. There is a good chance that, out of two fishing bags, you can put together at least one complete set of tackle. We sat beside the lake and did that.

It was cold and bleak. There is often something of a gap between the anticipation of fishing and the reality of the thing. This gap is never bigger than in March at 1400 feet up a Welsh mountain. And then Philip had a first cast into the waters of this little lake and a fish tugged at his fly like it had been waiting all winter to do just that and the gap miraculously disappeared.

That first little lake at the Teifi pools was the perfect way to start a trout season. The fish were eager enough to get you going but not so big that the rest of the season would be an anticlimax. In fact they were quite small. They weren't going to put any strain on knots tied with cold fingers and a winter's ineptitude. Ideal really. We worked our way round the shore of this shallow little lake. The fish kept coming and seemed to be getting a little larger but that may have been an illusion: it was just hard to believe that the one before could have been smaller. By the time we arrived at the miniature dam in the far corner we were ready for something bigger.

There is something bigger over a short, sharp ridge to the east. Llyn Teifi is the largest of the Teifi Pools and the source of the river itself. We came down from the ridge to the dam which controls Llyn Teifi as a reservoir. Arms of the lake stretched away in every direction and the water had the depth and promise of better fish. We told each other that. We fished up the coast, mercifully free from the insistent tugs of little fish. We told each other that too. On the first lake it had made no difference what flies we used. They had grabbed the first one to hand. This was more like it: we could plan a team of flies to search the water, a bit of weight here to probe the depths, a flash of gold there to grab the attention and a buggy little item for a trout to get its teeth round. This is the intellectual challenge that fly fishing is all about. We told each other that as well: there was very little else to do. Philip said he couldn't understand it: the place looked "*so fishy*". This is not a good sign. Philip's fishy instincts are uncannily inaccurate. We fished on around the top of Llyn Teifi without a tug or the sign of a rise.

We were strangely undaunted by the dourness of Llyn Teifi. The first little lake, a few hundred yards away, had been alive with rising fish: perhaps the next one would be the same.

It wasn't. Llyn Hîr is a long, narrow trench of water stretching south between the crags. There was not a sign of life. It was a cool, grey day in March and the Kelly Kettle, which should have been hard at it, reviving flagging spirits with piping hot tea, was languishing somewhere in a big sack labelled "swag" – along with a float tube, a pair of flippers and a tent. The tent we did not need.

At one time I quite fancied camping up here in the hills amid these little lakes. It is, after all, a long way from home: why not make a weekend of it? And then one day I went into the Talbot Hotel in Tregaron. There on the wall was an old newspaper cutting. It was the first I had heard of the *Beast of Bont*.

"Bont" is the mercifully short local name for the tiny town of

Pontrhydfendigaid. In the hills above the town, in the lonely country between Teifi Pools and the Elan Valley, farmers have been complaining for years that something had been killing their sheep. Several people reported sightings of a creature the size of a puma. The Telegraph reported: *"The Beast of Bont . . . is blamed for the death of a great many sheep around Aberystwyth, their injuries typical of big cat attacks - frontal maulings with large claw marks on the neck and throat."*

The editor of the Fortean Times, Paul Sieveking, reported other, more alarming encounters. The closest came from *a trio of witnesses in Llanrhystud, near Aberystwyth, West Wales. Rhodri Shaw, Rhys Davies and Sion Evans, all 12, were camping near their homes on 29 August when they heard a noise and saw a silhouette of an animal on their tent. "We thought it was a small cat magnified by moonlight," said Rhodri. "But when we looked out, we saw this huge black cat 2.5ft [76cm] tall. We froze as it circled the tent."* Since then there have been numerous sightings of more than one big cat. And making our way amongst the lakes we had come across the remains of a prodigious number of dismantled sheep. So what with one thing and another we thought we would leave the tent at home. Besides, I have a note from my mother to say that I'm not allowed to camp at Teifi Pools.

Across another ridge the last of the Teifi Lakes came into view. Llyn Egnant is a big bit of water. The northern shore where we had arrived is broad and shallow, fringed with coarse grasses with their feet in the water. The vegetation gave a little shelter from the breeze blowing down the lake, creating a broad strip of calm water. And at the edge of the ripple a fish rose.

The trick is not to look at the rise itself or its ring: look at the water to one side. It is easier where the water is calm and easier still when there are reflections of trees or grasses – anything straight. A bigger fish moves more water out of the way. It has no choice. The rise may be quieter than a small fish's rise – it often is

– but the surface of the water will buckle to a bigger fish. It is hardly noticeable but it is there and the reflections of branch and grass stem will bend a bit. It is a better fish.

The first fish did not jump. It had taken the Golden Olive Bumble which is my first – and often enough my last and only – choice of top dropper on a wild mountain water. What it did was twist and turn, raffling the rest of the leader and flies into disaster. For twelve inches of trout that fish made a real meal of it. Philip was well into a second fish while I was still under the bonnet making repairs. And so it went on around the shore of Llyn Egnant. Mountain lakes, llyns, loughs, lochs – call them what you will – are an endless fascination to me. Philip and I had dabbled flies into four waters all within one mile of tumbled crags and moorland. Both of us, with different flies, had caught fish in the first and the last. On the first we caught nothing but tiny trout. On the last, nothing smaller than twelve inches. And not a thing, not a rise or a tug, on the other two. Why? It was early in the season and the fish we caught were in shallow water which might have warmed up in what passes for sun in those parts. It could have been the time of day but I doubt it. We made out way back to the car and had coffee from a flask which is a little bit like coffee from a Kelly but not much. We had sandwiches instead of a hot cassoulet on the camping stove. There was still some light left of the March day and so we strolled down to the little lake where we had started. They were still at it. The breeze faltered as the light drained from the sky and the surface was pocked with the rings of tiny trout eating whatever tiny trout eat. And we had another half-dozen or so on the dry fly.

Funny sort of day to start to the season. On the one hand there was the grievous loss of my kettles and flippers and so forth and the bad-toothache of a front offside drive-shaft. On the other was a fine day in wild country hills with quite enough fish and no *"frontal maulings with large claw marks on the neck and throat"*.

61

I'd call that a win on points.

Teifi Pools are now controlled by the Tregaron Angling Association, tickets are £13 – no longer from the cottage on the road leading to the lakes, but from various shops around the area. Best go to www.tregaronangling.com for details

9

Fishing on Sail

*J*ust a hundred years ago most of the world's fishing fleets were still driven by sail. And then some leaden soul went and invented the internal combustion engine and, little by little, the creak of rigging and romantic billows of canvas gave way to the thump of a Lister diesel and billows of blue exhaust. Until, by the last quarter of the 20th Century, sail had disappeared from every commercial fishery in Europe.

Except one. In one tiny outpost of Europe, like Asterix's defiant village holding out against a sea of grey Roman civilisation, one ancient fishery carries on as if the propeller and diesel engine had never been invented. The boats and sailing rig have not changed for centuries: the fishing gear has hardly changed since its development in Roman times. Everything is done by the power of wind and muscle. This singular fishery is not to be found at the pointy end of a remote Norwegian fjord, nor in some undeveloped scatter of islands in the Levant. You'll find it just off Falmouth, in deepest Cornwall.

Byelaws passed in the early 20th Century prohibit the use of motors, for moving the boat or working the gear, on any vessel fishing for oysters in the Truro Oyster Fishery between Truro and the sea at Falmouth. This splendid edict, passed by some long-ago local Luddites, has preserved the sights and traditions of Europe's only surviving commercial sailing fleet.

There are about 20 Falmouth Working Boats fishing the Truro oyster fishery in the estuary of the River Fal. At 8.30 on a cold, bright morning in late March I was standing on one of them. The *Boy Willie* has been fishing these waters for 150 years, worked for several generations by the Vinnicombe family. Tim Vinnicombe had hoisted the massive gaff mainsail, run the jib out to the end of the prodigious bowsprit and was preparing to slip the moorings. He pressed a button and the Lister diesel chugged into life. Hang on - what about all that romantic sound-of-the-wind-in-the-sails stuff? Motors, it seems are all right to get out to the fishing grounds. From 9 o'clock, when fishing starts, they are verboten.

It was one minute to nine. We had reached the banks on the far side of the Fal. We were preparing the oyster dredges and their lines on the side decks as *Dolly*, another oyster boat, passed ahead under full sail and rounded to. She was a magnificent sight under her gaff cutter rig. And within thirty seconds she was a wreck.

That's what it looked like. The jib had fallen, slumped to leeward of the bowsprit: the staysail was lying on the deck: the main gaff had dropped drunkenly, collapsing the mainsail in half. She was drifting with the tide. I thought I ought to point this out to Tim - go to the succour of fellow mariners in distress and all that. I got a pitying look. That mainsail was *scandalised* - deliberately collapsed: Dolly was fishing. Oysters, it turns out, are dredged as the boats drift, the skipper steering the drift by a delicate balance of the collapsed mainsail and that scrap of jib.

By now Tim was hauling in the first dredge hand-over-hand. He levered the oyster dredge on board and spilled it into a tray. Somehow, I had imagined we would get oysters. Mostly we got *culch*.

Culch is the jumble of old oyster shells, stones and small debris that is the vital ingredient of an oyster bed. Culch is what the *spat* - the embryonic oyster spawn - must encounter and cling

64

to in order to grow into another oyster. And the trouble with culch formed from a millennium's worth of old oyster shells is that it looks an awful lot like the oysters we are searching for. There are other creatures in the culch. Scallops are prizes to be counted and the score called out to passing oystermen as a sort of side-bet. Any starfish is thrown in a bucket: starfish kill and eat oysters. I used to quite like starfish. But we oystermen hate them.

We aren't all that keen on slipper limpets either. These foreign invaders from America were everywhere amongst the culch, congregating in curious stacks on the oysters' shells and competing for their food. They glory in the scientific name of *Crepidula fornicata* and can grow a penis longer than the rest of their body. Which is nice. The stuff you find out on an oyster dredger. Occasionally you find oysters. The big ones go in the sack, the small ones go back into the culch and are slipped overboard. And then another dredge is hauled up, emptied and culled for oysters. Do that for another six hours and you may find that much of the romance of fishing under sail has escaped you.

But not quite all.

10

Three More in Norway

*I*t began a couple of years ago when a man appeared round the side of our house. It was a timely appearance because my son-in-law-the-teacher was in the kitchen taping an audio version of Cluedo for his junior class and we were short of someone to be the voice of Professor Plum. We asked the man if he would be Professor Plum. He said he would. Poor chap: he had been invited round for coffee by a mutual friend and found himself accused of murdering someone in the ballroom with the lead piping. And that was how I met Digby.

Digby is a fisherman. He lives a couple of villages away and the next time we met, at his house, he lent me a treasured book and urged me to read it. And I really meant to but somehow, by the time he phoned and politely asked for it back several months later, I just hadn't got round to it. In a fit of guilt I found the thing, opened it and began to read. Which is why Digby, Philip and I found ourselves the other day standing on a wooden jetty, gazing along a lake of an improbable turquoise, flanked by cliffs which rose sheer from the water and kept on going for two thousand feet.

The book was called *Three in Norway - by Two of Them*. Of course, it must be possible for someone to read this book and not have to go to Norway, to be where they had been and to fish the waters they fished - it just wasn't possible for me. I had to go. It is that sort of book.

Three in Norway is a journal of a sporting holiday. Three youngish men decide to spend the summer amid the peaks and glaciers of the Jotunheimen Mountains, the highest bits of northern Europe. The journey begins, for one of them at least, in London, transporting a vast mountain of supplies, rods, guns, packing-cases, tents and a Canadian canoe in a horse-drawn carriage to ribald jeers of "boat ahoy!" and the immense enjoyment of the populace. I was struck by the similarity to my favourite novel, *Three Men in A Boat*. Apart from the titles, both begin in the same way. There is the same banter between the three men, each complaining of the various character defects and idiosyncrasies of the others: there are the same accounts of mishaps and misfortune described with the same dry wit. *Three Men in Boat* has inspired many imitations over the years: I thought I had found another, perhaps the finest, in *Three in Norway*. And then I looked at the publication dates in the front of the book: *Three in Norway* was published in 1882 - seven years *before Three Men in Boat* appeared in print.

I was intrigued. It seemed that one of the greatest comic novels in the English language had, as its model, an obscure and forgotten fishing book. I delved a little deeper into the book and its history. It was not obscure at all: *Three in Norway* had been something of a best-seller in its day, already in its fourth edition when *Three Men in a Boat* was written.

The account begins on 8th July 1880 in Hull where Esau and the Skipper board a steamer bound for Christiania (now Oslo). These two would travel into the mountains where they would be joined by John. They transported their mountain of luggage, including "four guncases, seven rods, a bundle of axes, a spade and other necessary tools" and the two large Canadian canoes, by train to Eidsvoll where they loaded the whole lot onto the paddle-steamer

Skibladner for the journey along the length of Lake Mjøsa to Lillehammer. (Incredibly, that ship is still in service on the same route - the world's oldest steam ship). At Lillehammer, on 14th July, the tough stuff began in earnest.

They were heading for Gjende Lake in the heart of the Jotunfjeld. Roads are not thick on the ground in these parts now: they were largely non-existent then, just a series of tracks between farmsteads and villages. They walked between these, hiring local men to haul the load on wagons. When they reached one of the long, thin lakes of the region they piled the luggage into the canoes and paddled themselves onwards. In the late afternoon of the 15th July they landed on the shore of Espedals Vand. They unloaded the canoes, pitched the tent and cooked "a simple dinner of bacon, eggs, and jam, the last dinner during our trip at which trout did not find a place". That evening the two of them fished for the first time. As Esau left the shore he noticed:

"the Skipper's rod in the familiar Norwegian shape of a bow, and found him struggling with two on at the same time, both of which he landed, and found to be over 1lb each".

It was round about the time I read this that I realised I would have to see this place for myself.

Jotunheimen is now a national park. I did not know if fishing would be allowed there. I phoned the park's tourist information office to ask about fishing. I explained where I wanted to fish and told the man about finding a forgotten book, *Three in Norway*. I was about to outline the story when he asked, "Would you like to see their tent?"

I was stunned.

"Do you know this book?" I asked.

"Of course. In Norway it is very famous," he said.

Three in Norway - by Two of Them, it seems, though long forgotten in England, is still venerated in Norway where it has hardly been out of print in the century or so since it was first published. In Norway it is a well-loved classic, its authors still regarded as important figures in the history of Norwegian mountain sports. One of the prized exhibits of the Norsk Fjellmuseum - Norwegian Mountain Museum - is the tent that had been their home and that figures in the many of the book's illustrations.

Well, of course, I had to see their tent. And so it was that three of us, Digby, Philip and I, planned a fishing pilgrimage to Memurubu, the little oasis set amid the forbidding cliffs of Lake Gjende, where they had camped and fished for a month, 123 years ago.

Lees, Clutterbuck and Kennedy, the three in Norway, were away for three months in all. How times have changed: now, surrounded by every labour-saving appliance devised in a century of progress, we could only wangle a week away from wives and work.

We, too, were starting at Oslo: our mountain of luggage reduced to 75Kg, the baggage allowance for three on the Norwegian Air Shuttle flight from Stansted. We didn't bother with the spades and axes. Or the canoes. We landed an hour before midnight: by daybreak we were two hundred miles further north and the terrain was becoming distinctly lumpy with large bits of Norway disappearing up into the clouds.

We had not known what weather to pack for. England was enjoying the best summer I could remember but we would be fishing amid glaciers. And it can rain a bit. A hundred years ago it had rained for most of July. On the 18th it . . . *"continued raining in a keep-at-it-all-day-if-you-like kind of manner, so we resided in the tent and read, and indulged in whisky and water for lunch to counteract any ill effects of the reading - for some of it was poetry"*

We had come prepared for the rain: Digby had brought a bottle of scotch. Since a regrettable incident in April 1965, I am unable to drink scotch so I had brought a bottle of gin. In Lom, at the last supermarket before the mountains, we found tonic water and a lemon. We were ready for the wilderness.

It was difficult to feel intrepid in the warm sunshine as we drove along the eastern flank of Jotunheimen - the "Home of the Giants". The road vaulted a small river which barrelled out of a cleft in the rocks to rattle beneath the bridge and swing off through the trees. We felt like a break and pulled the car in beyond the bridge. It is hard to resist the temptation to put up a rod and flick a fly over a stream like this. So we didn't bother. Resisting, that is. Within a minute a flashing little trout rose to grab Digby's dry fly. It was our first fish from Jotunheimen. We packed the rods away and carried on to Gjende.

Lees and Clutterbuck had arrived here on the last day of July. *"Gjendin"*, they wrote, *"is perhaps the most beautiful, certainly the wildest and grandest, lake in Norway . . . It is eleven miles long; very deep; very blue; and on all sides rising sheer out of the water for from 1000 to 4000 feet are vast black mountains with snow clad summits; for it lies in the very heart of the highest mountains in Norway . . . along the greater part of its length there is no level place large enough to pitch a tent; no vegetation except berries and moss; and no possibility of scaling the frowning cliffs by which it is surrounded . . . although its first appearance is almost repellent, every moment of gazing seems to increase its beauty and awe inspiring grandeur."*

One week and 123 years later, Gjende was much the same. Except for the car park. It is a large car park and it was crammed with cars for it lies at one end of Norway's most popular hiking trail. And Norwegians dearly love to hike. The Besseggen trail follows the knife-sharp ridge above the northern shore where Ibsen had the eponymous *Peer Gynt*, riding a buck reindeer, leap into the blue waters of Gjende, two-and-a-half thousand feet below. There is a single break in these forbidding cliffs where the tumbling melt waters from the Memuru Glacier have carved a notch down to the lake shore. Here Lees and Clutterbuck could land their canoes.

"It is about halfway up the lake on the north shore, and is a very pretty little valley, profusely supplied with edible berries, surrounded by a thick birch covert and with more grass than we ever expected to find at this altitude"

Here at Memurubu they made their camp. The next day they were joined by the local hunter they had engaged. Öla *"produced the sack of potatoes and the cook, like a conjuring trick, from somewhere behind him, out of his hat or his coat tails . . . Öla is a big good-looking man, rather too much of a gentleman, we fear: but Ivar is without doubt a perfect ass, and will never be able to do anything in the way of cookery, except perhaps boil a potato, and even in that enterprise we consider it would be six to four on the potato".*

They made an extension to their tent for the hired help but Öla and Ivar preferred *"living in a wretched little stone dog-kennel . . . built by drovers, or some other dirty people . . ."* The stone hut, built into the hillside and roofed with turf, belonged to the family which each year brought cattle across the mountains to graze that precious grass. The hut is still there. And so is the family.

Kjetil Sveine and his family own and run the Memurubu Turisthytte, a cross between a hotel and youth-hostel, which accommodates and cossets the thousands of hikers that stagger down the other end of the Besseggen Ridge. There is another way to get to Memurubu. The Three had paddled their own canoes but there was then a boat ferrying people and supplies to Gjendebu at the other end of the lake. There still is. A modern ferry ploughs across the blue waters of Gjende, carrying hikers from Memurubu and Gjendebu. It was waiting beside us as we stood on the jetty at Gjendesheim.

We had bought our fishing licences in the kiosk beside the jetty. They were remarkably cheap: a week's fishing on most of the lakes and rivers around Gjendesheim costs just 100 Kroner - around £8. And we had made two other notable discoveries at the kiosk: fishermen hereabouts wish each other luck with the call of *"shit fiske"* and the beer we were drinking was called "arse". And so we set off.

The ferry was packed with bronzed folk in shorts and walking boots. Digby stood at the front of the boat with his GPS gizmo and announced that we were at Gjendesheim (which we knew) and that we were travelling at 9.4 knots (which we didn't). There were times in the next week when it might have been useful to know where we were and how fast we were walking but this was the last occasion that Digby and his GPS were in the same place at the same time. The boat cruised down a blue lake unruffled by rising fish and drew into the wooden dock at Memurubu.

We humped our 75kgs of baggage up the short incline to the hotel, dug out rods, reels and flies from its depths and made our way excitedly along the lake shore. Three hours later we slunk back, dejected and defeated. Much the same had happened to our first three fishermen:

"After dinner we tried all this portion of the lake for fish without success, and coming back received the awful intelligence from Öla that there are no fish in any part of Gjendin except the extreme ends. This is a dreadful blow to us . . ."

They were to prove Öla spectacularly wrong within a week - but we were to be there only another five days. That evening we poured over the map with Kjetil. Close to the forbidding shore of Gjende we could see a pattern of smaller, more manageable, lakes. Did they hold trout? Kjetil grinned. He used the word "Eldorado" a lot. The first little lake didn't seem to be more than a mile or so from Memurubu and less than two hundred yards from the shore of Gjende. Then we looked more closely at the map. There seemed to be an awful lot of brown contour lines packed into that two hundred yards. There were one-and-a-half thousand foot's worth - straight up.

Tomorrow we would start climbing. Ain't that always the way

with Eldorados?

"The Norwegians call their mountains either 'Tind', which means a cone, or 'Hö', a round top . . ."

I was reading from "Three in Norway", the book that had brought us here to the Jotunheimen mountains. It was written a hundred-and-twenty-three years ago but the mountains haven't changed. Some are pointy, some are roundy: they are all high. We were off to fish a pattern of lakes that lay a couple of miles from the hostel at Memurubu. We could see the track: it climbed steeply from the river beside us and straight over the top of *Sjugurdtinden* - one of the pointy ones. And so we began to climb.

It was a stiffish climb and blokes like us find themselves doing a lot of puffing and breathing heavily and stopping to admire the view. At every stop another peak of the Jotunheimen mountains came into view. The forbidding cliffs that enclose Gjende are streaked with torrents of white water that tumble two thousand feet into the lake. As we climbed higher we could see their source in the snowfields and glaciers above the cliffs. These cliffs are slightly lower on our side of Gjende: here the cascades are fed by mountain tarns. One of them appeared before us as we made our way around the top of Sjugurdtinden.

It is something they put in the air here - or perhaps something they take out - because it is extraordinarily clear. This makes it very hard to judge distances. We were to find this time and again. Now, we looked down on a tarn that appeared to drain into the blue waters of Gjende just a short drop below. In fact it was a fall of 1000 feet. The tarn looked much like any lochan in the mountains of northwest Scotland, set in a hollow of moss, lichens and rock. The water was frighteningly clear. The high clouds chose this moment to open and then shrink, revealing shallows and sharp drop-offs around the tarn. And so we got down to fish.

The writers of *Three in Norway* are very coy about the flies that caught all their fish. One day they caught twenty fish totalling 44lbs:

"All were caught on two patterns of fly, namely - No, philanthropy has limits and no man can expect to be told patterns of flies".

So we all began blind, each of us picking favourite flies. My trusty team of Black Pennel, Cinnamon and Gold and Golden Olive Bumble failed utterly, so I put up the dapping rod and dapped daddies - which also failed. Philip did no better and we were wondering whether such high lakes might freeze solid in winter and be devoid of fish when Digby called from the far side of the tarn. He was into our first Gjende trout.

I was expecting something small and dark from these high tarns. This was a magnificent creature of 15½ inches, deep-bodied and boldly speckled. So we kept fishing. It was well past noon under a cloudless sky. We caught no more fish on that first tarn and worked our way down along others that lie in the hollows of the high ground between four and five thousand feet. Beside the largest of these, Langtjonne, we found the remains of a large clinker boat and tried to imagine how on earth it got here. And why. On Langtjonne, Philip began to catch fish and I began to envy the pair of them.

The original Three in Norway had camped on the tiny patch of level ground at Memurubu. For three months they fished these waters, stalked the elusive mountain reindeer and dined on venison and trout. Digby, keen to recreate their experience, had his first fish cooked and served to us in the hostel restaurant that evening. It was shared by an elderly German hiker at our table. His name was Herr Fischer. Between guffaws, he pointed out that everyone at our table was a "fisher". On gales of such Teutonic wit the evening swiftly passed.

The Three in Norway had amused themselves at mealtimes by inventing elaborate, whimsical menus to describe their inevitable trout and occasional venison. This dullish diet improved immeasurably when "Esau" (James Lees) constructed an ingenious bread oven in stone and turf with a flue leading up a steep bank behind the camp. That evening we went in search of this relic of their visit.

Digby was in a state. He was fretting, emptying every bag and rummaging through the debris. He had lost his moustache, he said: we wondered if that was all he had lost. He had found his sideburns - he held them up - but the moustache had vanished. In his fervour to re-enact the Victorian visit of the Three in Norway, it seems, Digby had laboured long over a hot fly-tying vice. He had constructed false sideburns and a luxuriant moustache. He wanted to look the part when we photographed the oven. Now he was sure it must have fallen out when we bought our fishing licences at Gjendesheim. That missing moustache would come to haunt our days in the mountains.

The lake where the Three had caught that prodigious bag of trout was private fishing then and is private fishing now, but a phone call from Kjetil, our host at Memurubu, got us permission to spend a day on Russvatnet. Russvatnet lies two miles over the hill from Memurubu but that hill is one-and-a-half thousand feet above Memurubu. It is the beginning of the popular hiking trail along the Besseggen Ridge and we trudged up the track, being overtaken by young children and wiry old couples - even a dog carrying panniers went past us as we panted upwards.

Russvatnet, when we got there, daunted me. The wind had dropped away to nothing under a cloudless sky. Russvatnet is not as dramatic as Gjende, cliffs do not fall sheer to the water. It is just the scale of everything that intimidates. At this height there are no trees to give a notion of size and distance. In the clear air, the eye does not register the vastness of the surroundings - it just shrinks any human into insignificance. I cannot say I loved Russvatnet. We arrived in the late morning - around the time, the Three noted, that any morning rises stopped. We stared across the lake with the mountains beyond mirrored in its surface. Casting into that lot feels awfully foolish. We did it anyway.

After a fruitless few hours I wandered around to the other side of the lake where a river flowed across a gravelly delta. The water was ice cold from the snowmelt above. I *think* I saw a fish turn as I cast into the outflow. Digby was doing no better, even when the shadow cast by Besshoe crept across the water and a slight breeze ruffled its surface. Philip had all but disappeared into the distance: we could just make out a tiny speck of white that flickered as we watched. It turned out he was waving. Philip had just caught the three best wild mountain trout of his life, all between 1½ and 2lb.

It can happen like that. In the bumper bag the Three in Norway had taken one day on Russvatnet, "Esau" had fifteen fish, "The Skipper" had four and John only one. I wish I had read the book more closely before we went. They landed this bag, totalling 44lbs, in the last week of August. There is a footnote at the bottom of the page: "*We have found as many as three mice in the stomach of a Rus Vand trout.*" These "mice" were probably lemmings who inhabit these upland parts (we saw numerous holes between the mossy rocks). They migrate in autumn but the migration can become a tide, crossing lakes and rivers, in the cyclical "lemming years" when their population explodes. When something similar happened in New Zealand four years ago, prodigious number of huge trout were taken and angling records smashed as the fish feasted on migrating mice. In the late summer of 1880 the trout of Russvatnet were huge, averaging over 2lbs and.....

"*nearly all were caught in water so shallow that the dorsal fin of the fish was often visible in his mad rushes hither and thither; this made it extremely difficult to prevent the tail fly being hung up on a rock whenever a fish was hooked on the dropper, and not a few were lost in this manner.*"

I fancy those huge trout were hunting mice.

Long hikes into the mountains had left us knackered. We decided on a rest day and a trip up the lake to Gjendesheim. Digby was still fretting about his lost   moustache and, when we got to the village, he asked Greta, the woman who issued our fishing licences, whether she had come across a moustache. It was an ill-advised enquiry and capable of misunderstanding: things got quite unpleasant until the situation was explained. Digby perked up when one of the hikers who had overheard the question and got embroiled in disentangling Digby from the mess, told him that Norwegians made false moustaches from a hairy growth found on certain birch trees in the forest. Somehow, we don't seem to get this calibre of conversation round our way.

It was another cloudless day. A hundred and twenty three years before they had written: *"We have got quite tired of writing 'Another beautiful day,' and in future shall bring notebooks to Norway with these words ready-printed at the top of each page."* It was not a day to fish another lake of clear water.

The Sjoa River which leaves the lake at Gjendesheim has a quiet renown. The Three had splendid fishing here in 1880. Other Englishmen followed. And Americans: I was re-reading Negley Farson's classic "Going Fishing" the other day and found he had been there in the 1930s. It even has its own fly - the Gjende Fly - a small black number which hatches in vast clouds on the few hundred yards at the start of the river and which, we were told, we were a fortnight too early to experience. What with the mice and the Gjende Fly, a trout hereabouts in late August must be spoilt for choice.

The fishing had been hard under clear skies. We fancied something a little easier on our day off. I don't know if you remember - I certainly did - that on our way into Jotunheimen we had crossed a small rocky river. We had spotted the river from the road as it came tumbling out of a narrow cleft in the rocks. We had stopped for a few minutes to stretch our legs and we had caught our first fish. As simple as that.

The River Veo begins in the next-door glacier to the river that roars into Gjende at Memurubu. Why the Veo does not roar, I don't know: it just doesn't. Why the Veo is not the same colour of dirty soap-suds from glacial melt I don't know either: it just isn't. It is a crystal stream fussing between smooth boulders. It has probably done a fair amount of roaring in its time because those boulders are very big and very smooth. But in the first week of August it bounced jauntily from pool to pool. There is hardly room on a stream like this to fish together. Digby went downstream towards the junction with the majestic Sjoa. Philip began at the cleft in the rocks where we had seen the river emerge. I went upstream, following the rim of a narrow gorge which steepened as I went deeper into the forest. The track climbed higher and higher above the water which ran unseen beneath overhanging cliffs. I was beginning to despair of ever getting near the stuff when a bend threw the river into view far below me. I was looking down at the perfect pool.

The sunlight showed every detail of a gravel bottom where the waters pulled between small rocks. Upstream the pool deepened until, at the narrow neck, the water tumbled white into the deep shadow of a vertical cliff. Trout would be lined up along that wall. I could smell them from all the way up here. I eased my way down towards the rocky wall of the gorge and found a gully where I could lower myself down on roots and saplings. At river level the gorge was easy going, scrambling over smooth boulders. I settled myself near the tail of the pool and cast up between two rocks. A small shape detached from the bottom and shot to the surface. There is nothing difficult in this sort of fishing: it is pure pleasure. There will be fish wherever a current flows over any depth at all. I edged up the pool. I had taken seven fish when I heard a scrambling behind me and Philip arrived at my perfect pool. We shared the fish that lay along the wall, each one a little larger than the one behind until we reached the white water at the neck. Then we scrambled between the rocks and found ourselves at the tail of another perfect pool. We had taken fifteen fish from those two small pools when more scrambling heralded Digby's arrival.

And so we went on, leapfrogging our way between the boulders. We worked up both sides of the river. Sometimes the stream widened and split into several channels and there were pools enough for all. At other times there was a single channel but a second angler, casting from the other side would pull out fish the first had not spotted. Where the sunlight reached we could follow every move of the fish but the better fish lurked in the shadows of overhangs where a bobbing fly would disappear in a swirl.

And so it went on. When the cliffs closed in on one side we could make our way across the boulders to the other side: when they closed in from both sides we just waded into the water, shoes, socks, trousers and all. We were off duty. One day I will follow that splendid stream until one of us, the trout or I, gives in but the last boat back to Memurubu left Gjendesheim at 2.25pm and all too soon we were clambering back up the side of the gorge and legging it back through the forest of pine and birch. We all agreed we had just fished the perfect river.

Digby had not fretted about his moustache for some hours but the birch wood brought it all back to him. Hanging from a branch he found a tuft of the mysterious curly "hair". It was extraordinary stuff. Digby was delighted. It was better than the original, he declared, and stuffed some in his pocket. That evening a tangle of the stuff was lurking beneath Digby's nose as he posed alongside a curious construction of flat boulders built into a mossy bank, hidden in a thicket of birch and willow.

We had found the bread oven, built by "Esau" a century before.

There is a curious postscript to this tale. The next day we left Gjende for home. As we settled into our seats after take-off, Philip and I were playing dice and Digby got out the "The Spectator" magazine he had been reading on the flight over. He gave a small cry of discovery. The cover illustration was a cartoon of a reclining lady, wearing a louche smile and not a lot else. Stuck to her lower abdomen, like some bizarre, free-gift merkin, was Digby's missing moustache.

Three In Norway - by Two Of Them is published by the Flyfishers Classic Library. There is also a paperback edition, tel: 01654 702837

The Turisthytte at Memurubu offers every level of accommodation from a place to pitch a tent to en-suite double bedrooms with bunks and dormitories in between. For details, visit www.memurubu.no or phone Kjetil Sveine, tel: 0047 6123 8999 or (mobile) 9154 2620. Kjetil, like everyone else, speaks excellent English. The ferry from Gjendesheim to Memurubu costs 120 Kr return. Last scheduled sailing is at 2.25pm. Details at www.gjende.no

The Tourist Information Centre for the Jotunheimen National Park is in Lom, tel: 0047 6121 1600 or visit www.fjell.museum.no

There used to be English language versions of these last two. Now they are automatically translated by Google which may give you a laugh. Or a headache.

11

Unnatural Practices

*I*t is a well-established tradition that an Englishman must travel abroad in order to indulge a penchant for practices long-outlawed and reviled in his native land. He seeks more lenient lands where his depraved urges will be tolerated if not actively encouraged. That's what I did last summer, anyway. Not to Thailand or Algiers, though: I went to Norway.

Norway is not a land renowned for licentious libertines but then, on this occasion, I was not seeking bizarre sexual liaisons. I just wanted to catch some trout. Trout fishing is, by and large, an innocuous pastime but the method I was using, if used in Britain, could land me in chokey for up to two years.

It all began innocently enough, as such tales of degradation and depravity often do. There were three of us: Digby, Philip and me. We had driven through the night to arrive at the little town of Lom, on the flanks of the Jotunheimen Mountains. We were following the footsteps of three sporting-type Englishmen who had hiked and fished and shot their way through these mountains in 1880. I have already described their journey - and ours - in these pages. You may have read it. Your maiden aunt may have read it and she would have found nothing therein, with the possible exception of Digby's false moustache, that could offend that lady's delicate sensibilities. But that, Gentle Reader, was the expurgated version of the trip. I had glossed over the regrettable events at Lom.

We had no business going to Lom. The three sporting gentlemen of 1880 never visited the place in their travels. But their tent had. Lom is the home of the Norwegian Mountain Museum and one of the prized exhibits is the much-patched tent used by Lees, Clutterbuck and Kennedy during their months in the mountains. We just had to see it.

So we did. The Norsk Fjellmuseum is also the tourist information office for the mountains. Here we could get the licences to fish the mountain lakes that our predecessors had fished. It was our first time fishing in these parts: we were also hoping to get some local advice. A small blue leaflet at the information desk urged us to "Try your fishing luck" and advertised the services of Lom Fiske Guiding. Which is how we met Odd Erik. I am not making this up: that is his name.

We arranged to meet Odd Erik in the museum car park. A turbulent river was thrashing past the place and bursting over a waterfall. It didn't look at all fishy. It looked frightening.

The map in my 1884 edition of "Three In Norway", shows Lom lying beside the long ribbon of water - "Lake Vaage". The map on the back of Odd Erik's leaflet describes the same water as the River Otta. They are both right. The Jotunheimen Mountains are the highest bits of Northern Europe: glaciers and snowfields lie amid the peaks throughout the year. In winter and early spring, when the place is locked in ice, the Otta river winds a sinuous course across a broad valley bottom. In the warmer months the ice-melt from the glaciers swells the tributaries, and the river spreads across the valley as a shallow lake. But the whole lake is flowing, swiftly in places where the water is shallow or in the winding river channel hidden beneath the surface. It was a warm day in the first week of August and the ice-melt was tumbling from the mountains, carrying the sand and silt scraped off the pointier bits of Norway. We parked the car on a beach of this sand and wondered where, in this expanse of moving water, to start. Which is why we had asked Odd Erik along.

We launched his dinghy and motored across the river, tying up to a rocky outcrop on the other bank. By climbing above the water it was possible to spot subtle differences in the water. The deeper channel of the hidden river was slightly bluer with ice-melt: the shallower water was a shade browner. The trout and grayling of the Otta are conservative creatures. They could roam where they wish but they tend to stick to the submerged river channel. The trick is to find it. From above we could see that the channel ran close to our shore, swinging around the rocky outcrop. The problem was that, as soon as we lowered ourselves into the water, the differences in colour disappeared. We edged nervously in waist-deep water, feeling for the channel. The wading was simple enough: glaciers grind exceeding small and the bottom was a fine silt. The channel, when we found it, was sudden and the silt edges decidedly slippery but once we knew where it was we could fish along the channel with a heavy nymph. Odd Erik was doubtful about our nymphs. In this high summer water he favoured trundling a worm along the channel. But we had principles - or Digby did, at any rate - and we stuck to our nymphs. Ah! How high-minded and unsullied we were then.

Digby was the first into fish. It was a trout of half a pound or so. This first small fish had a sprinkling of tiny red spots on its flanks. Larger fish from these glacial waters are silver, flecked with black and very handsome.

Odd Erik was next. Working the channel with his worm he was taking fish after fish. Digby had got his eye in as well: his goldhead was taking fewer fish than the worm but they were bigger with one or two close to a pound. He was catching grayling, too. Philip and I had not had a touch. Odd Erik took pity on me and lent me his worming tackle. I rather wished he hadn't. I didn't get a touch with that either.

We moved up river. Above the town the water (I don't know whether to call it a lake or a river) broadened. It was a little unnerving to step out of the boat in the middle of the thing. We knew there were channels: we just didn't know where. We shuffled along looking for an edge. The contrast was greater here, the shallows were shallower, the drop-off sudden and obvious. We stood in the browner bits and fished into the bluer bits. And we caught fish.

We could have left Lom then. We could have fished in the mountains and I could have returned home without a stain on the family escutcheon. It was true that I had experimented with a worm - but I hadn't actually inhaled. Perhaps we should have gone but we didn't. Like many another slide into sin, it began with a drink.

Alcohol is fiercely expensive in Norway so I had bought some gin in the duty free at Stansted. What was needed now was tonic and a lemon. There is a supermarket in Lom. Downstairs it is the usual sort of supermarket, with the usual sort of lemons and tonic water, but there are stairs to another floor with clothes and hardware and gardening stuff. And at the top of the stairs, on the left, there is fishing tackle.

There were the usual sorts of tackle: racks of rods and assortments of spinners and spoons. There were reels and waders. And there, amid the lines and flies, was a curious device. I had a notion what it might be. It was an otter.

This otter is not the playful creature that takes lumps out of Virginia McKenna in "Ring of Bright Water": it is an ancient and cunning device for catching trout. Though somewhat illegal, otter fishing is not unknown in Britain. I have found the remains of an otter amongst the driftwood beside a Hebridean loch. It was a crude affair of rough wood and rusty wire. In Shetland I was promised one in action but the friend of a friend of a friend didn't turn up: it was probably just as well. But here, on open shelves, within reach of maiden aunts and young children, there were five different models for sale in one small supermarket, including a handy, folding version. It was like finding a display of whips and bondage rubber-ware in Sainsburys.

In Norway, it seems, the otter is a traditional and legitimate piece of fishing tackle. It is not a complex piece of kit: a bevelled wooden board around two feet long is weighted with a metal strip along one edge. A wire frame, like a small curtain rail, runs along one face and a ring slides along this rail. And that is about it. Just how this contraption was going to catch trout I didn't quite fathom. But I was standing next to a man who did. That evening Odd Erik agreed to take us ottering.

We had driven up into the mountains, to a smaller variation on the thin-lake-wide-river theme. It was flat calm. Digby and Philip went off to fish their flies. They wished no part of these proceedings. Odd Erik lifted his otterboard from the car. I had missed an essential part of the kit. He was holding a fishing line wrapped like a kite string around a plastic frame. He attached the end to the ring on the otter rail and, unwrapping some line, he launched the little vessel into the shallows.

The metal weight ensured that the board floated edge-upwards. It worked just like a kite: as Odd Erik walked along the shore towing the line, the otter pulled away from him, out across the water – just as a kite would climb up into the sky. He paid out more line as he walked, pausing now and then to detach a fly on a dropper attached to the main line. Soon the otter was thirty yards or so offshore and straining away like a dog on a lead. Ten flies on droppers hung at intervals along the line between the otter and the fisherman. By raising or lowering the line Odd Erik could make the things swim through the water or dance across the surface.

I was fascinated: I couldn't wait to have a go. And so we

walked on round the shore, two blokes walking a rather reluctant dog on a longish lead, whilst behind us a rake of flies was fishing a great swathe of the lake. The first thirty yards of a lake are usually the most productive and it was not long before a splash at the surface was matched by a sharp tug of a fish on the line. I had caught my first trout on the otter.

It was then that I spotted a problem with this admirable system: pulling on the line sends the otter out into the lake. How could I get the fish in? This was the cunning bit. Odd Erik gave a firm pull on the line: the otter surged ahead but, because we had stopped walking, the water resistance on the line pulled the sliding ring to the other end of that wire frame on the side of the otter. Now the otter changed direction and a steady pull sent it surging towards the shore. Odd Erik wound the line and flies back onto the handle and we retrieved the fish. It was so cunning and yet so simple. And so effective.

Just how effective we would discover later that week. From Lom we went on to Lake Gjende, a vast trench of deep, cold water, high in the heart of the Jotunheimen Mountains. Fish are to be found at either end but they are rarely taken in the body of the lake. Certainly not by us. We had tried and failed with the fly on several evenings. On our last evening we fished with Kjetil, our host at Memurubu on Lake Gjende. He launched the daddy of all otter-boards, a huge contraption with outriggers, swimming twenty spinners across this forbidding stretch of water. With the otter we caught six fish, up to two pounds, in thirty minutes.

Now, of course, this is all very wicked and depraved. You might suppose that it is the sheer number of lures a fisherman can deploy whilst ottering that so offends the vaunted British sense of fair play. But that can't be the whole answer: the traditional, and perfectly legal, char tackle of the English Lake District trails up to twenty spinners on two long lines reaching down into depths of ninety feet or so - much the same as Odd Erik's otter board but arranged vertically rather than horizontally.

Perhaps that is the problem with ottering: we British know instinctively that there are activities which, when done vertically, may be innocent enough but which are sordid and sinful in the horizontal.

Particularly when they are as much fun as ottering.

This story, the third from a memorable trip to the Jotunheim mountains of Norway, should have appeared in Trout and Salmon in July 2004. It was never published. Shortly before it went to the printers, the editor had a dream – I am not making this up, either. In this dream the righteous indignation of the angling world was roused to damaging fury by my account of fishing with an otter, which gave details of the making of an illegal piece of kit. It was like publishing bomb-making instructions in the Woman's Weekly, I suppose. "I can't ignore a dream like that," said the editor.

This editing by oneiromancy (the interpretation of dreams - I've just looked it up) was a new one on me. I could see its appeal: so much cleaner than picking through the entrails of sacrificed chickens. But I cannot say I was not miffed. So miffed, indeed, that in the article I wrote to replace it, I inserted an obvious and ludicrous fib. The editor had always prided himself on picking up other's mistakes. Well, we would see if he could pick up this one before he sent it off to the printers.

He didn't. To my quiet satisfaction, it duly appeared in this next story, about Lake Vyrnwy.

See if you can spot it.

Not All Beer and Bezencenet

Fishing the River Otta in Lom was surprisingly cheap for such excellent sport. DT: 40 NOK (£3.50), WT: 120 NOK (£10), available from tourist offices. A licence to fish with an otter costs about half as much again.

Odd Erik Aukrust runs Lom Fiske Guiding, Tel: 0047(from UK)61211024 or 99725138 (mobile). He speaks excellent English (as does everybody else).

12

Snooker Break

*I*t was an early morning in late spring. We drove through narrow lanes, getting narrower by the minute as dazzling billows of hawthorn blossom pressed in from either side. Bluebells fringed the steep meadows beyond the hedges and buttercups peppered the lush grass like a rash. The membership of the Dun's Tew Snooker Club is not noted for its poetic bent but even these lumpen souls felt something stirring somewhere beneath their knitted cardies: it was that sort of morning.

Beyond the twee half-timbering of Llanfyllin we followed the Nant Alan upstream, climbing out from the bucolic cosiness of the Welsh Marches towards the sterner stuff of the Cambrian Mountains. A sharp hairpin dropped us down from the first ridge and we descended into the deep valley of the Vyrnwy and the small village of Llanwddyn. One hundred and twenty years ago we would have had to travel another three miles to reach Llanwddyn but, in 1888 or thereabouts, the City Fathers of Liverpool saw fit to move the village and all its inhabitants three miles closer to England. Around the next bend we came across the reason why: the colossal structure of Britain's first masonry dam rose from the trees, stretching its massive bulk across the Vyrnwy valley. It was quite a sight. Even the membership of the Dun's Tew Snooker Club was stirred to something like awe.

"It's a big bugger, all right" said Terry. He was right: it is a big bugger.

A few moments later the membership was not just stirred: it was shaken. Lake Vyrnwy opened in front of us. It, too, is a big bugger - one thousand, one hundred and twenty acres stretching away to the north west and every one of those acres was mirror-calm beneath a cloudless dome of blue sky. It was enough to shake any fly fisherman.

The Dun's Tew Snooker Club was on its Annual Fishing Outing. The entire membership had turned out - as it had on the previous occasion in 1999 when the three of us had fished the hill loughs of County Cork. Today we had come to fish Lake Vyrnwy.

There could hardly be a finer setting for a fishing hotel. Lake Vyrnwy Hotel sits on a wooded ridge, high above the eastern end of the lake. The view from the terrace was breathtaking. The hand of man is not, by and large, a lovesome thing, God wot! It is hard to believe that the lake has not always filled this valley, so perfectly do its wooded shores tumble down to the water. If its Victorian builders had stopped there, Lake Vyrnwy would have been a beautiful corner of the Cambrian Mountains. But they didn't stop there. They had to go and add a Gothic castle, replete with battlements, arrow slits and pointy turrets. And, by some miracle, the thing works. That quixotic pump-house with its arched causeway invests the place with mystery and Arthurian romance. Its reflection rippled as a small boat inched across the mirror surface, heading for the boathouse hidden beneath the trees. Nick had been out fishing before breakfast. We loaded electric motors, batteries, rowlocks and Nick into the car and set off for the far end of the lake where the first hint of a breeze was creasing the surface.

Four miles away to the north-west we found the boats nestling into a tiny beach of grey sand. We hefted engines and batteries onto a couple of boats, loaded rods, bags and sun hats and pushed off onto the lake. The electric motors catch the Arthurian spirit of Vyrnwy, shoving boats and fishermen silently across its waters as if propelled by unseen forces. Which, I suppose, they are.

Nick and I turned left beyond the fringe of trees. The valley sides are so steep that the dense woodland tumbles down to the water and, unable to stop, trees and bushes stand up to their ankles in water, shoved forwards by those behind. Much of the shore shelves steeply and trout lie beneath the overhanging branches, dining on the drizzle of life that trips and stumbles from their leaves. Trout do rise in the middle of Vyrnwy but they only do it to annoy. They don't mean it. They take turns to go out there and lure unsuspecting fishermen into long and fruitless drifts down the middle of the lake. The real stuff is going on beneath those trees.

Anthony Rosser, manager of the Lake Vyrnwy Hotel, had presented the Dun's Tew Snooker Club Annual Fishing Outing with a small booklet - "The Lake Vyrnwy Fishing Book", by Victor Westropp. It was written a quarter of a century ago but the lake and its trout can have changed little in that time. He lists the flies that are successful on Lake Vyrnwy. There are patterns from Alexandra to Zulu, of every size, shape and colour. That is not surprising. Any trout that makes a living grabbing whatever falls from the trees is likely to grab anything that does just that and ask questions later. We tied on Black Pennells and Green Buzzers and anything that looked like it might live in a tree.

We proceeded to stalk the bushes and branches along the shore. An electric motor is ideal for this sort of stuff. With tiny bursts in forward or reverse, the fisherman at the business end can keep the boat drifting along the trees so that both rods can cast into every break in the canopy, under each branch bending low over the water. And when that cast is an inch or so too long he can edge in to unhook the fly. This is fascinating fishing. Every cast is aimed: anything within a foot of a bush or branch anticipates a tug as the fly is inched back towards the angler. And there it was. Our first fish of the day was a scrappy individual of ten inches, full of fight and indignation until the moment he was slipped back into the water.

Philip and Terry had turned right at the beach, towards Rhiwargor Bay at the head of the lake. We found them there an hour later, drifting serenely across the open water, casting to right and left as fishermen do on their first visit to Vyrnwy. Nick and I had fished here once before and we knew about the trout and the trees. We had told them before we started - but folk do not always listen to the Sage Advice of other folk who Have Been There Before, particularly if the first folk are Philip and Terry. I was gliding our boat closer in order to repeat the Sage Advice, when I was stopped by a mysterious force. You know the scene where Captain Kirk of the star-ship "Enterprise" is about to lay hands on the strangely calm, blond-headed, blue-eyed alien of indeterminate sex and he runs into an invisible force-field? It was like that. The boat where Terry and Philip sat was surrounded by an unseen but impenetrable shield of smugness. You could taste the stuff. On the seat between them were two fine fish. They didn't say anything: they didn't have to. Besides, they were preoccupied with another trout towing them around the bay on the end of Terry's line.

And so were we. No sooner had we started a drift across the bay than Nick's line straightened and we had our very own one-pounder. And so to lunch.

Lake Vyrnwy Hotel had done us proud. On the little beach where we had found the boats there were now four wicker baskets and Anthony Rosser. He had the sort of look Ratty might have worn when Mole asked him what was in the picnic basket he had packed for a day up the river: "There's spicey chicken," replied the Rat briefly; "marinadedolivescoldbeefinciabattasmok-edsalmonclaretcheesesbiscuitsandstrawberriesandcream-"

"O stop, stop," cried the Mole in ecstasies - only, of course, we didn't. We just tucked in.

The electric motors had to work a lot harder to shift us that afternoon: there was so much more of us to shift. Like us, the trout of Vyrnwy had lunched heavily when the valley was first flooded in 1889, leaching nutrients from the rich farmland of the valley bottom. The average weight was just under a pound in those first seasons but fell to just half this within fifteen years. The thin soils of the valley sides were soon washed away, exposing the hard and unproductive Cambrian rocks and shales. The best food - and the best fish - were often to be found where the numerous streams, destined to fill the baths and lavatories of Liverpool, spilled into the lake. Rhiwargor Bay, where we had filled our boots that morning, is fed by two streams, Afons Eiddew and Nandroeth. A third river, the Eunant, runs under a picturesque bridge into another large bay at the head of the lake. Which is where we headed after lunch

The valley sides around Pont Eunant are steeper and more dramatic than the north shore. Huge oaks and pines cling to rocky ledges and hang far out across the waters. Rhododendrons ready to burst into bloom lurk between the mature trees, remnants of the grander sort of Victorian garden. They are all that remains of Eunant Hall, home of Sir Edmund Buckley, that once stood where the Eunant and Vyrnwy rivers once met near the head of the valley. I have always pictured these drowned mansions and villages as rather romantic spots, dappled with dim light when the sun is high, with fish cruising through gaping doors and windows. Folk near such places are forever hearing the church bell toll when the wind sets the waves rolling down the lake. So I was saddened to learn that this is total tosh. Eunant Hall, it turns out, was thoroughly demolished before the waters rose, along with the old village of Llanwddyn and the small settlement of Pant-y-Lleinr. A total of ten farms, 37 houses, 3 pubs, 2 chapels and the parish church of St Wddyn were abandoned to the waters as the inhabitants, past and present, left the valley for the last time - even the remains of the dead were removed from the churchyard and reburied next to the new church three miles down the valley.

But perhaps one building in the valley survived. Nick and I had caught nothing in Pont Eunant Bay. We were heading back across the lake to the northern shore: we would carry on fishing beneath the trees where we had caught that first wild fish. We drifted east with the gentle breeze blowing down the lake, casting up to the wavelets slapping against the grey rocks. A violent tug came to nothing but then, on the next cast, the rod lurched forward again and I had my best fish of the day, another beautiful specimen of fourteen inches. I slipped it back into the water and looked up to see a wall and a roof of grey slate amongst the trees at the water's edge. It could have been a boat house but the door in the face was too small for any boat. We were intrigued. I nudged the boat into the rocks of the shore and we clambered out. It was a single square room with a fine floor of square flagstones. Two large windows high in the wall lit the interior. They seemed a bit over-the-top for a store shed, besides, the walls had once been smooth-plastered and white-washed. Much of the plaster had fallen off but where it clung to the stone walls it was covered in hand-written messages, some scratched into the surface but most written in pencil with the fine, flowing letters of an earlier age and a sterner regime of primary education. They dated from every era of the Twentieth Century.

It had once been a chapel, one of those abandoned as the waters rose but miraculously not demolished. In the century since the lake had filled, visitors to Vyrnwy have found this quiet place, hidden in the forest, and recorded their thoughts on its cool walls. "Final Victory will be ours" reads one poignant line: it is dated "The Second Great War 1939-?" Were we winning or losing when that was written?

It was cooler now. The sun still shone relentlessly but there was no malice in it. The fish seemed to appreciate the change. In the following hour another half dozen splendid trout came to our boat. The breeze was falling with the sun, leaving great swathes of the upper lake flat calm. Trout rose sporadically in these calms: perhaps they had been doing that all day but such gentle rises had passed unnoticed in the ripple. The serious stuff was over for the day. Now we began a graceful ballet, gliding towards a rise, casting vaguely in its general vicinity until another was spotted and then heading towards that. And so on: pleasant but pointless, like any other ballet. We didn't need another fish: between us we had caught thirty trout to around a pound and lost a few more.

It was just the last dance of four old fishermen who were enjoying the sun and didn't want to go home quite yet.

Did you spot the deliberate falsehood? It's more obvious if read out loud. If you didn't find it - and you really want to know, give me a ring on 01295 758221 or email jon.beer@tiscali.co.uk

The Lake Vyrnwy Hotel controls all fishing on Lake Vyrnwy. The fishing is fly-only and only from boats: life jackets must be worn and, alas, the boats are no longer electric-powered. There are just 10 boats on Vyrnwy's 1120 acres. A boat and fishing for two rods costs £55 per day (one rod: £40). There are several "two nights" packages including dinner, bed and breakfast at the hotel with fishing, boat and packed lunches included: from £155 (for 2 persons) per night. For other details tel:01691 870 692 or visit www.lakevyrnwy.com

13

Laird Of The Rings

Married men may have reason to revile the name of John Young of Comrie in Perthshire. Men merely proposing marriage have even more cause to curse the man. He's certainly not popular with the blokes round our way.

His crime has been to set a standard of romance that leaves the man with a bunch of roses or a box of chocs delivered on skis simply nowhere. Before his wedding, John Young set out to pan the gold for his wife's wedding ring. How does that make the rest of us look?

He found the stuff an hour down the road in the Cleish Hills near Dunfermline – which may lack the two-fisted *chutzpah* of the Klondike but is a lot more convenient for the shops.

Gold has been turning up in the burns of Scotland for centuries. In 1239, the monks of Newbattle Abbey discovered gold in the Lowther Hills of Dumfriesshire. This area around the headwaters of the River Nith became known as "God's Treasure House in Scotland" providing much of that country's wealth – and its crown jewels – in the Middle Ages. The tradition continues: the mace for the new Scottish parliament was decorated with gold panned from these streams, the same water where, three years ago, George Paterson panned a nugget of 6g, enough for a wedding ring in a single lump.

Traces of gold, it seems, can be found almost anywhere and by anyone who is prepared to sift through the gravels of these icy streams. Quantities worth the hard labour of panning are rarer and are usually found by those with an eye for likely features and geology. There is gold in the hills of the west: there has been puff of a gold mine at Tyndrum, north of Loch Lomond. Perthshire has several gold-bearing streams including "The Birks of Aberfeldy", a beauty spot (and now a country park) immortalised in song by Robert Burns. It was while we were fishing together on another tributary of the River Tay that John Young told me about his wedding ring and gold panning in the streams of the Cleish Hills. My mistake was to tell this story to my wife when I got home.

I blame myself (32 years after my own wedding, I find it saves time): a story like that is bound to make a girl compare and contrast. I know the signs. She wasn't disgruntled, exactly - but then she wasn't exactly gruntled, either. So, rashly, I made a sort of promise and, last autumn, set off for the hills myself.

GOLD! Just the word can unsettle a man: I was all for selling up the farm, taking ship to Skagway and heading up the Yukon Trail. Happily that would not be necessary: the 8.40 sleeper from Euston, changing at Inverness, would get me to the gold-field just after lunch. Helmsdale may not have quite the pizzazz of the Yukon but it's a lot handier if you have not quite given up your day job.

It was a shame about the mule: I had set my heart on a mule. And one of those shovels with a long handle and a pointy blade. And some chewing baccy and a knife for whittling. I could grow myself a stubbly chin, no problem, but I needed to get me some gold-panning gear.

I found the craft shop and information centre by the harbour in the little town of Helmsdale in north-east Scotland: there wasn't a mule in sight. Nor even a spittoon. Inside there were tweeds and knitwear and jars of local honey - but beneath a table of Celtic jewellery and Rennie Mackintosh silverware, I spotted a collection of more agricultural items: a small cache of trowels, sieves and pans. I had hit pay-dirt. The sign said I could hire a set of panning tools for £2.50, a trifling sum when riches beyond the dreams of avarice were in the offing. All I had to do now was find out what to do with them. And where. "Where" was eight miles up the road.

It was a very British affair. In 1868 a local man, Robert Gilchrist, returned home from working the goldfields of Australia. Half a century before, a gold nugget had been found in the river and Mr. Gilchrist got permission from the Duke of Sutherland to pan the river gravels for gold. He found the stuff everywhere. The news spread as such news will and by the following spring there were 500 licensed prospectors churning up the bed of the river and its tributary, the Kildonan Burn. By that autumn £12,000-worth of gold had been panned – a fortune for the panners but loose change for the local sporting gentry who were not happy: the gravel-washing was ruining the salmon fishing and the *hoi polloi* milling around the strath were disrupting the deer-stalking. It just wouldn't do. They complained to the duke who promptly withdrew all licences: the Kildonan gold rush was over.

But not for me. I might be 135 years late but I was eager to start. We were standing at *Baille an Òr* – the "town of gold" - where a shanty town of wooden huts had once stood on the banks of the Kildonan Burn. Now it's a pleasant patch of turf ringed by rock and heather. I was not alone. Ronald Sutherland, a local fishing guide and golf instructor, was about to initiate me into the arcane secrets of gold-panning.

This is how it goes.

Gold is the heaviest stuff to be found in the Kildonan Burn: when everything in the river is shaken up by storm and flood, the gold settles first and deepest. In time it works its way down through the sand and gravel until it reaches bedrock. And there it stays, waiting for Ronald and me. Or you.

We climbed down through the heather into the deep gorge of the Kildonan Burn. Ronald examined a boulder in the river bed. He tugged at it. It didn't budge: it had not been moved recently. There was a chance that the riverbed beneath had not been disturbed by other panners. He dug down to bedrock behind the rock and sloshed a spadeful of sand and gravel into the garden sieve he had balanced on the pan. A couple more spadefuls from the riverbed filled the pan. Was there GOLD amidst that unpromising mud pie? Ronald grinned: "Let's see".

He put down the spade, picked up the pan and stood to his knees in the river. He lowered the pan just beneath the water and began to rotate it, shaking the pan until everything inside was moving and fluid. Gold is the heaviest stuff in the gold pan: when everything is shaken up and fluid the heavy gold will settle first and deepest, gradually migrating to the bottom of the pan. Ronald lifted the pan, tilting it forward to spill a little of the cleaned gravel back into the river. One side of the gold pan is deeply ridged, holding back all but the topmost layer. And so he went on, alternately swishing and spilling, until the just finest and heaviest sediments were left in the bottom of the pan. I peered over his shoulder: it still looked like sand to me - and pretty sludgy sand at that.

Ronald tilted the pan gently away from him, just a little. We were both staring now. We were both excited now but only one of us knew why. As he tilted the pan back towards him, the spoonful of sand stretched out across the bottom of the pan, leaving a tiny fringe of the finest black sand sticking to the bottom.

And there, like bright stars in a black sky, were flakes of gold. GOLD!

Ronald touched a finger tip to a tiny flake and then touched the finger to the surface of a tiny bottle of water. The gold flake plummeted, glittering, to the bottom.

GOLD!

It seemed incredible to me then - as it seems incredible to me now - but on my desk is that small bottle and the flakes of gold that Ronald and I gathered from the Kildonan Burn.

At the end of a back-breaking afternoon I had collected forty of these tiny flakes. It was going to take a long time to pan a whole ring. This does not bother me: the gold for the Queen's wedding ring came from this same Kildonan burn.

And I bet Prince Philip didn't get it all in one go.

Astonishingly, gold is to be found in many places in Britain. Curiously, most sites are around the 4°W line of longitude, from Kildonan in north-east Scotland, through Wales and into Devon. Scotland is particularly auriferous (a splendid word you get to use when you look for gold).

The 4°W longitude passes close to the village of Wanlockhead in the Lowther Hills where, five centuries before, a huge nugget of 1.13 Kilograms turned up. Nowadays the village is home to the National Gold-Panning Championships which take place over the Whitsun weekend each year. The Museum of Lead Mining at Wanlockhead tells the history of Lowther Gold.

The Welsh, as we know, dearly love to dig and Welsh gold has usually been mined rather than panned. A Roman gold mine at Dolaucothi is owned by the National Trust: an underground tour tells its history from Roman times. Gwynfynydd Gold Mine in Dolgellau started in the 1860's and was one of the richest mines in Britain. Gwynfynydd, along with Clogau Gold Mine near Barmouth, closed in 1999. Charles and Diana's wedding rings were made of Welsh gold from these mines – but then, so was Michael Douglas's.

The 4°W line crosses the Bristol Channel but English gold is decidedly iffy. It was once mined at North Molton on the fringe of

Exmoor and is widespread in South Devon but finding enough to make a wedding ring may take longer than most fiancées are prepared to wait.

John Young of Comrie, by the way, is one of the nicest blokes I know. He is the fishery manager of Lochlane and Laggan Fishings on the River Earn. If you'd like to fish the Earn with John visit www.country-pursuits.com/html/river_earn.html

14

Down the Pan

I cannot pretend I wasn't apprehensive: I was. I was going to Northern Ireland for the first time. The day before, the back pages of the newspapers had been full of Ireland's win over Italy in the World Cup. The front pages were full of images of a crowded bar in the small village of Loughinisland that had been machine-gunned while the locals were watching the match. Six had died. While I waited in the airport I found Loughinisland on the map in my bag. Looking at the map was a mistake. My images of Northern Ireland had been built up over twenty-five years of news broadcasts from towns on the map: Belfast, Londonderry, Strabane, Enniskillen, Portadown, Newry. And none of this news had been good news. And so I was a little apprehensive.

I was excited as well. The Republic of Ireland has long been a Mecca for game fishermen: a lot of empty green space and an awful lot of rainfall has produced some of the best salmon fishing in the world and fishermen travel from all over the world to try it. Well, Northern Ireland has every bit as much rainfall and grass and salmon but, what with one thing and another, fewer fishermen have been visiting of late. We were on our way to take a look at one or two of the choicer spots.

I had another reason for feeling excited and apprehensive: I was going to Northern Ireland to lose my virginity.

I had never caught a salmon. I had come close: I had hooked salmon: I had played salmon: I had landed salmon. I just hadn't done all three to the same fish. It was beginning to be something of a joke amongst angling friends. It was beginning to be something of a joke in my own family: my four-year-old daughter had caught a salmon. She was beginning to patronise me. She was not alone. All right: this time I would break my duck.

But not that first day on the River Mourne. The Mourne is part of the River Foyle. As far as I could make out, the River Mourne *is* the River Foyle between Strabane and Newton Stewart - where it becomes the River Strule. Confused? I was. The name doesn't matter: the river is a gem. When I asked someone to describe it to me before I went they said it was "like the middle Spey", which may help you but meant nothing to me. For us trout anglers it is a broad, rocky river with a powerful current even after a week or so with little rain and there are no major obstructions in the twenty five miles between Newton Stewart and the sea at Londonderry. It was my first time on a proper salmon river. I was not sure what I should be looking for. There was the occasional small rise but that looked to me like the occasional small trout. And then something sounding like a bag of sugar thrown into the river crashed in the tail of the pool and we knew there were salmon about.

There was a certain amount of agonising over choosing the fly. This was harder for John and Sandy than it was for me. We had stopped at the tackle shop in Newton Stewart to buy fishing licences and ask how the river was fishing. David Campbell, the owner of this fine establishment, told us he had had three the evening before and showed us the fly that had done the stuff. This seemed a fair recommendation to me and I bought one. So did Sandy. So did John. I assumed we were going to fish with them. But that is not how these things are done. At the riverside they opened their fly boxes and picked up this fly and that before each settling on something that was similar but *not quite* the same as the fly from the shop.

We worked our way slowly down the river, feeling the way with wading staffs in the waist-high current. The bottom hereabouts is a tumble of large rocks that can slide away into deeper holes and I had my work cut out finding a foothold from which to wield the fifteen-foot rod Sandy had lent me. This regularly repeated rhythm of step-stumble-slip-balance-heave-cast-curse-recast and feel ahead for the next step had a fascination all its own and I was quite unprepared for the slow pull of something on the end of the line. It could have been a clump of weed in the strong current until I felt the shudder of life that spells *fish* to any fisherman. I leant into the fish a little and wondered why people made such a fuss about salmon fishing. And then the fish appeared and set up a commotion, thrashing at the surface: then it was gone. If this description is a little abrupt, that is exactly how it felt.

I turned round and shouted to Sandy: "What did I do wrong?" He answered that I had done nothing wrong - it just happens that way. This may or may not have been a truthful answer but it was certainly a wise one for within a minute or so Sandy was into a fish that stayed only marginally longer and a few moments later a second, bigger fish, had come and gone.

The salmon rivers of Northern Ireland, perhaps salmon rivers everywhere for all I know, are well-supplied with old gentlemen who have fished the rivers all their lives and now spend their days dispensing advice from the relative security of not having to follow it themselves. One such now hove into view. He sucked on his pipe and said our rod tips were too stiff. Sandy said that was rather a shame because he had only recently acquired his fifteen-foot Loomis and now he would, of course, have to put it across his knee and snap the thing lest he be tempted to use it again. Losing a couple of fish in five minutes can make one surprisingly bitter. We fished on. John had seen fish up at Burnfoot Pool but had touched nothing. The only action seemed to be here on Stralag Pool and it was here we concentrated during the afternoon, edging down the fast water, swinging the flies across the stream. Then John got a fish. And this one stuck.

Perhaps it was fitting that John had struck first. He is the local man who was showing us the rivers of the north. John Todd runs Gilaroo Angles, a game angling service, and it was his intimate knowledge of these rivers that had found us the fishing. Without the pressure of many visiting anglers, the structure of angling in Ulster sometimes appears a little tortuous. Many waters are privately owned and some, like this stretch of the Mourne, do not exactly advertise day tickets but they can be had if you know how and who to ask. John knows who to ask.

We had a fish. There was a mild celebration back in the homestead that evening. We were staying at Lough Beg Coach Houses. This is a set of newly, and lavishly, converted mews cottages in a splendid courtyard. They are self-catering - sort of: that is, if you wish, meals can be chosen from a menu and delivered to the cottage in a heated container. This is such a wonderful scheme that I am surprised I have not come across it before. It has all the comfort of eating at home without the fag of cooking: all the ease of eating out without the possibility of troubling the local constabulary. The local constabulary in these parts are extremely hot on driving when dappled.

If we had wished to become dappled we could hardly have chosen a finer spot to fish the next morning. The Bush is a small river on the north coast of Antrim. The first town up from the tide is Bushmills and boasts the oldest licensed distillery in the world. The Bush was a surprise: it was not my idea of a salmon river. I think of rugged torrents and falls and white water. The River Bush in June is a picture of pastoral tranquillity, slipping through waving beds of ranunculus into deep, slow pools twisting among the watermeadows. It is not a big river: the Derbyshire Wye at

Bakewell, perhaps. And yet at Portballintrae it has one of the most fascinating, infuriating pools I have seen in all my puff. At Portballintrae the river meanders, deep and slow within its high, reedy banks between the golf course and the sand dunes behind the Giant's Causeway. The river makes a last turn beside the second tee and slithers through a bed of ranunculus, sparkling with white flowers, beneath a small bridge and into a narrow pool. This pool is on the beach. At the tail of the pool the Atlantic rollers were crashing before a north-easterly gale: a majestic scene of nature in the raw. At the head of the pool the waterweed wafted serenely in the chuckling stream, as domestic and idyllic as maybe. In between there were barely forty yards of windswept pool separating these two scenes. Sea pools are fascinating places. This one could hardly have been six yards wide but it was full of fish that had slipped in on the last tide. Occasionally a fish would leap clear of the water at the head of the pool or a head and tail would slip through the surface. They were tantalisingly close. Sometimes a fish would follow the fly or swirl behind it, or leap in front of its path, disturbed by the passage of the fly. But never once did we touch a fish in that pool. It was infuriating. As the tide rose a larger wave surged in and stirred the pool and fish would show along its length for a minute or so but still they would not take. An enterprising child with a bucket and spade could have carved a channel in the sand and drained the pool in an afternoon: he could have taken his pick of the salmon in the thing. From time to time we gave up and moved into the deeper, stiller water between the reeds above the bridge. Here the flies had to be retrieved to give them movement and here Sandy got his first fish. There was a yell and John and I looked up to see Sandy's rod bent steeply down over the reeds as if a good pike had taken on an ancient gravel pit. It was a fine, bright fish, fresh from the sea - which was still pounding at the tail of the sea pool a hundred yards away. Still, we had another fish and another reason to celebrate back at the Coach House.

I was not anxious by this time, not really. But I could feel the other two willing me to get a fish. It is surprising how little that helps.

The next day we returned to the River Mourne. At the tackle shop in Newton Stewart, we learned that the river had fallen four inches and David Campbell had caught five the night before on a smaller fly, which he showed us. We all bought one. I was getting the hang of this. We talked pools. Stralag would still fish but the mood of the meeting was that The Pan had a good chance. Sandy thought I ought to start fishing on the Pan. At the time I thought this was because he had considered the conditions, weighed the advice and felt my best chance of a fish was on this pool. It later turned out that Sandy, a professional editor to his socks, had been thinking up captions to the photographs he would take. He thought there would be more mileage with "fishing down the pan" and "flushed with success on the pan" than with anything I might achieve on "Stralag". You could see his point.

I stepped into the water at the head of the pool and began the rhythmic dance I had learnt on the first day. Five minutes later the line went solid and moved upstream. I leant a little and nothing came loose. I leant a little more and the thing stuck. There were no heroics. It was not a big fish and either it would fall off or it wouldn't so I played it into the shallows like a trout with the comfortable knowledge of 10lb on the end of my string. And there it was, my first salmon. I had lost my virginity.

I will tell you the truth: it was perhaps a bit of an anticlimax. I am reluctant to write this because John and Sandy will read it and I am afraid they wanted it more than I did. But it is the truth. And perhaps that is often the way the first time. You have been told the earth will move and it doesn't. Why should it: the first time is rarely the best - it is just the first. If I remember anything of the first time it was just a feeling of relief: "Good, that's over and now, perhaps, I can get on with enjoying it the next time". And it was the same with my first salmon, that day on the River Mourne.

Another uncomfortable parallel struck me as Sandy and I grinned down at my first fish where it lay on a wrack of weed. It was not a large fish. We both spotted this but Sandy was admiring it and saying what a pretty fish it was. I think he was telling me size doesn't matter.

Who are we kidding?

15

Somewhere, Overrun With Rainbow

So, how do we feel about wilderness fishing? I love it. I don't know why. I would like to think that the solitude of the wilderness frees the psyche from the petty burdens of civilisation, sets the soul soaring above the mundane to contemplate the enormity and wonder of creation. I'd like to think that. But I think it's probably a sneaking suspicion that the fish there will be easier to catch because I'm the first fisherman they'll have encountered.

Also there is the vague notion that wilderness fish should be bigger, growing to a ripe old age without other fishermen hauling them out and eating them. So a wilderness, populated with large and obliging trout, has always struck me as a good place to fish.

The hard bit is finding one of these.

Don't bother to search in Britain: I've tried. I have searched in most bits of these islands from Cornwall to the Shetland Islands and I have found places where the soul can soar as much as it fancies - places, frankly, which could do with one or two petty burdens of civilisation – and most of them have trout but they are not the large and gullible kind of trout. They tend to be smallish and disconcertingly wily. The large and gullible ones went years ago.

When a man thinks of things large and gullible his thoughts turn naturally to North America. And when he thinks of the wilderness he looks to the parts that are not infested with Americans. He thinks of Canada.

Canada, it turns out, is mostly wilderness. We could see the stuff passing below us, hour after hour on the flight from London: the frozen seas around Baffin Island, across the treeless tundra of the Barrens of the North West Territories and the endless stunted forests of Saskatchewan and Alberta. Two thousand miles of wilderness without a road. And that's before you get to British Columbia and another five hundred miles of mountains before touchdown in Vancouver. And buried in the middle of that last little lot is Lake Eutsuk.

Lake Eutsuk lies in the heart of Tweedsmuir Provincial Park. This is not a park as we know it. There are no signs keeping you off the grass. It has two-and-a-half *million* acres of mountain forest and one gravel road. But the gravel road is 70 miles from Lake Eutsuk. You have to fly into Eutsuk in something that floats.

This mountain fastness between the Rockies and the Pacific is the natural home of the rainbow trout. I had come to the mother-lode of things large and obliging. One of them lay on the wooden pontoon where the float plane had set us down - a wild rainbow trout, fat and fin-perfect, of eight pounds. This gorgeous beauty got that way feeding on salmon, albeit a very small land-locked salmon, the kokanee, which infests the waters of Eutsuk Lake. And the best way to catch these predatory rainbows is to use something imitating a wounded kokanee which involves trolling a large plug on a down-rigger and that is quite enough of that. There are other ways.

Eutsuk Lake is a 50-mile-long finger of water gouged from the mountains by glaciers that don't feel all that far away in the middle of July. At the western end of the lake a tongue of snow and ice reached down the mountainside and plunged deep beneath the water. Fifty miles away, at the eastern end it was summer. Here the waters of Eutsuk narrow and shallow, gliding

110

imperceptibly into the Redfern River. The shallow water warms rapidly in the sunshine and the margins were pocked with fish rising to a hatch of mayfly.

About these mayfly: Americans call all members of the upwinged ephemerid family "mayfly". You can point out that some species don't hatch till October. Doesn't do a bit of good: to an American they are all mayflies. It is hard to blame them: we Brits don't have a word at all. We have a word for the family *Plecoptera* - we call them Stoneflies. We have *two* words for the *Trichoptera* – Caddis or Sedge. But for the *Ephemeroptera*, the flies most beloved of trout fishermen, we have nothing at all. "Upwinged flies" is a cumbersome handle: "dayflies" is descriptive of their short adult lives but it has never really caught on. "Ephemerids" has more than a whiff of the school swot about it. Someone ought to think of something before the American "mayfly" triumphs by default. These mayflies, though, really were Mayflies: great lumps of things, three tails, the whole package. And something was sucking them down with gusto.

We waded out towards the main tongue of current accelerating into the Redfern. I had put on a Klinkhamer Special which works very well as an emerging sedge and well enough as an emerging-anything-else. It floats wonderfully and, if you are careful to avoid getting floatant on the body, looks just plain fishy hanging down through the surface. And before five minutes had passed a splendid rainbow trout thought so too.

A wild rainbow from the wilderness waters of British Columbia is a bit like a stocked rainbow in a British river – in the same way that *Pâté de Foie Gras aux Truffes* is a bit like meat-paste. The colours shimmer as the trout twists in the clear water, from olive-green peppered with spots through every fin to a roseate silver that flashes in the sunlight. I slipped that first rainbow back into the water – barbless hooks are the rule here and all but one fish each day must be returned. I cast out again to the deep run where fish were still rising along the crease of the faster water. A minute or so later a second fish grabbed the fly and stuck. Two minutes later I rather wished it hadn't.

It was a grotesque parody of that first wild rainbow. It was a pantomime dame of a fish, something like a barbel with a huge mouth and lips, rising to pluck mayflies from the surface. It was a squawfish. To a man after squawfish it may have been a beauty but I was expecting flashing rainbows and it wasn't. Todd, the guide standing beside me, was disgusted: he was sorry I had to see that. I got the feeling that one of us, the squawfish, the river or I, had let him down. Probably all three. He took the fish from me and did something quick and unpleasant: catch-and-release does not extend to squawfish, apparently.

The hatch had all but petered out as the day warmed. At the lodge that morning I had studied the display of recommended flies for sale. There were the usual discreet dry and wet flies representing the creatures of the stream, with the usual sort of discreet names: the March Browns, the Coachmen, the Green-wells. Nothing you would mind your mother finding in your fly box. But alongside these were things that read like an Ann Summers catalogue of erotic gear: *Madame X, Bitch Creek,* and the *Stimulator.* Some of them looked a bit that way too, with plastic and dangly bits of rubber. On Todd's advice I had bought a handful of Stimulators and a couple of Madame Xs.

The Stimulator is a fearsome sight. For a start it is yellow, a sort of orange-yellow that can give you a nasty turn if you open you fly-box suddenly. It has a bushy tail and wing of elk hair and it is palmered about as much as a fly can be palmered. It looks like the sort of thing you might use to clean down the spout of a teapot but it would have to be a very big teapot: the one I had was about size four. It didn't seem to be the thing a trout would wish to get inside its mouth.

But I was quite wrong. We had been fishing where the lake is undecided about becoming a river. Around a bend it makes up its mind. The placid waters swing round a grand pool, accelerating as the rocky bed rises until the water plunges down two chutes around a rocky islet. A portage trail runs through the forest, bypassing the rapids. Todd and I followed the trail through the trees to regain the river. Here, below the chute, the water boiled around the rocks, fussing and bulging as it raced along. There was not a hint of a rising fish in this lot. Todd cast the Stimulator out into the current. It was not a long cast, just enough to get it out of the margins and into working water. The Stimulator rode the swirling current as it swept by until the drag on the line or a rogue wavelet pulled it under. Or a fish. The water where the Stimulator had disappeared exploded and a rainbow trout took to the air. A sixteen-inch wild rainbow in wild water can pull your string a bit. Todd fought the fish downstream before he could bring it into a quiet margin to release it.

The Stimulator was a revelation. That was the beginning of a perfect afternoon. The sun was hot now, an antidote to wading the cold, clear water. The river broadened beneath the rapids, sweeping across pebbly shallows threaded with deceptively deep runs. And in every run there were rainbows prepared to launch themselves at a Stimulator.

The night before I had been fascinated to watch humming-birds flitting around the lodge. Now a gentle breeze carried another small bird across the river. Where the hummingbirds were dashing emerald, these were straw-coloured and ponderous. One fluttered close: it was not a bird but a huge fly, the Big Golden Stonefly of the West. It stuttered on across the water, rising to drift into the trees. There were hundreds of them, wings flashing golden in the sunlight as they fluttered across the water to lay their eggs. The fussy hackles and tatty hair wing of the Stimulator imitate the struggles of a stonefly trapped in the surface, triggering the trout's explosive grab before the fly can escape. It's exciting stuff. Just like the name says.

Another day, another water, another fly. The trail to Willachuck Lake begins, romantically enough for a bloke from Banbury, beside a beaver lodge. No-one had walked this trail for a couple of years since it had become blocked by fallen trees after a forest fire. And they didn't use it much before that, two or three times a year, no more. So Willachuck Lake does not get fished a lot. There were four of us: Tom and Jerry, two brothers from Chicago, and I were following Brandon, our guide. He had a chainsaw and was clearing a path through the maze of fallen trunks. I resented the chainsaw shattering the peace of the wilderness - until Brandon pointed to a steaming pile of fresh grizzly bear poo on the trail. I quite liked the roar of the chainsaw after that: I missed it when it stopped. An hour or so later we made it over a couple of ridges to a reed-fringed lake amid the pines.

We had lugged float tubes up the trail and on a grey, still morning we pushed off from the shore and flippered out onto Willachuck Lake.

The lake was reputed to hold good wild rainbows and something with the heft of a large bag of sugar had just crashed in the margins on the far side of the lake so I decided I would work my way over there. I had no idea what to put on the end of my line. The Golden Stonefly is a thing of running waters: the Stimulator would be no use on Willachuck. My friend Philip fishes for rainbows in the reservoirs of England. He uses buzzers and nymphs and emergers and so forth and then, when he gets no joy with these, he sticks on a Whiskey Fly and starts catching fish. He isn't proud of this addiction to Whiskey Flies but, he says, he can't help himself. So what I did was stick on a Whiskey Fly and let the line trail as I flippered off towards the other side of the lake.

I didn't get that far. About halfway across there was a sudden shock on the line and the stuff started peeling off the reel at an alarming rate. Belly boats are fun. A good fish spins you round and a better one tows you along as you fight it. This first wild Willachuck rainbow measured 18 inches. It was as tight as a drum. I released it and carried on flippering.

It took some time to get to the far side of the lake. Fish kept grabbing the fly and trying to drag me back. I had had three by the time I made it to the margins. There were fish moving here and I cast to them in the prescribed manner but had no offers before the activity faded. I had put them down. So I paddled off towards another bay. As soon as I was under way a fish hammered the trailing fly and we were back in business. Fish were beginning to rise in earnest now and a hatch of flies was studding the surface: another hatch of Mayflies. Brandon called them Grey Drakes when I paddled towards him to ask. It took some time getting there, having to fight and shake off several fish that grabbed the Whiskey Fly on the way. At one time the fly was dangling in the water as I measured the fish on the apron of the float tube. You can guess what happened. I was well into the teens by the time I made my way across to Brandon. I took off the Whiskey Fly and put on an imitation of the floating dun. I knew it was the right thing to do: that's what the others were using. I was, frankly, a bit bored by just trolling around catching these splendid fish. Also, it seems Brandon wanted to borrow the Whiskey Fly.

The floating dun did take a couple of trout – but it was hard work and they did feel a bit fluky. I got a bit bored with not catching fish too. So I went back to the Whiskey and trolling and battling with wild rainbows fit as a butcher's dog up to twenty-one inches long. And eventually I just stopped fishing.

So here's the thing: on that day, in that place, the Whiskey Fly was far more effective than an imitation of the natural fly on the water. I can't be sure the trout I was catching were feeding on those hatching duns but I am dead certain they were not feeding on an insect with a silver-and-orange body and a hot orange wing. Worse: the better presentation was to troll the thing. I think I know why that might be: on the calm water that day, casting disturbed the fish more than a gently moving float tube – think of the trout that grabbed the dangling fly: it must have swum between my legs to get at the thing. There is something else: I was using a silk line. This floats when it is cast but can be made to sink gradually on the retrieve. Trolling on a long line allowed the fly to fish a little deeper and with less wake. The right fly and the right presentation. But I had a niggling feeling that I had done something not quite pukka.

No-one said anything, exactly, and Brandon was busy committing the dressing of the Whiskey Fly to memory, but there was a sort of something in the way Tom and Jerry politely declined my offer of a sample - which is a damned nerve coming from the nation that gave us *Madame X, Bitch Creek,* and the *Stimulator.*

But I know what they meant.

That trip to Eutsuk was the quintessence of American lodge fishing, a combination of sybaritic luxury, uninhabited wilderness and a lot of very large outboard motors. The lodge was staffed by two or three guides and a couple of startlingly attractive girls who cleaned and cooked. It was holiday work. One of the girls was studying to become a physiotherapist. As part of her course she had to complete so many hours of massage before the end of the vacation. Would we, she asked, allow her to practise on us in the evenings? Isn't education is a good and noble thing?

The company has changed but the lodge where we stayed and the places we fished remain the same. Take a look at www.redfernriverlodge.ca

16

Current Affairs

One day, perhaps, I will appear in court, hauled up in front of the bench for fishing without a permit. I shall defend myself, of course. I will pace about and bring in writs of Habeus Corpus, Magna Carta and Rex-versus-Wossname. Also some tort, if I can find out what that is. I will demand justice. And when I am convicted and the beak asks if I have anything to say before he passes sentence, I will ask for a dozen other offences to be taken into consideration, all on the little River Elan above Pont ar Elan. It lies beside my favourite route from the Midlands to the upper Teifi and every time I pass that way I stop for ten surreptitious minutes. I will throw myself on the mercy of the court and in mitigation of these crimes I will produce a photograph of the River Elan as it wanders in extravagant meanders across the valley bottom, winking in the sunshine, swinging close to the little road across the mountains only to swerve away again. The little tart. Who could resist the captivating little minx? I will also point out, m'lud, that I have never actually caught a fish in the little River Elan.

That is not strictly true. I was up there again last Friday. There were three of us and we caught, between us, six small minnows. It was Pete who did the actual catching: he was the one with the net, scooping them up as they drifted downstream after Vaughan had passed a hundred volts through their vicinity. They are easier to catch that way.

I had always wanted to go electro-fishing. It suits me down to my socks. Much of the joy of fishing on different waters is not knowing what's down there when you cast your first fly. I'm not terribly keen on getting to know every fish in the stream by name and spending hours laying siege to The Colonel who has lived under the second arch of the bridge since the year Old Tess was a puppy. Some blokes like that sort of thing. The only trouble with fly-fishing on different waters is that I'm not always sure what's down there after I have finished casting my last fly. I don't always catch every fish in the river. Or any of them, in the case of the River Elan. So when Vaughan told me he was preparing a report on the Elan and its fish, I asked if I could go along.

Vaughan Lewis is a fisheries scientist. He runs the Windrush Environmental Consultancy: he's a sort of watery Ghostbuster. *When there's something wrong with your aquatic invertebrate profile – who ya gonna call?* It's not quite as catchy a lyric as the original, but you get the idea. Vaughan was looking every inch the Ghostbuster as he shrugged the portable electro-fishing equipment onto his back. It's enormous. It has big red and green buttons and several knobs to twiddle and dials with needles whanging across hundreds of volts and amps and suchlike. There's a thick yellow cable that trails in the water and, at the end of another cable, Vaughan held the business-end, a black pole with its circular electrode. He stepped into the water with his two intrepid companions. Pete and I didn't get to wear any of this glamorous Ghostbusting gear: he got the net. I got a bucket.

At the end of 19ᵗʰ Century the little River Elan was dammed to form a series of reservoirs, the Elan Valley Lakes, to supply the growing population of Birmingham. It had always been a place for fishermen but they had been salmon fishermen: the Elan, and its tributary the Claerwen, were fine salmon spawning streams in the great days of Wye salmon. Craig Goch, Pen y Garreg, Garreg Ddu and Caban Coch reservoirs were opened in the first years of the new century and trout swam where the salmon had once spawned. After the Second World War another great expansion of Birmingham was expected and the nearby River Claerwen was dammed to cope with yet more Brummy flushings. Claerwen Reservoir was opened by the new queen on her first visit to Wales.

There are fashions in fishing as there are in everything else. There was a depressing era when stocked trout fisheries engaged in a debilitating arms race of size. There was a short, frivolous period when exotics were all the go – usually American brook trout crossed with anything that would have them – and then there was a time when everyone who could drive a JCB was digging a hole and announcing a new small stillwater. A sort of sanity returned, goodness knows how, when many river fisheries turned from huge rainbows to native brown trout which had at least a chance of reproducing without the aid of a bucket. And, with the coming of catch-and-release, many fishermen have rediscovered the value of a wild fish in an increasingly artificial industrial world.

Which was why we were standing up to our delicate bits in the chill waters of the River Elan while Vaughan pushed a hundred volts through them – the waters, that is, not the delicate bits. Could a wild fish survive in this particular bit of the industrial world? The answer, it seemed, was "no". The waters of mid-Wales have always been acidic, running off the uncompromising slates and shales of the region, but trout have lived in these waters since the last ice age: they can cope. The planting of conifer forests did not help. It was all too much for the upper Irfon, half-a-dozen miles to the south, where the waters running from the conifers are now too acid to sustain meaningful life. Happily the catchments of the Elan and Claerwen have little forestry: what they do have is rain. And when the wind is in the

119

wrong direction and someone is doing something unspeakable in Llanelli or Port Talbot that rain can tip the balance of the Elan from lovely to lethal. It may not not last long, just an hour or so: But an hour or so is quite enough for newly-hatched alevins and fry. The occasional acid episodes don't harm an adult fish in the broad waters of the reservoir but, at the wrong time, they are enough to wipe out a generation of young troutlings. After half an hour in the upper Elan, Pete had caught six minnows in his net.

Pete Jennings is the Head Countryside Ranger for the Welsh Water's Elan Estate. It had been his inspiration to turn the whole system into a self-sustaining wild trout fishery. It could be done, but only by extensive annual liming of those acid waters. The eastern reservoirs, fed by the River Elan, will continue to be stocked for the time being.

It is wild country up here. Peregrines nest in the cliffs above Carreg Ddu, red kite wheel in the sky and the screech of young buzzards echoes of the rock faces. It's surprising there are any other birds left alive. But there are. On the day of a sponsored bird watch in 1995, Elan's team of Countryside Rangers saw 67 bird species. One of these was the dipper. It was interesting where these dippers were spotted, fossicking around the stones and riffles of three streams, the River Claerwen and its two small tributaries, the Arban and the Rhiwnant. The sightings were marked on Vaughan's map of the estate. All the sites lie to the west of the Elan lakes. There is a reason for those marking on the map: the dipper makes a living from the aquatic nymphs and larvae of the stream. Streams that are too acid for trout hold few of these tasty items – and hence attract very few dippers. The dipper, it seems, is nature's little litmus paper. Somewhere in the hills between the Elan and the Claerwen there is a subtle change in geology, enough perhaps to make the difference. We were to find out.

At Llannerch y Cawr bridge the River Claerwen tumbles

Gordon with a triumphant trout from the Loch of Gutcher, seconds before the ferry to Unst departed. Another sunny day in Shetland. *(Man's Dog Ate My Trousers)*

A brace of arctic char, the loveliest of salmonids, from the depths of Coniston Water. Caught by Jeff and Bill on traditional Lakeland char tackle. *(Boys from the Deep Stuff)*

On a hidden cliff beside the River Eden, William Mounsey, "The Jew of Carlisle", carved this passage from Izaak Walton – with an ironic twist. *(Gothic Ghost Story)*

Straight off the Tide. Sandy Leventon fishes the fascinating, infuriating sea pool of the River Bush on the beach at Portballintrae. *(Down the Pan)*

Evening in the Arctic. On the Kaitum below Tjuonajokk *(Grayling for the Gourmand)*

Two sides of the Jotunheim Mountains. Philip and Digby climbing Sjugurdtinden, one of the pointy bits , to fish the high lakes among the peaks and glaciers above Memurubu. The glacier in the distance is the source of the River Veo (*below*), miraculously clear and full of willing fish under the summer sun. "We all agreed we had just fished the perfect river". *(Three More in Norway)*

Two sides of boat fishing for trout. One May morning we arrived at Lake Vyrnwy to find a flat calm under a blistering sun. Nick had got there first. You can spot him under the first arch *(Snooker Break)*. And a morning in June on Loch nam Brac in Sutherland with Ben Stack in the background. That day we would be visited by rain, sleet and hail – and a lot of trout. *(Onl-ly, Twenty-four Hours from Banbury)*

"I found him playing a splendid brown trout beneath a horse chestnut with the swelling chalklands of Salisbury Plain rising beyond the river" (*First Chuck on the Chalk*)

Chalk and Cheese – The rivers of Lozère.

In the south, the River Tarn has cut a spectacular gorge down through the limestone scenery of *les Causses*. Native *zebrée* trout lurk in its cool depths. A few miles north, the River Bès *(below)*, flowing over harder volcanic rock, has a rather more rumbustious, feisty character. So do its trout.

La Behottiere, on the Aclou reach of the River Risle. Charles Ritz considered this *"better than the finest reaches of the Test, the Itchen or the Wylye" (What I Did on My Hols)*

The quintessence of fishing for wild trout in wild places. ". . far below us a small saucer of loch nestled in a green hollow . . . the distant mountains of Skye floating above the horizon of a blue sea." *(Lost Luggage)*

through the trees and tries its best to sober up before meeting Dol-y-Mynach reservoir around the next bend. It looked a little large for ghostbusting so we decided on a more traditional method of looking for trout. We found them: within minutes a sprightly little trout had taken Vaughan's fly and was skittering towards the bank. I was just landing a second fish when Pete leaned over the bridge. He shouted down that we were on the wrong side of the bridge: I was fishing without a permit again.

We made our getaway in Pete's Landrover, following the River Claerwen upstream towards a huge dam. The healthy little trout we had found in the river ensure a splendid wild trout fishery in Claerwen Reservoir. From the dam, a track follows the indented north shore. It is the sort of track you would not hesitate to drive in a family car - as long as it belonged to someone else. It was a different world up here. Cloud and mist were driving in from the west and the wind that had rustled the trees in the lower valley was kicking white horses the length of Claerwen. It was also doing horrid things to my leader. Actually it was Vaughan's leader. He had lent me his rod and reel.

Vaughan is a serious stillwater trout angler. You know you have the a serious stillwater trout angler's rod in your hand when you hook the point fly onto the keeper ring and discover that there is still a fair length leader left on the reel. That leader was over twenty feet long. I don't know how many of you have experienced the quiet thrill of triumph at punching a twenty-foot leader, arrow-straight, into the teeth on an onshore wind: I know I haven't. I spent most of the first ten minutes flailing droppers around bits of the vicinity and most of the next ten minutes replacing the flies I had had to cut off in the first ten minutes. Vaughan meanwhile had caught a spanking little wild brown trout. And then another one.

They were fine fish, these little trout of Claerwen: each between ten and eleven inches and game as bantam cocks. We fished our way along that coastline until Vaughan tired of catching sporting little trout and I tired of picking my flies out of the scenery. The trout of the Claerwen, it seems, are thriving.

And, if I get time off for good behaviour, I will be back soon to fish for them. But with a shorter leader.

There are two permits for the Elan Estate available from the visitors centre below Caban Coch Reservoir (01597 810 880 or 898). I fished the Claerwen Wild Brown Trout Fishery: 20 Km shoreline of Claerwen reservoir and its feeder streams, the upland lakes, the River Claerwen above Llanerch y Cawr Bridge and the River Elan above and below the Elan Valley reservoirs. There is also the Elan Trout Fishery: 35 Km shoreline of the Elan Valley reservoirs (excluding Dol-y-Mynach reservoir and reserved areas) This holds stocked brown trout.

17

On-ly, Twenty-four Hours from Banbury

*I*t is a truth universally acknowledged that English towns are total rubbish for songs. No-one knows why this is so. No-one knows why Chicago is a toddling town and Chichester isn't. No-one knows why you can get your kicks on Route 66 - which *winds from Chicago to L.A.* - but not on the A66 - which winds, romantically coast-to-coast, from Workington to Middlesborough. It is not just that these are foreign places: the blokes writing all the songs about them are American and Americans get even more excited and dewy-eyed about these places than we do. It's just that their towns sound great and ours don't. *Twenty-four Hours From Tulsa* is a song of wrought emotions, chance encounters and wrecked lives: *Twenty-four Hours from Banbury* is about fish.

We were, I suppose, running away. It was seven o'clock in the evening of Wednesday, 6ᵗʰ June and the next twenty-four hours promised to be bunged up with Dimblebys and exit polls and swing-o-meters and the-returning-officer-for-thingummy-south-easts. I had a note from my mum saying could I be excused from general elections? Philip had one too.

So we got in the car and drove north, determined to be elsewhere for the next twenty-four hours. I will skip over the first nine of those hours. Nothing significant happened apart from the small discovery that you can't get your kicks on the M6 either. Nor yet on the M74, M73, M80, M9 and A9. Which brought us to Inverness around four in the morning. We crossed the Black Isle and headed north-west into the highlands. We saw the first red deer flickering through the trees beside the Black Water that follows the road as it climbs beyond Garve. Folk from Banbury get quite excited when they see a red deer: we don't get them round our way. We point them out to each other and stop and watch until they have disappeared. Just beyond Inchbae we saw a pair of deer across the river and thought about taking a photograph but the light was a bit murky at that hour in the morning. And then, round the next corner, there were a dozen of the things strolling up the road as if they owned the place and we had to slow up to avoid hitting them. It is uncanny how quickly the magical can turn into the mundane. Once, fishing in the watery wilderness of Assynt, I was sitting in the heather, knotting on a new leader when an otter came bumbling along the shoreline of the loch. I had only glimpsed otters in the past or watched them swim away from me but this otter was totally oblivious of my presence and was just fossicking along between the rocks and peat. It was magical and I was determined to stay still until it had passed on its way. But the thing did not pass on its way. It curled up and went to sleep. That was quite nice too for a while but after what felt like half an hour - but was probably only five minutes - I was wishing the thing would wake up, buzz off and let me get on with my fishing.

We were heartily sick of red deer by the time we reached Loch Broom and the west coast. The things infested the place. You get into a rhythm driving on the empty roads of the small hours and here we were creeping along with a foot hovering over the brake pedal as red deer lay in ambush round every turn and leapt out on us from the scenery. They ought to do something. It's outrageous how the wildlife is allowed to just roam around up here.

It was 5am on June 7th. The temperature was 2°C with the wind in the north and a dusting of fresh snow on the tops of Cul Mor. Neither of us had slept. A little north of Ullapool we stopped beside the road and had a brew of tea from the Kelly Kettle and reviewed the situation. We were making for Loch nam Brac for no better reason than that we had to make for somewhere. I had never seen nam Brac but I had always fancied it on the map. It sits beside a small single-track road that leads from nowhere in particular to the hamlet of Tarbet opposite Handa Island. It is about as far from Banbury and a general election as you can get on the mainland of Britain. The fishing belongs to Scourie Angling Club and you can buy a ticket from Mrs Mackay opposite the general store in Scourie, which is what passes for civilisation in these parts. The snag is that Mrs Mackay is not generally about at 5am. So we had a problem: how to fill three or so hours in a land containing little more than heather, rock and trout lochs. We didn't catch anything but Philip had a tug. It was a start.

At nine o'clock, and forty miles further north, we presented ourselves at number twelve, Park Terrace, Scourie and bought our tickets for Loch nam Brac and its boat.

Loch nam Brac is shaped like a distorted gauntlet with thin, watery fingers twisting off in all directions. You certainly get your money's worth of shoreline when you fish nam Brac from the bank. Which is what we would have done but the foot-and-mouth crisis three hundred miles to the south had put the willies up the crofters with sheep in the hills around the loch and bank-fishing was verboten. We bailed out the little grey boat tethered to a rather posh pontoon and pushed off. The wind which had dusted the tops of the mountains with snow was gusting hard from the north in a rather unfriendly way for June. On the other hand, we had to work so hard to row against the gusts funnelling down the narrow fingers of the loch that we didn't really feel the cold: it's wonderful the way nature compensates in these matters. It doesn't matter where the wind blows on nam Brac: you can always find a drift down one arm of the loch, through the little welter of rocks and islands in the middle and on down another arm. The problem is thrashing your way back again. After two fruitless drifts we were getting tired of all that thrashing. The shores of nam Brac are so convoluted that it is sometimes hard to tell what is an island and what a peninsula. Until, that is, you half-close your eyes and look at the colour. The vegetation on the mainland is the grey-green of grass and heather: the rocks and small islands, where the sheep have not grazed and the deer have not bothered, each sport a dense cap of thicker stuff, bright green with the new leaves of rowan, birch and willow. Which gave us an idea. There could hardly be any objection to our bank fishing on those islands where there were no sheep and, by the look of all that green stuff, never had been. We pulled into the lee of a small island and moored the boat. We crossed the islet through shoulder-high foliage and ferns and dropped down onto rocks reaching out into the loch.

The first fish on any water is a joy. The first fish on nam Brac was also something of a relief. It would be a hell of a drive for a blank. It was a nice fish, thirteen inches long with a small head and fine, fat body. But it was still only one fish. It was lunch time and we were starving.

Half-a-mile beyond Loch nam Brac, the single-track lane crests a ridge and drops steeply down to the sea and the Restaurant at the End of the Universe. That's not the name of the restaurant: that's just what it feels like. The tiny Seafood Restaurant sits above the jetty where a boat carries birdwatchers across to the nature reserve on Handa Island. Prawn creels were stacked on the jetty where the fisherman had just unloaded his catch of prawns. Jackie, his wife, runs the Seafood Restaurant. These prawns are *fresh*. They are also about five times the size of the biggest prawn I have ever caught in my little net at the seaside – and they have great big claws. I have just been looking them up in my daughter's book on the *Natural History of Britain and Europe* and I fancy they might be *Nephrops norvegicus*, the Norway lobster, "marketed as scampi or Dublin Bay prawns". So we tucked into a delicious a plateful of *nephrops* and discussed what might be done with the rest of the day.

Over lunch we had learnt something about nam Brac. On the long drive north we had consulted a book on "The Rivers and Lochs of Scotland". It was published in 1997 and described nam Brac as "..the largest and most productive of the Scourie Angling Association waters". And we believed it. What that book had not mentioned was that the loch had been home to a trout farm for a decade and that, in 1997, the loch had already been closed to fishing for two years due to a toxic algal bloom which had turned its waters orange. It was closed for four years and is only now recovering. We didn't fancy it so much after that.

There comes a time when a man needs fish and lots of them. That time had come. A couple of miles from nam Brac, hard by the road to Durness, lies Loch na Claise Feàrna. The fishing belongs to the Scourie Hotel but if none of the guests have chosen to fish it by 9 o'clock then anyone can get a day-ticket. It has a reputation for lots of smallish fish but it also has the chance of a salmon or sea trout so there is always something of a thrill when a tug is felt or a fly disappears. The boat at Claise Feàrna is moored close to the road so we would lose no valuable fishing time in a trek over the hills. Claise Feàrna was just what we needed. We raced back to the hotel and collected the rowlocks.

The wind was still gusting strongly out of the north. The boat lies at the southern tip of the loch so someone was in for a stiffish pull upwind before the first drift. Philip said he would do it: he said a man of my age ought to take it easy. That is the thing with Philip: willing, almost to the point of recklessness, for Philip is not as young as he believes himself to be and after thirty hours without sleep, and a life spent designing ladies frocks, he was, frankly, in no sort of shape for a long row to windward. It was decided we would make first for the lee of the small island in the middle of the loch. The rowan, birch and willow on the island in Claise Feàrna have been un-nibbled for so long that they have grown into large trees, hanging low over the water on all sides. We pulled into the slick of calm water in the lee of the island and while Philip got his tackle together and his breath back I tossed a cast under the trees.

The response was startling. The trees overhanging the water must drizzle a steady trickle of edible goodies onto those trout. In a wind, that just gets better. As soon as the fly, any fly, hit the water it was grabbed by one of the small but eager trout that patrol beneath the trees. I had caught and released four while Philip changed a tippet. We stopped counting after a dozen. It was just what we needed to get the juices flowing again.

It was a different story when we returned to the real world on the other side of the island. It was my turn to row. The wind had eased a little but we were now visited by a nasty little shower of sleet and hail as we made our way upwind. This was grim - but not so bad for the bloke doing the rowing: he wasn't facing that way. I think it got to Philip. He announced, rather dramatically, that he was going to dap. Philip had just been given a new dapping rod for his birthday and he was determined to use it. We began the drift from the head of a small bay in the northern shore. As I fished, Philip set up the dapping rod, delving in his fishing bag for floss and a fly like a small bottle brush. We were out into the loch before his preparations were finished. He raised the rod and the huge dapping fly disappeared into another squall of hail. These are not textbook conditions in which to dap.

No-one had thought to tell the trout. We were out in the middle of Claise Feàrna when a trout hurled itself out of the maelstrom of wind and hail and grabbed the fly. I had not had a touch on my team of wet flies so, when a second fish slashed at the dapping fly now dragging soggily across the surface, I abandoned the fly rod and set up a second dapper. Dapping is the only form of fly fishing I know that makes you laugh. It exemplifies, as perhaps few other forms can do, the essential haphazard nature of the thing. When fishing the wet fly, we change flies and depth and speed of retrieve and so forth and – lo! – a fish occurs and we are pleased to think it was because we changed the fly or depth or speed of retrieve or something else. It is hard to keep up this flattering pretence with dapping. Fish occur or they don't: the fisherman is practically an innocent bystander.

Fish occurred. Not many, but enough. The wind began to drop and grow fluky and the dapping lines began to waft about in an unsatisfactory manner. It was half-past-four. We telescoped the dappers and took up the fly rods again, drifting back towards the road with the gentle breeze. The trout couldn't get enough of us now and Claise Feàrna lived up to its reputation of an awful lot of fish around the ten-to-eleven inch mark. It was five o'clock. We were one dog and a couple of hearty girls short of the Famous Five but, like them, we were "tired but happy" as we drove down the road to Scourie, looking forward to a long drink at the hotel bar. Twenty-two hours ago we had been in Banbury: since then we had driven six hundred miles and fished hard on two lochs.

But it was not over yet. The road from Banbury to Scourie passes over Loch Duartmore. Passing that way in the cold of early morning, we had stopped on the bridge and looked down the loch. There we had seen the first rises of the day, dozens of them pock-marking the surface. We would have chosen to fish Duartmore but for two seemingly insuperable problems: a guest at the Scourie Hotel had already chosen to fish the loch that day and all that gorgeous rising had been deep inside the reed beds that fill much of the loch. As we walked into the hotel that evening the solution to the first of those problems was climbing out of his car. He was calling it a day after several fruitless hours in the reeds of Duartmore. And we thought we might have the answer to the second problem. We begged and borrowed the bloke's rowlocks, climbed back in the car and headed south.

It is a strange sort of reed. Not densely packed around the margins of the loch but a single thick stem every foot or so and a fair sprinkling of water lily and pondweed for good measure. It is quite possible to cast a fly into this sort of stuff – once: it will never come out again. Fly fishing is only possible in the patches of open water. The fish know this and they stick to the reedy bits, rising between the stems to suck in the insects which infest the reed beds. In this fortress of reeds the trout are all but invulnerable. But there is a way. In the faintest of breezes a dapped fly can drift between the reeds and dance over any pond weed. The leader can be man enough for pond weed and more because it never lands on the water to frighten the fish. This is not classical dapping on a rolling wave. This is *dibbling*.

Dibbling is a game for two. The man in the bow lowers the rod until the fly brushes the surface. Nothing much more than a light breeze is best for this delicate work. The man on the oars gently works the boat through the reeds: he is casting the fly, guiding it to the spot where a good fish has risen. Both of you are staring intently at the fly waiting for the reeds to rock as a big fish moves in. We did not have to wait long. The daddy-long-legs fly disappeared in a crisp "sploosh" and a fair fish was on. The oarsman backs into clearer water while the rod man holds the fish firmly. A fourteen inch fish was a good start.

We fished on for an hour in this fashion, taking turns on the rod and the rowing in this fascinating minor branch of the sport. Then the wind died away and the rises petered out.

It was seven o'clock. Only twenty-four hours, forty fish and one General Election from Banbury.

Scourie Angling Club has fishing on many lochs between the A894 and the coast by Handa Island, north of Scourie. Nowadays the tickets for the club's waters are available from the Scourie Filling Station, tel: 01971 502422 (open 9-1, 2-5, Mon-Sat). Day tickets are £10 and the boat on Loch nam Brach (from May) is £10

Scourie Hotel controls several hundred lochs and lochans around Scourie. The hotel residents will have chosen their beats by 9am. Any unused beats (and there are always some unoccupied) can then be fished by day-ticket: £10. Visit www.scouriehotel.co.uk or tel: 01971 502396

For a real treat stuff yourself with Nephrops norvegicus at The Seafood Restaurant, Tarbet by Scourie, tel: 01971 502 251. We did.

Alas, there is no fishing on Sunday in this neck of the woods.

18

Grayling for Gourmands

I have got *macros*. This is not an unsightly skin condition. Nor is it a tasty cheesy-flavoured corn snack. It is a thing on my word-processor. In the middle, at the bottom, nearest my tummy as I type, is the space bar. To the left of the space bar there is a grey key marked "Alt". I do not know what Alt means. There is another one on the right side of the space bar marked "Alt Gr" and I don't know what that means either. But much the same thing happens when I press either one - a menu of interesting things I might want to do with my document unfurls at the top of the screen. But the one on the left does something else. By holding it down and tapping on one of the letter keys, I conjure up a string of letters that I have assigned to that key - a macro.

This is terribly useful. For some reason, places that are good to fish are hell to spell. So if a tricky name is going to crop up a few times I make a little macro and when I need the name again the macro types it for me. My keyboard has become a scrapbook: press a key and get a memory. I have just bashed a few a random: Alt-L gets me *"Llanfihangel Glyn Myfyr"*, the little place I fished on the River Alwen last spring. Alt-M came up with *"Mhaolach-coire"* which is something you wouldn't want to type twice and a lovely limestone loch I'd fished in the hills behind *Inchnadamph* (Alt-I) last summer. Alt-T used to get me the *River Twymyn*, a tributary of the Dovey, but that has had to go. I need Alt-T for *Tjuonajokk*.

Tjuonajokk is north of here. If you start from Banbury, then the Shetland Isles would be about half way north. Tjuonajokk is comfortably within the Arctic Circle and about as far north as you can go in Swedish Lapland. It felt terrifically manly to be going fishing in the arctic.

From Stockholm I took a plane to the northern mining town of Kiruna. I looked the part. I was wearing a padded shirt in a loudish check, battered walking boots and a liberal coating of mosquito repellent on my exposed regions. The other passengers were wearing suits and ties. Except for one. Beneath a broad-brimmed hat the man wore tough-looking stubble and faded denims. Here was a man of the northern woods. I took the seat beside him. His name was Luc. He was from Paris. It was his first time in the arctic too. Like me he was heading for Tjuonajokk.

The next morning Luc and I were on the third leg of the journey. The small helicopter tilted forward over the stunted forests of the northern barrens and then climbed a slope to slip through the gap between a rocky ridge and the belly of grey cloud. Through the perspex beneath my feet I could see a scattering of cabins swimming up to meet us. We had arrived at Tjuonajokk.

It was Fredrik's first season as a guide at Tjuonajokk. He said he would show us around the wilderness camp and, by golly, he did just that. He showed us our cabin and we dumped our gear. He showed us the jetty and the boats, the spring for drinking water and the sauna, the bin to dispose of fish guts, the bin for waste water and the bin for food waste, the bin for burnable waste and the bin for metal waste. And he showed us where to drop our human waste. I know we had to know all this sort of stuff - but it is hard to take in the correct procedure for dealing with various categories of household refuse when standing within a longish spit of some of the best grayling fishing on the planet.

133

And then Fredrik asked if we would like to go fishing that afternoon. Do bears deposit ursine waste in the woods?

I will describe one of the world's great grayling rivers so you will recognise one when you see it. The River Kaitum at Tjuonajokk is undecided whether to be a river or a lake. It looks like a lake, a narrow finger of water stretching away between the hard old shoulders of Sweden's highest mountains. Luc and I scrambled aboard Fredrik's long, elegant boat and we curved away from the dock, heading into the narrower waters beyond a fringe of birches tinged with autumn on the last day of August. Large boulders stood out along the rocky shore: the Kaitum was low in late summer and Fredrik swung the boat in extravagant curves through a chicane of small buoys that looked meaningless on such a wide water - until he pointed out the huge rocks just below the surface. The buoys were leaning to a current that was growing as the Kaitum steadily narrowed. Half a mile below the cabins the boulders began to crowd towards us from both shores. A figure stood to his waist in water and another stood on the submerged rocks alongside the main channel. Fredrik headed for the shore and we ground to a halt on the rocky bottom beside another boat. We had reached Taivek.

Taivek is the first of the rapids where the waters of the Kaitum are squeezed to twist and boil between the boulders of the rocky shore in a series of deep glides and bouncing channels and pools. By stepping from boulder to boulder across the shallows we could reach the edge of the main current sweeping past. It all looked a bit big for a boy from Banbury.

I cast a small dry fly up into the bouncing water. I could see nothing in that lot as it swept past me. Neither, apparently, could the fish. A few yards downstream Fredrik was casting a fly into much the same sort of stuff. The fly was a Klinkhåmer Special which you had better have if you fish here. I'll tell you why. The thing rode the standing waves like a cork and its conspicuous white wing shone like a beacon in the maelstrom - until a great grey thing, slicing through the waves just upped and snuffed it out.

It was a grayling of 40 cm - 16 inches in old money and a thumping great grayling in any one's money. I was impressed by this fish. Fredrik slipped it off the barbless hook and slid it back into the current. He asked if I would like a Klinkhåmer Special. I had my pride. It lasted until Fredrik had caught another three fish. That wasn't very long.

What with one thing and another it had been a tiring couple of days. I took that Klinkhåmer Special and sat on a large, comfortable rock beside the tail of the last run at Taivek. In front of me the water accelerated smoothly towards the last plunge of the rapids. The broken water started at a submerged rock in midstream and as I tied on the fly I caught a glimpse of a rise in the bulge of water in front of the rock. I could cover the spot without moving from my comfortable seat. So I did. For the next hour or so I sat on that rock and cast at the fish which rose subtly and steadily within that little wave.

I never did catch that fish. Look: it is not easy casting a dry fly onto smoothly accelerating water. The leader straightens and drag is instant. So I cast the thing in coils and the fly would fall way short and ride the current magnificently or land yards beyond and tow the line through the lie like a mine sweeper. Occasionally I got it right and the Klinkhåmer rode up and over the little bulge in the prescribed manner and nothing whatsoever happened. And once, just once, as the fly swept over the rock, the fish rose at the speeding fly - and missed. It was difficult to feel too disappointed at the failure to hook this elusive fish: in the hour or so I was trying, those bungled casts and dragging flies had resulted in eight of the finest grayling I had ever caught. They had risen from everywhere but the spot where I was aiming.

On the inside of Fredrik's boat there is a scale. It shows the minimum size of fish to be taken. It is 35cm long. That is 14 inches, about a pound. I do not believe they make grayling that small in the Kaitum. We didn't see one during those days at Tjuonajokk. Those first eight fish were from 15 to 18 inches and built like brick sheds. An eighteen-inch grayling is comfortably over 2 lbs and a 2lb grayling leaping through the twisting rapids and leaning on the heavy currents of the Kaitum River does not say "it's a fair cop" and come quietly: it resists arrest.

We had all caught fish. Back at Tjuonajokk the boats of anglers were returning from the rapids upstream and downstream. Most fishermen had come in parties of three or four, sharing one of the cabins scattered amongst the trees. A network of narrow wooden pathways, looking like a child's first wooden railway set, meanders between the cabins, and connects to the sauna, the lavatories and the central log cabin that serves as dining room, office and shop. These raised pathways save the fragile arctic vegetation from the tramp of fishermen's feet. That evening the scent of wood-smoke drifted over Tjuonajokk as the outdoorsier types cooked their supper of fresh grayling in the camp's ingenious smoke stoves. Luc and I, the soft southerners, were eating in the restaurant, a bizarre combination of Lappish camp cooking and *Parisien haute monde*, the domain of Martin, the equally bizarre *chef de cuisine*, resplendent in apron and tall chef's hat fashioned in soft brown leather that would have one or two of my more colourful friends all of a do-dah.

As the light faded I made my way to the hot night spot down by the water's edge. The sauna is Tjuonajokk's answer to plumbing. First man in lights the huge old wood stove in the centre and the wood-fired boiler in the corner. The temperature rises towards unbearable as each newcomer splashes a beaker of water onto the coals on top of the stove, sending a searing wave of humidity rolling around the room. As each man reaches bursting point he fills a bucket with water from the open boiler and takes it out to mix with ice-cold water from the spring. Ladlefuls of this mixture poured over the head cleanse and cool the fisherman until he is ready to return to the sauna and resume the talk of the day's fishing. The Swedes were unfailingly considerate and switched into embarrassingly proficient English to include me in the conversation.

So I was a little taken aback the next morning when I met one of the sauna crowd on my way to breakfast.

"Moron!" he muttered as we passed.

I wondered what obscure rule of sauna etiquette I had unwittingly transgressed. The next bloke said the same, but with a smile on his face which was all the more unnerving. The same thing had happened to Luc so in the cabin we got out the Swedish phrase book. Turns out this is Swedish for "Good morning".

We met Fredrik at the boats. It is not necessary to have a guide to fish the Kaitum but an eloquent display of two dozen mangled propellers nailed to the cabin by the boat dock suggests it is not a bad idea for first timers. Besides, he had the mother-lode of Klinkhåmer Specials.

In the days that followed we watched late summer turn to autumn in the sub-arctic. The grey clouds slid down the mountainsides until they settled on the tops of the stunted birch trees at the water's edge. Spiteful little rain squalls whipped down the valley from the slopes of Kebnekaise, Sweden's highest mountain, now lost in the murk. And the fish rose with a demented urgency, sensing the freeze up of land and river just weeks away. I spent an evening by the gaslight of the cabin constructing a clutch of Klinkhåmers to replace the two Fredrik had given us which were now chewed beyond recognition. I held the first couple up to be admired by Luc. "Merveilleux!" he said, with just a touch of irony "....With these beauties we will be able to catch twice as many grayling as before." There was something of panic in the way he said it. I knew just how he felt.

137

For our final day we motored upstream to the Tjirtjam rapids, renowned even on the Kaitum river. Below the white tumbling waters the river is broad with the main channel of fast water hard beside the bank where we landed. We waded as close as we dared to the channel: the awkward, tumbled rocks of the bottom appeared deceptively close in the crystal clear waters. In the bouncing water beyond the main channel huge grey backs were porpoising through the waves - just beyond reach across the fast current: the fly would land thereabouts only to be snatched away by the drag on the line. Before long I gave up the struggle and cast shorter, into the main current where it swept down for a yard or two before disappearing in a crisp little rise. That weight of water can flatter a little fish, so you can imagine what it does for a grayling of 20 inches. I was a long time getting that fish in to land.

We ate the fish, my biggest ever grayling, spit-roast over a fire beside the river with a pot of coffee simmering in the embers and the hiss of raindrops on the hot stones as another shower drifted down onto us.

We had waded back into the rapids for our last afternoon when what we dreaded finally happened: Luc had finally found a fly that out-fished the Klinkhåmer. It was nothing to look at, a mottled-brown rag-tag of duck feather and hare's ear with long guard hairs leaking out both ends. Luc called me over when it had taken a couple of fish that had ignored the Special K. He caught another to show me what he meant. He handed me the rod and I had a go. We started giggling when it had taken three fish in three casts. I got a rise on the fourth cast and missed it, laughing. Things were becoming silly. I handed the rod back to Luc. He cast again and caught another. And another. And then we stopped.

I had waited years to stumble across just such a fly on just such a water and yet, when it happened, somehow there didn't seem much point in going on. Strange creatures, fishermen.

The fly Luc had rummaged from his fly box was "La Peute", a renowned French fly from the vice of Henri Bresson.

Tjuonajokk is a fly-in fishing camp beside the River Kaitum, 120 km inside the arctic circle. Accommodation is self-catering in comfortable log cabins, water from a spring and hot sauna by the shore. Boats, outboards and guides are available. So is a licensed restaurant but a can of beer is eye-wateringly expensive. Bring your own.

Tjuonajokk is famous for its grayling, averaging 1-1½ lbs with fish over 4½ lbs every year. The Tjuonajokk record is 2.7 Kg - 5lb 15oz! There are trout too: 5kg (11lbs), they say, are "not unusual" (who are they kidding?) but these are taken while spinning rather than on the fly. Also arctic char.

More details from: www.tjuonajokk.se but you'll probably need to get Google Language Tools to translate it for you. It works pretty well.

19

Putting on the Style

*I*n the summer of 1964 the Beatles appeared on *Top of the Pops* in some rather fetching pullovers. These were no ordinary pullovers: they were black, sleeveless, v-neck numbers with a front of black leather. They were so sharp you could have stuck a handle on them and used them as a razor. Not that I used a razor in the summer of 1964. Not every week, anyway. This pullover was clearly the business. A lad turning up at a party wearing something along these lines was pretty well bound to get off with Christina Brown.

A nasty surprise awaited me in The Marlowes, Hemel Hempstead's fashion quarter. I would have to deliver an alarming number of newspapers to buy a black leather-fronted sleeveless pullover. These things were not cheap: the Beatles must really have been coining it because they had a pullover each. By the time my paper-round had paid for just one leather-fronted pullover, Christina Brown could have been a grandmother and well past her prime. I just couldn't afford to wait that long.

Love, they say, will find a way. It did. In a shop window off the main street I spotted the very same garment – a snip at just 34 shillings. The front was not exactly leather – it was a sort of shiny black vinyl – and the back was not exactly lambswool – it was woven nylon and, frankly, it looked it. But in the sort of dim light best-suited to these enterprises, I fancied I would look uncannily like Paul McCartney at the party on Saturday. Stunned by my stylish clobber and a glass of subtly spiked fruit punch, Christina Brown would surely consent to become my partner on our journey through life. Or, at the very least, give me a snog.

I mention all this to illustrate that *style* has always been something of a gift with me. I can take no credit for this: I was just born like it. So you can imagine my interest when, the other day, I learned that the hand of style reached into the world of trout fishing.

The Clyde is not the first place you think of when it comes to style. Or trout come to that. For me, the Clyde has always conjured up monochrome images of dry docks and derricks, boiler-makers and plate-riveters in flat caps swarming like ants over the bare bones of a ship. But when a boiler-maker packed in making boilers for the week and the plate-riveter ran out of plates to rivet, they would catch the trains that left from Glasgow for the upper reaches of the River Clyde. Through Motherwell and Wishaw, Carluke and on past Lanark to Carstairs Junction the train went, scattering boiler-makers and plate-riveters like broadcast seed corn along the line. Twenty miles further upstream the line reaches Abington and Crawford. Here, barely five miles from its source beneath Clyde Law, the River Clyde is already a fair-sized moorland stream swinging through meadows of rough grazing over a gravel bed. The holiday anglers who had travelled from Glasgow would climb down from the train in Crawford and make their way the few yards to the river. And when they got there they fished *"Clyde style"*.

They had to. By 1885 David Webster of Lanark, author of *The Angler and the Loop Rod*, was already bemoaning the decline of catches on the Clyde. Anglers have talked like this since angling began and Webster still claimed to be able to catch well over ten pounds of trout in a day's fishing. Angling authors say things like that too. But details of fishing matches on the river in the middle of the century are very revealing: *the average size of these Clyde trout was just over two ounces*. The winners of the competitions were catching dozens of these tiny trout. The fishing pressure was not just from the holiday anglers of Glasgow. The same trains that brought these amateur fishermen down from the city collected nightly consignments of trout from the stations along the Clyde valley to be sold in the markets of Manchester. The trout of the Clyde did not live long enough to grow big. In order to take his expected bag of ten to fifteen pounds, Mr. Webster would have had to catch around 80 trout in his six hours' fishing. That's a trout every four-and-a-half minutes.

The need to keep up this prodigious catch rate on water as hard-fished as any in the land led to the development of the *Clyde style* of fly-fishing. The waters of the Clyde are crystal and shallow. The fish of the Clyde were small, fast and very, very scared. The fishermen of Webster's day used long rods with up to nine tiny flies strung along 16 feet of leader. To a Clyde trout every cast must have looked like a hatch of fly. Or the mother and father of all bird's nests.

A century has passed since Webster's day but the waters of the upper Clyde are just as clear and probably a little shallower. The trains no longer stop at Crawford and so I came by car along a newly-built section of motorway, a thing that can wreak more havoc in a trout population than many a train-load of industrial labour bent on pleasure. This is *Eddie Stobart* country: I slid out of a line of trucks coyly called *Marie-Theresa* and *Julie* and *Betty-Sue* and slipped down onto the old road through Crawford.

I had come to meet Ian Miller. That is what you do if you want to see the upper Clyde fished as it should be fished. Ian has lived and fished all his life around Crawford and the Clyde. We crossed the river and railway, following the line downstream to the meadows below the village. The Clyde runs north-south here, a broad highway from England into Scotland, and it has shared its valley with a succession of roads over the millennia. The remains of a Roman road hug the bank above the village with the railway just as close on the other bank. A century later the village was visited by the new A74 trunk road to the north, and finally, the motorway. And yet in the field beside the Clyde all this civilisation is hidden from view. The low, bare hills of moorland grazing spread away on all sides and there is an awful lot of sky. The banks are sheep-nibbled down to the margins and there are no trees to encumber a cast - which is just as well if you are proposing to swing nine flies around the scenery. All in all it is a lovely, lonely spot.

It is not always like this. In the early season the river is still fished hard: a fisherman every hundred yards is not uncommon at a weekend and they are there to catch fish. Clyde fishermen belong to a broad church and they will take trout with anything a trout will take. Worms, of course, and caddis larvae but they will also load a tiny hook with a single house fly or oak fly. Or a gadger – which sounds like a shipyard worker somewhere between a boiler-maker and a plate-riveter but is the nymph of the large stonefly and a very fine bait indeed. But by mid-May this feeding frenzy is over and the banks of the Clyde are left to the occasional fly fisherman and then the Clyde style comes into its own.

Ian does not use a team of nine flies. He fishes with five. Rod makers these days bang on about tensile modulus and casting a narrow loop. The last thing you want when you are waving a fistful of flies is a narrow loop: Ian fishes with a long rod – 12 feet – with a soft action that turns over a large loop to settle its swarm of flies gently on the water. This is not the team of flies of the loch fisherman, with its variety of rugged individualists to cover every angle from the small dark number, through flashy numbers in silver or gold, to the big bushy things that dibble in the surface.

The Clyde fisherman knows exactly what he is imitating in late June and his flies are all subtle variations on the theme of a little olive dun. The flies, like the naturals, are small – 16s and 18s – and slim bodied in quill or silk. The hackles are sparse, just a single turn either side of the upright wing of starling or snipe.

We began at Graveyard Flat where the Clyde runs in a long glide with a deeper channel under the far bank. Everything about this river and its fishing is subtle. There are no plunging falls and obvious pools: there are runs and glides and riffles but they merge one into the other so that one man's rocky run might be another's smoothish riffle. And the rises in amongst this lot are equally subtle. The fish that have survived the furious fishing of the early season are fish that keep their heads down. I couldn't see a thing when Ian pointed to a gently bouncing run along the far bank. He stepped into the shallow margin and worked his way above the spot before casting across and letting the team ride the current.

Nothing happened. Well, it doesn't always in fishing. He lengthened the line and began working down the run, letting the flies work round the subtle eddies and boils where the rocks beneath rumple the surface.

I didn't see the fish take the fly either. But there was the rod dipping and the line straightening off the surface and Ian was bringing in a Clyde trout. In the competitions of the 1860s there were sometimes prizes for the best six fish. These rarely reached half-a-pound each. Ian's first fish would have beaten them all. It was a foot long and in perfect condition.

Another trout, the twin of the first, came from that run before we worked our way upstream. Around the bend a stand of Scot's pine comes down to the far bank and black-headed gulls were wheeling over the river, dipping and swooping close to the surface. Over the past ten years the gulls have taken to plundering the hatches of fly like so many ponderous swallows and martins. It was a sign of good times to come. With a hatch of fly in the offing, Ian decided to switch to a single dry fly.

As he set about dismantling his swarm or flies, I was staring at the subtle boils on the surface. From time to time there was something a bit more definite about one of them. Not a lot but it was there with a momentary ring. It was a rise but only just. I was getting the gist of the Clyde. I put on a size 16 dun and worked out line to cover the spot. It looked ridiculously over-hackled, riding high on the smooth surface of the river. Evidently the trout thought so too. A splashy rise drowned the fly but the fish had reconsidered the whole enterprise at the last minute and turned away. A minute or so later Ian had changed his cast and that little twiddle of the feeding fish was back on the surface of the water.

This time the fly disappeared with no fuss at all. It was there and then it wasn't. A Clyde trout can do that. I had marked that tiny twiddle as a seven-inch fish of a couple of ounces. I was quite surprised how much bend a seven-inch, two-ounce trout could put in a twelve foot rod. When Ian brought the thing to the bank we could see it was twice that length and over eight times the weight. It was also quite the handsomest trout I had seen in a long time.

They do not run to red spots, these trout of the Clyde. Red spots, I suppose, would be too obvious. They are speckled. The dorsal fin is speckled, even the little adipose fin is speckled. The sun had come out sometime along the way and now the trout lay in the sun-dappled shallows, content to recover while we admired the shifts of colour in the light that lit up the orange pectoral fins. It did not dart as a small fish will: when it felt it was time to cruise back to the depths of the river, it cruised.

Keen students of the written word will have spotted that so far I have caught nothing. I was beginning to get the hang of this river. I removed half my leader and replaced it with the thinnest stuff I was carrying – something under five thousandths of an inch diameter. I got my smallest Easy Rider dun which has all the right stuff only rather too much of it and clipped the body as slim as it would go. I pulled out some of the hackles until the thing sagged into the surface. Upstream Ian had spotted a trout rising where the current was squeezed by a bank of gravel. It looked like a small fish - but so far everything had looked like a small fish and Ian had caught nothing below three-quarters of a pound. On the third pass over the spot the fly went down in a dimple. Finally I had scored on the Clyde.

Which is, incidentally, rather better than I did with Christina Brown on that Saturday in the summer of '64. The smell of warm plastic is not an aphrodisiac.

The United Clyde Angling Protective Association has around 40 miles of fishing upstream of Motherwell. This is mainly for trout and grayling but runs of salmon and sea trout are increasing. All legal methods are allowed. Catch limit: four 12-inch fish.

The United Clyde APA must be the best value river trouting in the country. A season ticket costs £40, day-tickets £10. These are available from tackle shops throughout Lanarkshire, Post Offices in Crawford and Abington (and elsewhere) and the Tourist Information office in the motorway services at Abington. Further information on their excellent website at www.ucapaltd.co.uk or contact the club secretary, J. Quigley, tel: 01698 382479

20

Leather

*T*wenty years ago I taught an adult evening class in the
Northamptonshire town of Brackley. The course was on
coastal navigation. Now, Brackley is about as far from the coast as
it is possible to get in Britain but folk thereabouts, it seemed,
couldn't get enough of tidal predictions and magnetic variation
and the cardinal buoyage system. I don't know why. Between talk
of Position Fixing by Horizontal Sextant Angle and the
Regulations for Preventing Collisions at Sea, we spoke of other
things. I told them that I was a bit keen on fly fishing. The next
week, sitting on my desk like an apple for the teacher, I found a
battered aluminium box. It was a dry-fly box. It was scarred with
a chalky corrosion and a few dents but otherwise it was intact.
One of the group - not a fisherman - had come across the thing on
a beach twenty-five years before. He said he didn't know what to
do with it. And then I had this really good idea: he could give it to
me. So he did.

It opened, after a fashion. Inside were the normal spring-
loaded little lids. The springs were a bit rusty and the transparent
windows were yellow, whether by design or age I couldn't tell.
Inside the lid, instead of fly clips or ethafoam, there were over-
lapping flaps of leather and a rusted pair of tweezers held in a
leather loop. And there were flies, lots of them, some on archaic

hooks with square bends, one or two with eyes of twisted cat gut and all of them rusted and ropey.

Look: don't bother to start writing in, pretending you lost a fly-box just like that back in '56. This is not one of those eye-moistening pieces from generous gentlemen that appear in the editor's letters page: *"last week I found a Hardy Perfect reel beside the Colonel's Pool on the Halladale. Would the person who lost it please get in touch . . ."* Forget it. If you lost a fly-box forty-five years ago, learn to live with disappointment. I cannot imagine how it ended up on a beach amongst the flotsam of the high-water line - but it's mine now.

Stranger things than my fly-box have been coughed up by the briny. In the early winter of 1786 a Baltic brigantine trading ship, the *Frau Metta Catharina von Flensburg* , left the Russian port of St. Petersburg at the end of the Gulf of Finland. She was laden with a cargo of hemp and leather bound for Genoa, then an independent republic amid the various duchies and kingdoms of Italy (you don't get this erudite sort of stuff in *Angling Times*). The craftsmen of Genoa were renowned for their boot-making: Russian leather was equally famous for its suppleness, resistance to water and a characteristic aroma of birch oil which seemingly made it repugnant to insects - something my wellingtons might consider.

On the 10th December the *Metta Catharina* was sheltering in Plymouth Sound when a violent gale struck out of the south-west. A local newspaper, The Sherborne Mercury of 18th December 1786, reported:

"Same night was drove on shore on Drake's Island the Motte Catharine of Flensburg bound from Petersburg, for Genoa, laden with hemp and leather; the vessel and cargo entirely lost; crew saved."

The ship and its cargo sank beneath the mud of Plymouth Sound. Nothing much happens in our story for 170 years, when some unlucky fisherman dropped his fly box on a beach, to be picked up by the bloke in my navigation class, an incident not reported in the Sherborne Mercury or anywhere else.

Seventeen years later, on the 20th October 1973, Colin Hannaford and Chris Holwill of the Plymouth Sound Sub-Aqua Club were searching the sea bed off Mount Edgecumbe, looking for the remains of *HMS Harwich*, a ship-of-the-line that had sunk in 1691. They did not find it. What they found was a ship's bell. When they winched the thing up through thirty metres of water they found that the bell was covered in writing, a ship's name, its home port and the date of launching: the *Frau Metta Catharina von Flensburg* was back in the land of the living. Returning to the spot a few days later, the club divers discovered a dense tangle of something-or-other sticking out of the mud. They brought a sample of the stuff back to the boat. It was leather.

From the name on the ship's bell and the archives in Britain and Germany they began to piece together the history of the ship and its cargo.

It's a good story, isn't it? I would love to pretend I carry that sort of thing around in my head. I don't. If anyone had asked me what the Metta Catharina was a fortnight ago I would have gone for high plateau in Argentina: either that or a bone in a horse's foot.

I only stumbled on the story the other day. I was chatting to a bloke who said he knew this other bloke who knew a bloke who made leather fly boxes. I had never really thought of leather fly boxes. I was intrigued. So I got a phone number and spoke to the second bloke who said he'd never met the third bloke – the one who made leather fly boxes – but he thought there was something special about the leather. It was meant to be two hundred years old. I was more intrigued. The second bloke rummaged about and found a phone number for the third bloke. I got through the next day. The third bloke's name was Rob Ross. Rob is a craftsman in leather, all leathers from fine goatskin to half-inch bull-hide – and two-hundred-year-old Russian leather.

He told me the story of *Metta Catharina*. Those strands of leather waving from the mud beneath Plymouth Sound were the beginning of an archaeological excavation that continues to this day. The first leather brought to the surface was decayed and badly stained but, as the work progressed, season by season deeper into the mud, the leather that began to emerge was in a remarkable state of preservation. Inside the tightly-wrapped bundles of half-a-dozen skins, much of the leather had escaped unscathed from two centuries of sea water. Year after year, the precious bundles were brought to the surface. The skins are scrubbed to remove any mud and then soaked in changes of fresh water to leach out the salt. While still wet they are rubbed with an emulsion of oils, mutton tallow and beeswax and then pegged out on a frame to stretch and dry. The result is a supple leather the rich colour of conker with all of a conker's subtly of sheen and shade.

It is with this gorgeous stuff that Rob encases the aluminium fly-boxes, hand-stitching each edge and seam. It was then that it struck me: if each box is hand-made it might be possible to have my own fly-box encased in this sumptuous stuff. I had just the thing in mind: the old box that, like this leather, had miraculously come in from the wet. They were made for each other. Rob thought it might be possible and so I arranged to drop it round on the following Tuesday.

I was standing in Rob's workshop in the little village of Caerwys in North Wales. It was full of the sumptuous smell of leather but with an overtone of something more aromatic. I was getting a tiny tang of the birch tar oil that had been infused into the Russian leather during its finishing (the process is known as "stuffing": you might want to drop this into the conversation at the next dinner party). This trace of birch oil had survived the dunking of two centuries. The heady aroma of birch oil was a vital characteristic of the fabled Russian leather. It was well-known to the fly-fishers of the time. Alfred Ronalds was a thoughtful fisherman who revolutionised fly dressing and fishing in the early 19th Century with his meticulous observations and illustrations of aquatic flies and their artificials. In his *"Fly Fisher's Entomology"* he advises the fly-tyer that *". . . as good feathers are valuable they should be guarded from the moth by camphor, Russian leather or other preservatives."* Rob Ross has taken this advice to heart and keeps his flies in the stuff: he handed me his fly-wallet, adapted from a traditional design, with leaves of felt and vellum pockets, made in the Russian leather. It glowed in my hand, its rich surface still bearing the characteristic diamond pattern that had been pressed into the drying skin.

The wall behind the bench was covered in the tools of the leatherman's trade, strange shapes of brass and steel with smoothed wooden handles, pointy bits and blades of strange purpose. A slim box, clad in the precious leather, lay on the bench awaiting stitching. It had dignity and gravitas: it could have housed a field marshal's baton. It was the case of a multi-piece rod. A box lay beside it, a fly box in the same rich dressing. It was dead posh. I fingered the battered old box in my pocket. All my fishing tackle seems to end up battered. I was not sure I could be trusted with anything as magnificent as an antique leather fly-box. I am not really built for the finer things in life: they intimidate me. I need not have worried. Every fly-box or fly-wallet in Russian leather comes with a potted history of the stuff printed on parchment. It is worth reading: it tells you just what this leather has been through since it was trotting around as a reindeer. I will be brief in case you are reading this over breakfast. It begins with a touch of putrefaction to remove the hair *". . . accelerated by sprinkling with urine"*. It moves on to the softening of the skins by immersion *". . . in a warm bath of bird's droppings or dog dung"*.

I stopped reading at that point. Suddenly I was quite glad the stuff had been soaking in Plymouth Sound for two hundred years.

Rob Ross still works as a craftsman specialising in leather sporting cases. The salvaged Russian leather is now in very short supply, but he still has enough for various small items, including the 6 compartment dry fly boxes, and leather-handled trout priests. Working in modern leather, Rob makes a traditional leather fly wallet with 4 felt leaves and various vellum pockets for casts, and can make anything from watch straps to gun- and attaché cases. Contact Rob Ross, 4 Llys Pendre, Caerwys, Flintshire, CH7 5BJ. Tel: 01352 720054.

The curious story of the leather and its history can be found in "The Wreck of the Metta Catharina" by Geoff Garbett & Ian Skelton, published by New Pages, The Cottage, Pulla Cross, Truro in 1987.

21

Disturbing Local Residents

I was loaned a book the other day. It was a first edition published in 1931. This sort of thing frightens the life out of me. I'm terrified that all the pages will fall out like autumn leaves as soon as I touch it.

The book is called "The Lakes of Wales". It lists well over 600 of the things from Aber-Hirnant to Ystwlan and contains much useful information for the fisherman such as *"This lake has now practically disappeared"* which is really rather thorough. Many writers would have left this lake out – along with the Kerry Pool (*"at present there is no pool")* – but not Mr Ward. He lists the fish to be found – if any – in each water and gives the meaning of the Welsh name and any legends belonging to the place. All in all this book is the business.

I was leafing through the thing and came across Llyn Idwal.

"In savage grandeur this magnificent tarn has no equal throughout the British Isles . . ." it said.

Now, I am rather a fan of savage grandeur. You don't get much of it round our way in Banbury. I read on:

". . . with the exception of Loch Coruisk in the Island of Skye."

I wasn't sure I wanted to settle for second best. If one is going for savage grandeur, one might as well go for the savagest and grandest. I was leaning towards a visit to Loch Coruisk instead and went to look that up in Sandison's "Rivers and Lochs of Scotland". Coruisk, he agrees, is *"one of the most dramatic and exciting lochs in Scotland."* Terrific: I was going all goose-bumpy at the thought of all that savage grandeur. I read on:

"However, be minded that to reach Loch Coruisk . . . you must negotiate the infamous Bad Step, a foot-narrow ledge above a precipitous plunge into the sea."

I have never been very keen on narrow ledges, particularly over precipices. To reach Llyn Idwal you must negotiate a pleasant, fifteen-minute path up from the café by the car park. And so it was that, on a sunny morning in late July, Philip and I set off for north Wales and the second-most savage grandeur in the British Isles.

It was sunny but there was an early morning chill in the air early in the morning when we climbed out of the car in the car park by Ogwen Cottage. Around us, chaps in climbing boots and long socks were pulling ropes and harnesses and helmets out of cars and looking round at the ring of mountains. We went over to the café. More climbers were standing around the counter drinking tea and eating thick bacon rolls. We tucked our trouser bottoms into our socks and went and hung about with them, squinting up at the ridges of rock across the valley in the way we climbers do. It is only a morbid dread of heights that stops me actually climbing. I'm quite good with the big cups of tea and the bacon rolls.

We looked a lot like rock climbers when we set off up the path that begins behind the café. We were draped in volumes of bright blue and orange nylon with any number of D-rings, shackles and clips hanging off strategic corners. Even the rods might have passed for collapsible ski-poles. It was probably the flippers, though, that gave us away.

I think they call them "rangers". Not the flippers – they call those "fins" nowadays, it seems – this was a bloke that yelled at us before we were barely two strides along the path, past his hut. He asked us what we thought we were doing, where we though we were going and what we thought we were carrying. We told him. Fishing. Llyn Idwal. Float tubes. He said we weren't. We assured him we were. It was not a promising start to a conversation.

The spectacular surroundings of Llyn Idwal and large slabs of Gwynedd around and about are owned by the National Trust. The Trust can be a bit sniffy about their fishing – and they own a lot – but some bits are leased to angling clubs. This bit is. Llyn Idwal and several other lakes in the area are leased to the Ogwen Valley Angling Association. And the Ogwen Valley AA sells day tickets. Philip and I had our tickets. We had checked with the club secretary that we might float our tubes. We explained this to the ranger bloke. He said that they didn't encourage fishing. We had begun to get that impression - although what they thought the Ogwen Valley Angling Association would get up to other than fishing is a mystery. He said that fishing might disturb the birds that nested on the slopes and crags around the lake. Just then a sort of scream rose from the direction of Capel Curig. It became a deafening roar and a jet fighter came screaming down the valley at rooftop height, flipped onto its side to make the turn around the shoulder of Carnedd Dafydd, and barrelled off down the Nant Ffrancon pass. We clapped our hands over our ears as a second jet deafened us and shook the scenery. We promised not to disturb the little birdies and left him to it.

It is a spectacular place. Llyn Idwal lies in an amphitheatre of cliffs and crags sweeping 2000 feet up from the small lake. It is actually a fair-sized lake but it is so dwarfed by those brooding walls of rock that it appears little more than a pond until you spot the figures, tiny dots of blue and orange. They are climbers clinging to the cliff face across the water. It all looked very benign in the sunshine. It is not always like this. In "The Lakes of Wales", Frank Ward describes the place in a storm when "*. . . it is*

*impossible to stand against the wind, and water is literally torn in sheets
from the surface, almost hidden by a cloud of spray covering the lake to a
height of 20 or 30 feet."* I bet that disturbs the birds more than
somewhat.

Today the wind was just a gentle breeze from the north-west,
slipping up the valley from the café and ruffling the surface of the
water. It was about perfect. We found a spot opposite a tiny,
heather-topped islet and began blowing up the tubes.

There is a strange and delightful moment in float-tubing. My
tube is the old-fashioned sort: it is modelled on a tractor tyre that
you sit inside. There is a dilemma with this design. Do you step
elegantly through the hole and then have a bulky doughnut
round your waist for the tricky business of putting on the flippers
– or do you put your flippers on first and then have tricky
business of threading them, and you, through the tube? Either
way is awkward. You then stand up, holding the tube around
your waist like a bulky tutu and shuffle gingerly backwards over
uneven stones into the margins. You usually forget your rod so
you have to shuffle back and get that. You shuffle and stumble a
little deeper: it is about as awkward a way of entering water as
can be devised. And then, with the water above the knees, you sit.
In that moment you are transformed from a stupid, encumbered,
stumbling thing into a stable, floating thing of grace and elegance.
All tubers smile a blissful smile at this moment. They can't help it.

We finned a little way out into Llyn Idwal. There may be better
places to be than afloat in a crystal lake on a sunny summer's day
within a ring of spectacular mountains, but I can't think of one
offhand.

And the water really is crystal. And surprisingly shallow. With
those steep walls towering on three sides I had imagined the shore
would plunge away into unfathomable depths. It doesn't. For the
most part it is a bright green carpet seemingly just beyond the tips
of the fins but depths are hard to judge in all that clarity.

We drifted apart. In these moderate depths you could expect a fish to be found anywhere on Llyn Idwal. But with the sun bright and high in a cloudless sky I did not, frankly, expect to find a fish at all. And for a time we didn't.

It was Philip who found one first. We had seen nothing rising and so he had decided to go down and find them. A green goldhead nymph had been sucked in by the trout that was now splashing on the surface. It was a first, fine fish of half-a-pound – but then any first fish is a fine fish. It was a lot better than I had expected. Back in 1931, Frank Ward put the average fish at 4oz with a half-pounder considered good. Nothing has changed in the years since then: Bryn Evans, the secretary of Ogwen Valley AA had told us to expect much the same. Under such a bright sky we were happy to get anything at all.

I was drifting down the lake before the light breeze, deeper into the encircling crags. The rock wall at the head of the lake is split by an immense cleft, Twll Du or the Devil's Kitchen, and it was down this terrifying chasm that young Prince Idwal was hurled by his foster-father, Nefydd Haradd. Something similar was going on to my right. The summer sun had produced a rash of towels and picnics along the small shingle beach at the lip of the lake and as the day grew hotter children were whooping and hurling themselves into the water from a rock on the northern shore. I hoped they weren't disturbing the birds.

I was drifting down towards a scattering of rocks in the middle of the lake.

There are in this world certain things which, although pleasant enough on their own, cannot realise their full, sublime potential until chance brings them together. Bacon and baked beans, for example. Tomato and freshly-ground black pepper. Wilson, Keppel and Betty. Things like that. And so it is with the float tube and dapping.

No-one daps these days. There is now only one dapping rod

on the market and no-one stocks it. But dapping is a fine way to fish and huge fun. It also has the happy habit of bringing up the better fish, fish that would not normally stir their stumps for anything on the surface but when offered an insect the size of a lavatory brush find they cannot resist. The problem with dapping is, I suspect, that it does not lend itself to precision (or the illusion of precision). It is all too obvious that the fisherman just sits on the end and waits for something to happen.

All that changes with a float tube. With a tube the fisherman is able to move around, hither and yon, and drop his dapped fly exactly where he wants it to drop. The fisherman's legs hang down into the water and provide a perfect drogue to slow the drift: by paddling gently against the wind, the tube can be made to hover in one spot so that a dapped fly can give a tasty lie a thorough going over. I was slowly bearing down on just such a spot.

The shores of Llyn Idwal are thoroughly lumpy, as if lorry-loads of assorted rock had been dumped and forgotten. This is more or less what has happened. When the glacier that once lived here melted, it carelessly dropped all the debris it had gouged from the walls. Most of this stuff was dumped at the edges but one load was dropped in the middle. A few rocks break the surface, surrounded by the dappled shallows that trout love and no-one can reach but a man in a tube. I wafted serenely on before the light breeze.

It is often thought, by non-dappers, that you need half a gale and waves like an advert for aftershave before fish will come to the dap. In fact a slightly fluky breeze is ideal. The fly sticks in the surface and then tumbles off across the ruffles in a thoroughly natural manner. I'd have grabbed it too if I were a trout.

It was a trout of thirteen inches, a comfortable three-quarter pounder. That's the real problem with dapping: the fisherman can't tell you how he cunningly caught the thing, how he placed the fly just so and moved it thusly – in dapping it is all too apparent that the fish does all the work.

And what a fish it was. Years ago, long before Frank Ward fished Llyn Idwal in the twenties, there was a vogue for stocking trout to improve the strain of a natural population. Rivers throughout the country were stocked with trout from the Test and Itchen in the forlorn hope that stony little streams in the West Country would turn out the bruising trout of the chalkstreams. For stillwaters the fashion was for something silvery: lakes, llyns and lochs were stocked with the famous fish of Loch Leven. When Frank Ward wrote "The Lakes of Wales" there were two distinct strains of trout to be caught in Llyn Idwal: the silvery descendants of Loch Levens and *"the golden trout native to the water"*.

The trout that had leapt into the sunlight to grab the huge dapped daddy was a butter-bellied bar of gold.

We had a splendid day on Llyn Idwal. Later in the afternoon we walked back to the café. It was shaping up to be a fine evening and we thought about fishing Llyn Ogwen. Besides its natural population of wild brown trout, the lake has a regular stocking with chunkier rainbows. Several stolid citizens were parked on camp chairs along the bank. They were ledgering for the rainbows of Llyn Ogwen but nothing had been caught for several hours. I wasn't surprised: it was still warm and bright. I was happy to sit in the sunshine but Philip, undeterred, launched his float tube and began to fish his way downwind, past the line of anglers. It was generally agreed he had no chance. Then he hooked a good rainbow. He brought it to hand and released it. There was some muttering from the line of stolid citizens. Then he hooked another. A good deal more muttering occurred. He released that. Things were beginning to get ugly when he hooked and released a third rainbow. They were shouting things now. They were not nice things. Something had upset them. It was hard to tell what annoyed them most: Philip

159

catching the fish or Philip releasing the fish. There is no pleasing some folk.

Shortly afterwards I was informed that there had been an addition to the rules of the Ogwen Valley Angling Association: "The use of a float tube on any of the waters is strictly forbidden".

Ogwen Valley Angling Association (www.ogwen.net) has fishing on 4 miles of the River Ogwen (salmon and sea trout), Llyn Ogwen (rainbows and browns) and several smaller mountain lakes including Llyn Idwal (wild brown trout). Day-tickets are available from the Ogwen Falls Café, by Llyn Ogwen. Also from Ogwen Bank Caravan Park and W.E. Jones (grocer), Bethesda.

"The Lakes of Wales" by Frank Ward, published by Herbert Jenkins Ltd (1931) is a gem - if you can get hold of a copy.

22

Coming Soon, to a Riverbank Near You

*P*aul Clark works in the Department of Zoology at the Natural History Museum. His e-mail is P.Clark@nhm.ac.uk - I should jot it down because one day soon you may need it.

You will be fishing on the Thames or one of its lower tributaries, or perhaps on any river flowing into the North Sea. You will reel in your line to find you have caught a crab. Not a huge crab, two inches or so across the shell, dark brown and with a distinctive "fur" covering the claws. Don't bother to jot down the description: there are no native freshwater crabs in Britain. If the thing is a crab then what you have is a Chinese Mitten Crab. You will want to tell someone. Tell Paul. He's part of the team monitoring the spread of the Chinese mitten crab with the help of Britain's fishermen.

The first Chinese Mitten crab arrived in the Thames Estuary in 1935, probably in the ballast of a ship from the Far East. Other isolated specimens turned up during the 70s but it was not until the 1992 that they were known to be breeding in these waters. The late 90s saw an explosion of the population. Suddenly they were turning up everywhere along the tideway and its tributaries. And suddenly environmentalists were worried about the impact of this alien species on native freshwater habitats.

They have good reason to worry. What little has been reported of a mitten crab's interactions with other species is alarming: it eats them. The mitten crab is the James Cagney of crustacea: small but very tough, violent and voracious. Do you remember the American Signal crayfish? That foreign marauder went over the wire from commercial crayfish farms and has spent the last decade or so displacing our smaller native crayfish and generally trashing the river fauna of southern England. But even the large signal crayfish may have met its match. A 2½ inch mitten crab is reported to have dismantled and eaten a signal crayfish in minutes. An adult freshwater mussel is safe from any native predator except the otter - but a mitten crab can open a mussel like a tin-opener. Mitten crabs, it seems, will eat anything and everything. They will even have a go at a chap's tackle. Several specimens have been found with nylon fishing line in their guts. The questionnaire from the Natural History Museum asks anglers if the crabs have attacked the fish in their keepnets. The impact of this formidable eating machine on our freshwater ecosystems is, at present, unknown.

What *is* known is the damage it can wreak on the scenery. The mitten crab burrows into river banks. The burrows are about the size and length of a vacuum cleaner hose, and in suitable soils up to 28 burrows have been found in each square metre of river bank. The honeycombed bank simply collapses. Chiswick Eyot, the picturesque island in the Thames, landmark of Varsity boat races, is under attack, its banks undermined and crumbling at an alarming rate. Anglers finding mitten crabs are also asked to report any burrowing.

You do not have to be an angler to find these things. Folk in Kew or Richmond could find them in their gardens. They have been reported crossing cricket pitches and garden lawns as they leave ponds and streams, migrating in late summer and autumn to the sea where they breed. This year they have been found as far west as Staines but they will certainly not stop there. In China they are called the "Hairy Mountain Crab" and have been found 900 miles from the sea. Nowhere in Britain is more than 100 miles from the sea.

The Chinese mitten crab may be here to stay but in China, ironically, it is disappearing. In China, where they - or more specifically, their gonads - are a delicacy, the voracious little beast is receiving some of its own medicine: it is being eaten to death. Hunting for the table has reduced the population so much that some rivers have to be re-stocked from hatcheries. And it could happen here. Mitten crabs destined for London's Chinese community are reportedly fetching £15 a kilo.

A word of warning before you start looking in the back of the cupboard for the wok and checking if there is an "R" in the month: in its native waters the mitten crab harbours a pernicious little parasite, a lung fluke, which has infected 3 million people in Asia. Amongst almost everything that isn't yet known about this little beast in Britain is whether our mitten crabs carry this parasite.

So get that wok good and hot.

This appeared in the Daily Telegraph thirteen years ago. Not a lot has changed. The liver fluke has not been found in British crabs and there is talk of commercial fishing of the beasties to control their spread. You can read a lot more about the mitten crab on the Natural History Museum's website, http://www.nhm.ac.uk/research-curation/research/mitten-crab/index.html

23

Two Cheers for the National Trust

In 1997 I had a look at fishing in National Trust properties. I had to delve. What I discovered was, I thought, rather shocking. Some gorgeous, and very desirable, water was fished only by the National Trust staff and their friends. Others were let to small private syndicates. There was a fair whiff of graft. I was incensed. I had to be careful how I reported all this because I was writing in the Daily Telegraph and rather fearful of litigation. Here's how things stood then.

The National Trust owns over 1% of the United Kingdom. This makes it comfortably the largest landowner in the country after the state itself. The main purpose of the Trust is to promote permanent preservation of this large chunk of the prettier bits for "the benefit of the nation". Of course, it is jolly nice just to know it is preserved for us but sixty years ago it was acknowledged, in the National Trust Act, that the purpose of the Trust should include the promotion of "access to and enjoyment of" these places of natural beauty and interest.

We all enjoy ourselves in different ways. The Trust lists over 25 different leisure activities that occur on their land from ballooning to windsurfing with shooting and hunting, hang-gliding and motor-cycling in between. With me it is fishing. The thought of "access to and enjoyment of" of the bright waters that flow through the Trust's lordly acres and the serene lakes that dot the Trust's parkland had me all of a do-dah. I telephoned the National Trust and asked for details of their fishing waters.

They could not tell me. There is no such list. Nor could they tell me which of the Trust's properties had rivers or lakes. They didn't know. Their regional offices might have that information. The National Trust is divided into 16 regions: I would have to ask each region. So I asked each region. The North West Region provides a single information sheet on fishing and boating in its waters of the Lake District. The other fifteen have none: that sort of thing was dealt with by the land agents of the various properties - if I knew which properties had rivers or lakes. I didn't - that's why I was phoning. Several regions offered to collect the information and send it to me.

In 1995 the National Trust published "Open Countryside", the report of the working party into access to Trust properties. The report establishes principles and makes recommendations of policy and practice. The second half of the report looks at the provision for individual activities. Fishing is something the Trust feels it does well. The report asserts that "this activity (*fishing*) is generally well controlled by the Trust" and later that "the level of use is . . . almost total". But *use* and *access* are not the same thing at all. The level of use of my garage is almost total: the access, I hope, is severely restricted to me and the wife, otherwise all those locks are a waste of time.

There is a simple test for access to a National Trust water: can you or I fish there?

The Severn Region sent details of their game fisheries. They have trout fishing on the River Windrush and the Sherborne Brook: it is let to three private individuals. There is salmon and trout fishing on the River Wye at the Weir Gardens. The fishing on one bank is let to a private syndicate. You and I once had access to the fishing on the other bank: until recently it was let weekly with a National Trust holiday cottage. Now the cottage is used for staff accommodation and the fishing is unavailable. We can fish on the River Coln at Bibury where the fishing is let to the Swan Hotel.

It is a similar story in Northumbria. The Trust's waters on the rivers Coquet and Wansbeck are let to a private syndicate. The lakes at Crag Lough and Cragside are let to small angling clubs who do not issue day-tickets. You can get a weekly permit to fish the South Tyne at Bellister Castle. But this is not all the water the Trust owns in Northumbria: it is all they told me about when I enquired about their fishing. The properties of the National Trust are listed in a book called just that. In there you will find "Allen Banks", 200 acres of hill and river scenery along the banks of the River Allen, a tributary of the South Tyne. I spoke to the agent and enquired about this fishing. I was told that the Trust's water was not fished, had not been fished, in accordance with the donor's wishes. This is curious. Allen Banks was given to the Trust in 1942. Also, one of the clubs that leases water from the Trust was asked to tender for the Allen Banks fishing but were told their bid was too low. They believe it has gone to a private syndicate.

In the guide to their properties the Trust gives a list of abbeys and other religious establishments, always a good place to look for fine fishing. Mottisfont Abbey in Hampshire has some of the finest. The River Test is arguably the most renowned trout water in the world. The Test and its side streams flow through the abbey grounds but you and I do not have "access to and enjoyment of" any of this fishing. Not unless we are being entertained by one of the companies that leases this water from the Trust. The Abbey Stream in front of the priory is not leased: it is fished only by members of staff.

Fountains Abbey has nothing so grand as the River Test. The River Skell is a small stream channelled into water gardens and a large lake in one corner of Studley Park where the anglers of

Ripon once enjoyed splendid sport before the Trust acquired the abbey and closed the fishing.

They closed the fishing at Belton House too. For many years Lord Brownlow leased the trout fishing on the River Witham and the carp fishing on the lake to the Grantham Angling Association. They were asked to leave when the Trust took over the property. The lake was subsequently let to a small syndicate and is now run by the Trust on annual membership. The River Witham is not fished at all despite a yearly plea from the Grantham Anglers.

The catalogue goes on: properties where the waters have been closed to anglers, properties where waters are leased to individuals, private syndicates or closed clubs. It does not have to be done like this.

Happily, on many Trust properties, it is very different.

In Devon the visitor can fish the wooded valley of the River Teign, the rocky gorge of the East Lyn and the lovely little Plym. These waters are all leased to clubs that issue day-tickets as well as annual memberships. In Cornwall, the Trust issues visitors' permits for its stretch of the River Fowey.

In Cumbria the Trust owns vast areas of the Lake District and fishing on many of the lakes, hill tarns and becks is available to the visitor - with the exception of some choice salmon fishing on the Derwent at Dunthwaite which is privately let. There is, uniquely, a National Trust leaflet with details of all their Lake District waters.

You and I can fish much of the Trust's waters in north Wales and parts of Yorkshire, either with a permit from the Trust itself or through day-tickets from the clubs that lease its waters.

The "Open Countryside" access report gives guiding principles for the management of many activities on Trust land. It recommends that special conservation clauses should be incorporated in any lease of fishing - "preservation for the benefit of the nation" is the Trust's primary purpose. But "access as a fundamental way of providing this benefit" is a principal purpose and access clauses might equally be incorporated into leases. There might even be an Angling Membership to cover all of the Trust's waters just as members can visit any of the great houses. Something similar is being considered for other activities.

Meanwhile there are more private leases and more closed fisheries. The reasons for this are not hard to fathom. Years ago I ran the library in a large secondary school. Believe me, a library would be much easier to run if only people would not keep coming in and borrowing the books.

And there can be other reasons: some of the books may be just too good to be loaned.

"Properties of the National Trust" describes a small wood in the west of England. The wood includes a stretch of a pleasant little trout stream that was not mentioned in the list of waters they had sent me. I phoned the regional office and was passed on to warden for that property. It was only a short stretch, he said, a few hundred yards. They don't allow fishing here "because of the otters". We are a sentimental race: anything that has been cuddled on camera by Virginia McKenna and Bill Travers is sacred to we Brits so I assured him that I quite understood and said goodbye. "But", he said, "if you're passing this way and fancy some great fishing there is a small lake on the estate - about four acres - stuffed with carp and hardly ever fished."

Was it open to the public? Was it fished by an angling club?

"No, no, just by me and the Head Forester. Come and try it"

Now, that's what I call access.

The National Trust was frightfully nice to me after this article appeared. I was invited to a meeting of a committee where fishing management and access policies were to be discussed. I went along with Vaughan Lewis who was there as a fisheries consultant. Things changed.

Not a lot – but in the right direction. Three years later I could write in the Telegraph . . .

Three years ago I was ranting in these pages about the National Trust. The Trust owns over 1% of the country, making it easily the largest landowner after the state itself. This probably makes it also the largest owner of fishing rights. It was hard to be sure: when I tried to find out just how much of this lovely fishing they were preserving for the benefit of the nation, it emerged that the Trust itself had no means of knowing how much water it owned, which bits were being fished or by whom. Who, exactly, was getting the benefit of all this preservation? Leases and licences had been arranged *ad hoc* by individual property managers, some of whom may have been red hot on Georgian facades and Jacobean plasterwork but didn't know their River Axe from their River Ebble on fisheries. The result, in some regions, was a muddle with little apparent policy on fishery management or access by the public – access, that is, by *me*: I take these things very personally.

But then, incredibly, things began to change. The National Trust is not swift but it is thorough. In 1998 Vaughan Lewis of the Windrush Aquatic Environment Consultancy was commissioned to produce an independent report and fisheries management plan for Trust waters. It arrived last year. The result, for us fishermen, will appear before the end of this year. It is, in part, a booklet.

Enjoy Fishing With the National Trust is a little masterpiece. In its own small way it is a thoroughgoing counterblast to the unthinking antis that would ban all field sports, including fishing. The Trust has no axe to grind about fishing: it can – and does – ban it on waters where it believes it conflicts with its wider aims of the conservation of rare animals and fragile habitats. Elsewhere, though, the Trust positively welcomes fishing at its properties, recognising that *"Fishing can also encourage good environmental management of watercourses and their associated habitat . . . This can benefit a great many species, not just fish"*. Which is what fishermen have been saying for years. The booklet goes on to outline the sort of fisheries the Trust aims to provide. These are essentially wild, self-sustaining stocks of indigenous fish in natural densities and species. A set of National Trust Fishery rules has been produced to lessen the impact of fishing on these waters. They re-establish a closed season for all types of fish, limit the number of anglers and their catch, discourage mountains of ground-bait and ban live-bait altogether. It is, in short, a model of responsible, low impact fishery management.

The bulk of the booklet is given over to what I had been waiting for all these years, a catalogue of National Trust waters with details of the fishing and phone numbers.

The range of water is staggering, everything from small ponds to broad rivers, from mountain tarns to lordly chalkstreams. Most of them are managed by fishing clubs and quite a few of these are restricted to members only. In future, I am assured by the bloke in charge of such things, new leases should include some day-ticket provision for visitors. It cannot be too difficult: the National Trust is in the visitor business. But some of the tastiest waters do not appear in the list at all. The River Test at Mottisfont Abbey is leased to several companies for corporate entertainment and several other stretches of tasty trout-stream are leased to individuals and small private syndicates where there is no public access. Other waters do not appear in the list because this is the Trust's first stab at cataloguing their waters and they have just missed them out. Read the thing when it emerges: if you think the Trust has some fishing they have not listed then ask for an explanation. All this water is, after all, preserved for you and me. Let's enjoy it.

* * *

And that year I did enjoy one of those changes. The waters in the booklet were arranged by regions of the National Trust which gave bits of it a charming whiff of the dark ages: would I find Morgan-le-Fay rising out of the water I went to find in Wessex?

You know you're arriving somewhere posh when all the places have double-barrelled names. A mile or so beyond the road to Sixpenny Handley and Tollard Royal there are turnings to Gussage All Saints and Moor Crichel. I was in deepest England, the England of soft pink brick and tile, of fragrant, bee-loud villages inhabited by eccentric vicars who get themselves foully done to death in the billiard room with the candlestick: a country-side infested by batty old spinsters played by Margaret Ruther-ford or similar who have the whole case solved and sorted in time for high tea at the big house. At Tarrant Hinton I turned off the A354, skirting around Blanford Forum on the lanes through Tarrant Launceston, Tarrant Monkton and Tarrant Rushton. At Tarrant Keyneston I turned onto the road to Wimborne Minster. I didn't get there: a mile or so before the town I reached my destination. I had arrived at Kingston Lacy.

Kingston Lacy is the big house and as fine a spot as you could wish to get yourself beaned by Colonel Mustard in the study with the lead piping. It is that sort of place, a 17th Century pile designed for Sir Ralph Bankes by Sir Roger Pratt (I've been reading the National Trust handbook). It stands in 254 acres of wooded park and is stuffed to the gills with Titians, Rubens and Van Dykes. There is, apparently, a fine collection of Egyptian artefacts. Which is nice. And, tucked out of sight in a fold of the chalk lands on the other side of the road, there is a stretch of the little River Allen. Which is even nicer.

The River Allen? *It's a chalkstream, Jim, but not as we know it.* The chalkstreams of southern England are rare and special beasts.

171

They are not rare in southern England, of course: in parts of Dorset and Hampshire you trip over the things at every turn. They positively get in the way. And they are not rare in fishing literature. For various reasons, not entirely unconnected with an excellent train service from Waterloo, these few streams have dominated the literature of English fly-fishing: at times you might think that no right-minded trout would be caught dead in any other sort of stream. But in the overall scheme of things the chalkstream is a rare beast: well over half of the world's total supply of chalkstream runs through these few soft valleys and villages of southern England. And the thing is, it's a discontinued model: they aren't making any more of them.

The enduring image of an English chalkstream is familiar enough from a thousand illustrations in books and magazines. A stream of bright water hurrying, bank-high through lush water meadows. The surface is not smooth but bulges gently with the wafting of luxuriant weed that trails downstream and twitches to the lively current. And in between these banks of weed lies the pale gravel, the very stuff of the chalk downs, shining in the summer sunshine, highlighting the darker shapes of trout and grayling that hover and swoop in the channels between the weeds.

The River Allen is not as other chalkstreams. There was precious little swooping to be seen on the River Allen that day. The water may have been bright: it was hard to tell. In places it was hard to spot water at all through the dense reeds that choked the stream. Between the reeds the water moved sluggishly, deep and dark and uninviting. Altogether it was the sort of place you might find Humphrey Bogart, floundering along up to his shoulders, with the *African Queen* on the end of a rope. It was not hard to imagine - particularly as, at that moment, a bloke up to his shoulders in the River Allen came floundering through the reeds. It was not Humphrey Bogart - it wasn't even close – it was

Vaughan Lewis.

Vaughan is a fisheries consultant. Amongst other things he mends broken rivers. And the poor old river Allen had certainly received several nasty dents in the past.

It all started to go wrong for the Allen sixty years ago. It was 1940 or thereabouts, the darkest days of the war, when England was living under the threat of imminent invasion. In deepest Dorset there was a numbing realisation that even a crack battalion of formidable lady sleuths in tweed suits and sensible shoes was unlikely to stop a Panzer division that had fought its way from the Ardennes to Sturminster Marshall. Something Had to Be Done. They decided to deepen the River Allen. Whether this drastic measure would have saved Hinton Parva from being crushed beneath the Nazi jackboot we shall never know. It certainly wreaked havoc on the River Allen. But not nearly as much havoc as the diggers and dredgers of the Wessex Water Authority would wreak in the years that followed.

It was a pattern that would be repeated on rivers the length of the land. In the lean years after the war farmers were exhorted, encouraged and entreated to bring more land into production. The water meadows around the brimming chalkstream were too lush for crops - but what if they could be drained? So they dug a little more out of the Allen, spreading the fertile spoil on the banks, raising them a little more. The high waters of winter that had once spread out across the meadows now hurried on down the channelled river, arriving in a heap at Wimborne and threatening to dampen its doorsteps. So they dug a little more out of the Allen. As the little river deepened, its summer waters slowed and the reeds that had once been kept to the margins encroached, choking the river and threatening to undo all the splendid efforts of the dredgers. And so, to remove the reeds, they dug a little more out of the Allen. And so it went on.

They were still at it in 1982 when the last of the Bankes of

Kingston Lacy left the estate to the National Trust. The following year the River Allen played its last card when the beat at Kingston Lacy produced a grayling of 3lb 10oz, a fish that would hold the official British record for the next five years. By now the waters were leased to the Wimborne and District Angling Club but ever-increasing weed growth, and bore-hole abstraction to flush the lavatories of Bournemouth, persuaded the club to give up its lease. The fortunes of the little river had bottomed.

And then, five years ago, the little River Allen began to get lucky.

Fishing has never been high on the list of priorities for the National Trust. Their interests lean more towards Titians, Rubens and Van Dykes: they go goose-bumpy at a fine collection of Egyptian artefacts. And then Marcus Brown became the National Trust's property manager at Kingston Lacy. And Marcus Brown is a fisherman. And there was more: not long after this the National Trust began to show a quickening of interest in the thousands of waters it owned. Realisation dawned that they might do a lot more than simply reflect a Georgian facade or carry the eye towards an avenue of trees planted by the third earl in memory of a favourite spaniel. As part of this review of National Trust waters, Marcus and the little River Allen received a visit from Vaughan. A plan was made.

Mending rivers is not cheap: it depends on what is broken. The Allen was only dented: its water quality remains superb, bubbling cool and clear from the chalk around Gussage St Andrew and Monkton Up Wimborne (I'm not making these up). The Bournemouth and West Hampshire Water Company has agreed to a reduction of abstraction from the chalk, easing the recent low flows of summer. The water company is also stumping up nearly half of the £30,000 needed for the first phase of the river's restoration. The other half of the funding has been provided by the National Trust itself, the Environment Agency,

The Wild Trout Trust and the Salmon and Trout Association.

Thirty thousand will buy you a lot of stuff. Amongst other things it will buy you two-and-a-half thousand tons of assorted stone and gravel. Most of this was standing on the river bank as Vaughan pushed through the reeds and hauled himself out of the water. The solution to the ills of the Allen is relatively straightforward: for sixty years people had been digging stuff out of it. Now they were about to put a load of stuff back.

It is not, of course, quite as easy as that. Dumping 2½ thousand tons of gravel can do some damage, particularly if you are standing under it - if, for example, you are a crayfish. The River Allen still has a thriving population of white-clawed crayfish, the native species that has all but disappeared from southern England. It is very, very illegal to dump gravel on a native crayfish. A survey had identified several crayfish hotspots: they would be spared the gravel. The water voles were more of a problem. Before the gravel was dumped beside the river the banks were strimmed to the bone to persuade the voles to decamp to the other bank for the duration. Both the voles and the crayfish would be coming home to splendid new accommodation, thanks to the faggots. Have I mentioned the faggots?

The years of dredging had deepened and widened the river in places. The gravel would make it shallower, new banks of hazel faggots would restore its original width. Chestnut stakes are driven into the bed on the line of the new bank. The faggots are secured to the stakes and the space behind this faggot wall is back-filled by slicing off the over-high river bank, forming a broad margin just above river level. This reproduces the brimming, bank-high water of the typical chalkstream with its damp, rich margins. The voles and crayfish find snug homes in the nooks and crannies of the faggot bundles along with the infinite variety of creepy-crawlies that fill out the rich menu of a chalkstream trout. And when the winter rains flood the river the water will spill out across its new, broader margins, dissipating its power and sparing the doorsteps of Wimborne.

The digger roared into life. Marcus and I watched as the bucket dug deep into the gravel and swung the first load out across the reeds of the Allen, dropping it with a crash into the waters. The water turned milky with chalky earth from the gravel and an ugly scum of foam was carried onto the reeds downstream. So Marcus and I headed upstream to go fishing.

There are parts of the Kingston Lacy water where the reeds have not taken over, that have been spared the worst of the dredging over the years. Here the river runs a little swifter and shallower although still sunken below high banks thick with reed and nettle. Marcus pushed his way through the vegetation and slithered into the river. I followed. It was slightly eerie down there between the high banks. Nothing was moving on the water. We could hear the digger thrashing away, two bends downstream and I had my doubts that there was a fish left within half a mile of where we stood. Marcus cast a lightly weighted nymph upstream. And nothing happened.

Nothing happened for another half dozen casts. And then there was a bulge in the water beyond the line and something big and frantic burst through the surface. I don't know why I was so surprised: it was, after all, the reason we were standing there in the river throwing flies about. I just was. I was less surprised when a second fish fell for Marcus's fly a few minutes later. By the time the third fish came waltzing downstream from that same bend on the River Allen I was getting some idea of the potential of this little river.

Look: this is the story of a river. It is not a story of fishing with Marcus - who was meant to be on leave and at home painting the living room and who, if his wife ever reads this, is going to be in a spot of bother. We fished. Trout up to fourteen inches occurred. Also big grayling although not nearly as big as 3lb 10oz. And after a while we climbed up from the water and walked back down the river towards the sound of the digger.

One vast heap of stone and gravel had disappeared from the bank. A staggering transformation had taken place. I had expected a scene of devastation that would take a season or so to soften. Not a bit of it. Where, just a couple of hours before, a deep, dark bend had been choked with reed, the River Allen was spanking down a brand new, shiny bright riffle. It was magnificent. A deeper run had been left under the far bank where the water bounced beneath the overhanging grasses. We stood and gazed and marvelled at the difference a few hundred tons of mixed gravel can make. And as we stared at the cheerful riffling of water over bright stones there was a subtler movement under the dancing surface. It hardly seemed possible. But it was happening. A trout had eased down from the deeper, darker water and was edging downstream onto the riffle. It slid across the current until it found a deeper scrape in the gravel and there it hung in the current. I watched it for a while and missed the arrival of a second fish which announced itself by rising flamboyantly at the head of the riffle.

The new, improved River Allen was already open for business.

It was too. In 2000, the factfile at the end of this article in Trout and Salmon read:

"The National Trust has just under a mile of the River Allen at Kingston Lacy . . . Day tickets are available from the Kingston Lacy Estate Office, Tel: 01202 883402 and cost £15 (National Trust Members), £25 (non-members)."

But old habits are hard to kick, particularly if you weren't all that keen to kick them in the first place. Recently I learnt that the National Trust at Kingston Lacy has let this tasty piece of water, much improved with help from the Environment Agency, the Wild Trout Trust and the Salmon and Trout Association, to a private syndicate.

So much for the assurance that "new leases should include some day-ticket provision for visitors".

But I do have some good news to pass on. The fishing at Allen Banks – remember the bit I was told could not be fished "in accordance with the donor's wishes". Well, I've just spotted this bit of water as a beat in the Tyne Rivers Trust angling passport.

24

First Chuck on the Chalk

We don't have much geography in our bit of the country. I remember doing geography in 3a with our form master, "Bert" Owen. We did about volcanoes and the formation of coral atolls and synclines and so forth. Also glaciation. To this day I have a working knowledge of *moraines* (lateral, medial and terminal) and an easy familiarity with the likes of a *bergschrund*, the large split or *crevasse* at the back of a *corrie* or *cirque* where the newly forming glacier begins to move downhill. But you don't see a lot of this sort of geography round Banbury. To be frank, we don't have a lot of geology either. We just have soil.

It was two weeks after the end of the trout fishing season and father and I were driving west on a misty morning. Half an hour or so west of Banbury and you are in the Cotswolds which are something of a puzzle for chaps who have learnt their geography from "Bert" Owen. The Cotswolds are limestone but they are not limestone as we know it in 3a. Where are the Limestone Pavements? Where are the swallow holes and extensive cave systems? Where the flora typical of a Karst Region? Where the typical river gorges? Cirencester is pleasant enough in its way but it could really do with something like the gorges and luminously clear waters of the Dordogne and the Tarn.

From Cirencester we swung south as the morning mist began

179

to burn off. Through Malmsbury and Chippenham it was turning into another of those splendid days we had last October when the sun shone like June but you enjoyed each moment all the more, knowing that it could be, had to the be, the last improbable balmy spell before the blasts of autumn and winter proper. It was a day suffused with that sort of desperate nostalgic enjoyment of a last fling: we were heading for an area of the country where a quirk of fate has extended the trout fishing season to the middle of October.

Wessex. Even the name is nostalgic, vaguely Arthurian. I imagine Offa, or some such, clapping a rudimentary knighthood onto some local chief who had slaughtered an unlucky band of Vikings caught snooping round his henhouse. "Henceforth", he says, putting an arm like a country ham round the chap's shoulder, "and for all time, your children and your children's children shall bear the name 'Daneslayer'. Also, you can have an extra fortnight's trout fishing at the end of the season". Something like that.

(I *know* that the waters to the east, in Hampshire, Sussex and Kent, have even later trout fishing but this area is the NRA's "Southern Region" - a name with no romance at all and smacking of "the cancellation of the 07.43 from Carshalton Beeches due to a shortage of rolling stock".)

At Westbury you come face to face with more geography than you can shake a stick at. From here the great swelling of Salisbury Plain spreads to the east with its rolling curves of sheep-nibbled turf under a huge sky. There are also satisfactory amounts of geology just beneath the thin turf of the downland. On the slopes above Westbury the huge white horse cut in the hillside announced that we were in chalk country. We had done chalk downlands in 3a, the winter rainfall on the dry uplands percolating through the permeable chalk, re-emerging as springs along the base of the downs: that sort of stuff. From Warminster the old A36 runs along the southern edge of Salisbury Plain, connecting the ancient villages that grew up along this line of bright springs: Norton Bavant, Heytesbury, Upton Lovell, Codford St. Peter, Codford St. Mary. And beside the road flows the bright stream that collects the steady flow from these chalk springs. The River Wylye.

I have never been a great fan of chalkstreams. In the same way that I have never been a great fan of Lobster Thermidor: we have not run into each other often enough to form any attachment. Frankly, I have never been able to afford it. Not for a season, anyway, and day-tickets on the famous chalkstreams of the south are rare indeed and consequently of the sort of price that has me calculating the price I would be paying for each cast and the cost of the time it takes to untangle a tippet and put on a new fly. That's how I know I can't afford it.

And then, a year or so ago, I was flipping through a catalogue of hotels. In the index of the Johansens Hotel Guide there are some pretty nifty establishments and they are grouped in various categories: "Hotels with heated indoor swimming pools", "Hotels with golf (on site)" - and "Hotels with salmon and trout fishing". So I looked this last one up. There were all sorts. And one, Bishopstrow House near Warminster, had "access to fishing within the hotel grounds, on the banks of the River Wylye". So last month I phoned them. Did they really have fishing on the Wylye? Well, sort of. They have a hundred yards at the bottom of the garden. We agreed that was not *really* fishing. "But", she said diffidently, "if we do get someone who wants to fish the Wylye we can always get them a day-ticket on the Sutton Veny Estate water upstream".

It was true. In this magical spot at the top end of the beautiful Wylye valley, nestling under the southern skirts of Salisbury Plain, Alex Walker farms the Sutton Veny Estate with its four miles of fishing along the river. And, along with season rods that have fished this stretch for twenty or thirty years, there are one or two day tickets.

Mixing season rods with day tickets can have its problems but these have all been avoided (or at the very least overwhelmed) by retaining the ancient, and arcane, beat system that has died out elsewhere along the river but which ensures that everyone has an equal crack at all stretches of the water. It is fiendishly complicated. If I have grasped the thing, it ensures that a full-season-rod would fish a different beat every day for a week and a half and would fish the same beat on the same day of the week only every other month or so. The situation with half- and quarter-rods is not nearly so straightforward. And interlaced through all this are the day-rods which dance to the same tortuous tune.

That morning we were to fish beat SV1. We approached the river through the riverside hamlet of Norton Bavant in the last decade of the twentieth century. The Wylye runs just out of sight behind a dilapidated and deserted old mill - and about a century or so earlier. You see the sort of thing in those paintings of rustic poverty that the Victorians were so keen on: tumbledown houses beside a charming stream with some flaxen-haired urchin feeding ducks. A week ago I would have put money on the last disused mill on an English chalkstream getting its oil-fired AGA and fitted Smallbone kitchen sometime in the late seventies. But there it was in front of us, slipped tiles, gap-toothed windows, weeds and all. The track led between the buildings of the old mill and over a rickety bridge of railway sleepers to a small glade in a stand of poplars beside a magnificent weir pool.

I would not kid you: as I backed the car between the trees we caught sight of a rod curved against the sky. On the footbridge across the weir there was a figure in the act of fighting a big fish.

There have been some appalling films come out of Hollywood in the last fifty years. One of the worst is a musical starring Gene Kelly and some other bloke. *"Brigadoon"* - the title is the name of a small village which Kelly and the other bloke stumble across whilst wandering lost in the mist of the Scottish Highlands. A strange place, this Brigadoon. For a start the inhabitants have the worst Scottish accents ever unleashed onto innocent cinema-goers. Also they have no modern appliances or knowledge of the present day: their clothes are strangely old-fashioned. It turns out that, for some implausible reason that I forget, the village comes into existence for only one day every hundred years and Gene Kelly has fetched up in Brigadoon on that very day. Climbing out of the car beside the Wylye at Norton Bavant I knew just how he felt. I hurried around the weir pool to the footbridge. The fisherman was still playing his fish. He was an elderly gentleman. He was dressed for fishing in pristine corduroys, an immaculate checked shirt and tie beneath a smart tweed jacket. A gold chain led from the buttonhole in his lapel to a pocket watch in his top pocket. You don't often see these sartorial standards by the riverside these days. Not on the rivers I fish, anyway.

And then I noticed his hat. It was one of those comfortable tweed things. Now, these are common enough: what made me uneasy was what was on the hat. Several spare leaders, each with a different fly on the end were wound around the hat in exactly the fashion I had come across in a description of a professional Tweed fisherman of the last century. Now, I am as rational as the next man and I realise that these things cannot happen. On the other hand, that's just what Gene Kelly thought and it caused him no end of trouble before he worked the thing out. Better be on the safe side. I was just wondering how I could casually ask the gentleman the name of the reigning monarch when I noticed he was holding a palpably modern carbon fly rod.

Mr. Collins first fished the Sutton Veny water on the Wylye twenty-five years ago, some time after taking up fishing "rather late in life". He showed me the small fishing book in which he records every fish he has taken since those days: and another entry was added as the fish he had been playing when we arrived had by now been netted, dispatched and weighed. For once, I was in no great hurry to start fishing and we stood on the bridge and chatted, looking into the deep waters of the Wylye above the weir. A huge shape drifted across a pale patch on the bottom. A leviathan trout. But then it drifted back and the shoulders were just too broad, the wrist of the tail too slender and its twin followed it across the pale patch: a pair of splendid carp.

It is pleasant to see other species tolerated in an English chalkstream. Too often such prestigious waters are vacuumed into an artificial trout monoculture.

While I tackled up, Mr. Collins set about fishing the rushing waters of the weir pool, coiling the leader with its discrete dry-fly carefully around his hat and uncoiling something a little more uncompromising and visible. He had selected a Feather Duster, an admirably bushy number I have used myself since I started fishing. It was invented many years ago for the turbulent waters of the West Country. Invented, it turns out, by two fishermen staying by the Barle who pinched the original feather to be palmered along the length of the hook from the hotel maid's feather duster. And one of those larcenous fishermen was Mr. Hubert Collins, whose nephew was now landing a small grayling from the weir pool in front of me. I am rather fond of these ancient angling connections.

I can only watch so many fish being caught by someone else before I have to start fishing myself. Two is so many. I left Mr. Collins at the weir at the bottom of beat SV2 and walked upstream to find father.

The next beat upstream begins as the ponding of the mill weir runs out. Here the water is shallower and swifter, running over bright gravel, pushing through a kaleidoscope of water weeds ranging from bright green to bright green with half-a-dozen shades of bright green in between. Nothing was rising in view.

Now, small rainfed rivers are my meat and drink. I can stand by one of these and spot the places where a trout must be sitting, the places where he might and places where he won't. I often get these completely wrong. But at least I think I know where to start. Faced with my first vibrant chalkstream I was somewhat at a loss: every run between the weeds looked like it would hold a fish and I couldn't see anywhere that looked like it wouldn't. How do you know where to cast? It took some time for the obvious answer to hit me over the cranium.

I suppose I might have stood there all day with a dozen tasty little weed channels in front of me, unable to decide which one to fish. I hope not. As it was, a small twiddling under the surface called attention to a feeding fish and I bunged on a smallish Pheasant Tail nymph and cast it up thereabouts. The first cast of the day, like the first pancake, does not count: I missed the channel by some way. The nymph drifted down further into midstream and then twitched. So did I. I was astonished to meet some resistance. And I bet the grayling was too. I was fairly sure that this was not the fish I had seen feeding so I slipped it off hook and cast again as originally intended. I don't recall how many casts it took - probably more than I think - until the line twitched again and there was another grayling.

Do you find this? I see more rises when I am fishing than when I am looking for rises. Perhaps I am looking harder at a smaller area. While I was casting for the second fish, I had noticed another rise across the stream and so as soon as the second grayling had been released I cast up and across. Again the cast did not go where I had seen the movement. It didn't seem to matter. The third fish was not a small grayling. The surface bulged as I struck and a vast thing moved off upstream gathering weeds like a cyclist through a back alley full of washing lines. It was a rainbow, one of those stocked in the first weeks of the season when the local browns are still a bit lethargic. I think the weeds took some of the stuffing out of it. They took some of the stuffing out of me. We were both exhausted when I got it into the bank. Three fish without moving a yard. And the first inkling about a healthy chalkstream in the flush of youth began to seep though: there are fish everywhere.

I went upstream to pass this notion on to father. He already knew. I found him playing a splendid brown trout beneath a horse chestnut with the swelling chalklands of Salisbury Plain rising beyond the river.

We fished on through that splendid absolutely-the-last day of trout, each cast and rise and fight relished all the more for being possibly the last of the year. A lovely day, perhaps the best of the season. I think so.

And if that magical little corner of England by the mill at Norton Bavant does exist for just one day every hundred years, well then, they chose a good day for it.

That day was, I think, my first fishing of a chalkstream. Glory be, you can still get a day ticket on the lovely waters of the Wylye at Sutton Veny. Twenty years on they are even lovelier because, deep joy, the fishing is now all for wild fish. The cost is £60 and booking is essential: for details phone 01985 212325 or email roz@chalkstream.co.uk.

25

What I Did on My Hols

*A*ny child will tell you. When I was at primary school there were two stories beloved by all teachers. The first was "A Day in the Life of a Penny". The other was "What I Did on My Holidays".

We will deal with the first. Whenever I change my trousers I transfer any folding money into the clean ones. I throw the change into my top drawer. Pretty soon I go back and pick out the silver when the folding stuff runs out but the brown boys could stay there till doomsday. A day in the life of any of my pennies consists of sitting in my top drawer. And so to the other sort of story.

The best week of the year is the last week of May. The rivers are in the best shape, the flies burgeoning and the trout up and doing before the heat of the summer. But my wife is a teacher and my girls are in school and this is half-term. We go on holiday.

This is not a fishing holiday, you understand. When I become rich and crusty and get my own way I shall go on a fishing holiday for the last week of May. Meanwhile I go on holiday and fish.

Fishing away from home, on unfamiliar waters under unfamiliar conditions, teaches you a lot. Fishing abroad, for unfamiliar species with strange methods and even stranger companions, teaches you a lot more. Each year I learn more about fishing in that one week at the end of May than in the rest of the season.

The first thing I learnt, many years ago now, was that fishing on holiday is not the same as a fishing holiday. Wives know these things instinctively: husbands have to learn them. My idea of a holiday is to go north to the cool waters of the Lake District or Scotland, or west to the mountains of Wales or the moors of Devon and Cornwall. Judi's idea of a holiday is to head south for the sun. We compromise. We head south for the sun.

The second thing I learnt was that there are trout to be found just a few miles from the sun-baked Mediterranean beaches from Spain to Turkey and all points between. There are trout in the mountains behind Malaga, in the hills of Cyprus and on the slopes of Mount Olympus. It is a quirk of geography that has Britain's trouty highlands to the north and west. Europe's highlands are predominantly to the south along the Mediterranean where the ancient collision of Europe and Africa buckled the continents into towering mountain chains.

And what trouty mountains they are. The limestone of Yorkshire's dales is the basis of the fine fishing in the Ure, Wharfe, Swale and Eden. Much of the mountainous mass from the Cantabrian Mountains in northern Spain, through the Pyrenees and Alps, to the Balkans and beyond is made of this magical stuff. And the trout and flies are there too.

The trout and grayling in these rivers are similar throughout Europe. The range of methods and techniques employed to get them out onto the bank can be very different. The English can get a bit sniffy about this: perhaps the way a nation's fishermen set out to catch fish is as good a reflection of a nation's psyche as any other. If so, there could be no more revealing contrast than that of the prestigious chalkstreams on either side of the English Channel.

The chalk lands that spawn the manicured waters of the Test

and the Itchen re-emerge across the Channel to underlie the famous trout streams of Normandy, the Risle and its tributary, the Charentonne. At Aclou, close to the confluence of the two streams, the Risle divides around a mill and the glorious fishing lodge of La Behottiere. Charles Ritz, who had fished all the very the best waters, regarded this stretch as *"the finest in the world and better than the finest reaches of the Test, the Itchen or the Wylye"*. This makes it pretty fair by any standard. By a fluke of good fortune I was able to fish on this spot for one day. It was hot and lush with luxuriant weed trailing under fronds of weeping willow (sounds quite good, doesn't it?). On a bright morning I started in the deep shade of the small stream below the mill. Within a minute or so a fine chub sucked in the fly. I was incensed. Would he have done that to Ritz? I thought not. Upstream a few dace were coursing across the fast water at the tail of a pallid pool. There was worse, or perhaps better, to come. In the pool a large shoal of sleek roach circled gently in the current. Were we not on a celebrated chalkstream? Why then all these cyprinids? I was nonplussed. Not so my host who cast a nymph to the edge of the shoal where the rotating water swept hard against the bank. The pool exploded, scattering roach hither and yon. In a minute or so a beautiful brown trout was netted, a wild fish of the Risle with a pale halo to each spot against a background of slate grey that gave it almost the light-on-dark apparel of a char. There were several more of these stunning fish in the slow water above the mill race. As I lay in the meadow grass to watch them a great slab of carp slid into view to hog the limelight. That celebrated beat in Normandy pulsated with variety and life in the way no famous, manicured and monocultural beat of the Test has done for generations.

But fishing Ritz's favourite water at Aclou is not without its worries. At one point in his great book "A Fly Fisher's Life" Ritz lists and classifies "the various accidents that can overtake the fisherman". Along with the familiar barbed wire, overhanging banks and holes in the bottom, he lists "ricochetting bullets". This may be some local method I've yet to come across.

Local techniques and methods are always worth learning. They can be devastatingly effective on their home waters, if not exactly according to Hoyle. Many years ago, through an accident of fate, I spent a week with a French lock-keeper on a remote upland canal above Dijon. He had only just become a lock keeper. His previous trade had been, as far as I could gather, a petty thief in Lille but the bottom had dropped out of the petty thief market and he was trying his hand at lock-keeping. Old habits die hard and although opportunities for wrong-doing are hard to come by on a small rural canal he had hit on an effective and satisfyingly illegal method of catching the multitude of small fish needed for a "friture". I was dragged in to help.

The two of us, in the half light before dawn, stretched a net across the canal below Bernard's lock and pegged it taught between the banks. A scaffold pole had been threaded through the bottom of the net and that was secured by ropes secured upstream. The canal was netted off. It seemed harmless enough. It was dawn on a still and peaceful morning. Then I was sent to open the paddles of the top lock-gate. Bernard swung the wheel that opened the bottom gate paddles and the water roared through from the pound above, bulging the net downstream. After a minute or so we shut the paddles. The water was still rocking as we hurried down to haul out the net. Thousands of small silver corpses were plastered against the fine netting like rotting flock wallpaper. Vive le Sport!

Gathering information on tickets and tackle can be a little daunting if one has just the flimsiest toehold on schoolboy French and little else (*but see the stuff at the end*). Some years ago, when I was still bright-eyed, I came across a leaflet advertising a free introductory lesson to Esperanto. It seemed to me then (indeed, it seems to me now) the perfect solution. I would wander my cosmopolitan way across the boundaries of the world, engaging in bright and improving conversations about *"trutoj"* (trout), *"musoj"* (flies) and *"fiskanoj"* (fishing-rods) with like-minded *"fisistoj"* (fishermen) beside sparkling *"riveroj"* (rivers - getting the hang of it?) It was not an unqualified success. For two reasons: first, I was encouraged to join a local Esperanto group. I did, and discovered there a motley collection of humanity with but one thing in common: no-one in the room seemed to have both oars in the water. They were all a bit odd. Was this a requirement - or a consequence - of Esperanto? The second drawback was more daunting: nobody else I ever met spoke the stuff. Anywhere. Except, curiously, Abergavenny.

I was once fishing the Usk near Abergavenny and, strolling into the town, came across the annual international Esperanto *"Kongreso"*. There was a lot of folk-dancing going on and they appeared every bit as odd as the home-grown variety. But the encounter did have some promise. I discovered that there existed a central register of Esperanto speakers throughout the world, together with their hobbies or areas of expertise. I cast my net wide. Realising that I was doomed to spend every Whitsun holiday in search of the sun, I asked for the names of all Esperanto-speaking fishermen in the countries bordering the Mediterranean. There was just one. He was a trawler skipper in Greece.

Perhaps I should have got in touch. I have learnt things from Greek fishermen before. On a holiday in Corfu I was taught by a local fisherman to fish with six handlines simultaneously. I will pass on this knowledge in case you ever have occasion to use such skill on a Scottish loch. You sit in the middle of a small rowing boat. You have no shoes on. The six baited handlines are gently lowered to the seabed and secured inboard. Now, one of the handlines is run between the toes of one foot. The same with the second line and the second foot. Two more lines sit beside you.

Each is looped over an ear. The third pair of lines pass through the fingers held out over each side of the boat. All six lines are thus held just off the sea bed. You strike when anything twitches.

Such is the joy of holiday fishing. What you will learn most is the similarity of all fishermen, a similarity high-lighted by the differences. All fly-fishermen are enthusiasts. But nowhere have I seen fishing fanaticism as in France. I met André in a tackle shop along the Moselle. A whirlwind of a man who arrived at the gîte that evening, talking fishing with me, advising the girls on restaurants and places to visit and doing card tricks for the children. Simultaneously. I'm sure he could have fished six handlines at the same time if he'd a mind to. We parted with promises: if ever we returned to the region he would show us his house and pond. Well, the next year we *did* return to Vosges and André did show us his house.

The house that André built is unexceptional - until we went through the innocuous green door to the basement. It was like entering the secret laboratory of a mad professor. Or the Bat Cave. A room the size of a small department store was stacked from floor to ceiling with immaculate tackle for taking all manner of fish in all manner of ways. Scores of rods lined the walls, and racks of reels designed to throw a kaleidoscope of baits and lures. There were other contraptions whose function I could only guess at. In the middle of the room, a long work bench was occupied with the production of a thousand "boilies". You will say that there are rooms like this in Britain. And so there may be. But I'll bet there is no garden pond like André's garden pond.

It is not a particularly large garden pond. It is formal, rectangular, with paved sides and one tree. Three springs, gathered from the surroundings, lead to the pond. Each trickles into its own concrete basin divided from the pond itself by a concrete barrier. And in each crystal basin there is a different selection of fry and fingerlings to be reared and released into the main pond or to be used as bait on André's many expeditions. The pond itself stirs to the combined convulsions of giant carp, huge pike, roach and tench, a school of rainbow trout and huge specimen browns.

And there, in André's garden pond, I caught my first Arctic char. Bizarre.

WORDS FOR FISHING IN FOREIGN

If you don't speak the language, getting tickets, tackle and information is a great deal easier with a little preparation beforehand. Look up the words for downstream, upstream, hooks, fly fishing, trout, grayling and so on – and write them down.

Then try this: I have great faith in the phrase "is it possible to...." *in any language. It has three huge advantages for the linguistically-challenged fisherman. First, it is followed by the infinitive of the verb (the bit listed in the dictionary - so it's easy to find)* ". . to buy a ticket here?", ". . to fish here?" ". . to pay with this?" *And so on. Secondly, it is immensely polite - if rather archaic. This is exactly what the rest of the world expects of an English fly-fisherman. Thirdly, and most important, it requires the answer* "yes" *or* "no".

Even I can understand that - as long as they nod or shake the head.

26

Chalk and Cheese

The most magnificent moustache I have seen in many years lurks beneath the nose of the mayor of Bagnol-les-Bains. It is a dense privet hedge of a moustache. Michel Genolhac is a fisherman and, for a fisherman, Bagnol-les-Bains is not a bad place to be mayor of.

Let me tell you about Lozère. It is not a big place, a small departement lost in the middle of the *Massif Central*. It is one of the most sparsely populated places in France - but not by trout. Several of the great trouty rivers of France are born within a few miles of each other in the hills of Lozère. The Allier and the Truyère flow north, the Lot and the Tarn flow west and if you hadn't seen the birth certificate you would never believe they all had the same mother. And, in truth, they don't.

Can you still get Battenburg cake? I haven't seen it for years. Lozère is half a slice of Battenburg. The northern half is made of the pink cake: the southern half is yellow cake. The village of Bagnol-les-Bains lies on the border.

The three of us met in the village playing field beside the infant River Lot. Michel had invited his friend, François, to help show me the rivers of Lozère. I felt rather sorry for them. You want people to think well of your girlfriend, to see her at her best, bright-eyed and dressed to kill before the party - in May and June,

194

say. Not *after* the party. Not with bags under her eyes and make-up slightly askew after a long night. It was mid-August after a long southern summer: the river was low and her dark roots were showing. The infant Lot is a beautiful crystal stream over a bed of bright gravel and bedrock and we did not catch a trout that morning. Michel and François took it hard. I tried to reassure them: I knew all about mid-August. Any man with a non-fishing wife and small daughter of school age knows all about holiday fishing in mid-August. Tomorrow would be different, they said. Tomorrow we would fish *le coup du soir* on the River Tarn.

And so the next day I set off with N-F wife and D of S.A. and headed south towards the Tarn, deep into the yellow cake.

The yellow cake is limestone. Southern Lozère is the land of *les Causses*, a vast wild region of rolling limestone uplands with a unique flora and fauna. Now, I don't know how you feel about unique flora and fauna: I know they are a Good Thing and I am delighted that they are there - but they don't thrill me, if you know what I mean. I know the little specks in the sky are a special sort of vulture or warbler but they are still little specks. I know I could not find these things that look a bit like sickly daisies anywhere else, but they still look like sickly daisies. I'm sorry. And then I realised what was missing from the Causse. Water. There are no little streams on the Causse, no pools, no babbling brooks. The rain that falls sinks quickly into the porous limestone and disappears.

It turns up in the River Tarn. I have never seen the Grand Canyon - I understand it is quite something - but, until I do, the Tarn gorge will do very nicely. It is stunning. One minute you are carelessly bowling across the endless sweep of the Causse, the next you are staring down into a giddying void and making sure you have hold of someone's hand. And far below, a river winds between overhanging cliffs of white limestone. We twisted down the side of the gorge to the village of La Malène and lunch.

We were not the only ones to be visiting the Tarn gorges. It is a popular place and the small road that shares the bed of the gorge for 50 km carries a steady stream of tourists, drivers and passengers gazing alarming upwards at the towering walls. The best way to the see the gorge is from the river. There were several hours to spare between lunch and the *coup de soir* so we decided to reconnoitre the river from one of the traditional punts that drift down the river for that very purpose.

The punt drifted, suspended above a pebble bottom by something like water only less so. The clarity is startling. Large fish hung in the current as we drifted into the shadows of the limestone cliffs. I asked the man with the pole what they were. *"Truite"*, he said. They were not. They were chub. They were very big chub. From time to time the bottom soared up to meet the punt and there were fish holding station across the slope. They were even bigger. I asked the man what they were. *"Truite"*, he said. They weren't. They were barbel. I put it to the man with the pole that these fish were barbel and those other ones were chub. He shrugged. He gave me the sort of look that said, if I knew what the fish were, why had I asked? He had a point there. We drifted on, sometimes scraping over shallows and small rapids, then hanging over another deep. As we closed one wall a fish held station in the shadow. It was eighteen inches long and marked like blotchy perch with three dark bars. It looked nothing like a perch. I asked the man what it was. He looked at me. *"Truite"*, he said. And, by golly, he was right. It was a *"zebrée"* trout, a native of these limestone rivers. They were all round us now. I had seen them in the River Ain of the Jura mountains and had assumed they were just a local population - the stocked trout did not have the marks. But here they were in the limestone again, hundreds of miles south on a river that flows to the Atlantic rather than the Mediterranean. Water chemistry? I don't know.

The evening came. The canoes that had drifted in shoals down the gorge all day had stopped: boating is banned after six o'clock. Michel and François met us in the village of Les Vignes with the familiar ritual greeting of "Jon, you should come here in May and June", and we set off to fish the River Tarn.

The light was fading rapidly as we changed into chest waders on the road above the river. The Tarn is fast but wadeable below Les Vignes with a strong central current. Much of the water that disappeared up on the Causses emerges through the bed as underwater springs in this section of the river, cooling and refreshing it through the summer. Down by the water it was darker still. I wanted to get a photograph of a *zebrée* trout but nothing was rising. Michel and François changed to nymph and worked up either side of the big river. François is a fisherman to his socks. He wears a beret pulled low over his eyes as he stares intently ahead, watching for a movement of the line. In common with many fine French fishermen he uses a line of natural silk which is regarded as expensive but superior: it is more supple and less conspicuous than a plastic line. His reel is a feather-light semi-automatic Italian job, a Vivarelli. I tried one on this trip and fell in love with it. I fish with nothing else now. If I could afford a silk line I would get that too.

The light had almost gone when François straightened and pulled into the first trout. He brought it to hand to show me. It was not a big fish but the distinctive diagonal bars of a native *zebrée* were already visible on its flanks. I had my photograph. Fishing in France stops 30 minutes after sunset. So we stopped.

There are bigger fish in Lozère. That evening we ate at a restaurant terrace overlooking the Tarn and talked of fish. While François was at the bar Michel showed me a reference book on the freshwater fish of Europe. Under the heading for brown trout was the European record, a brown trout of 14.30 kg. That is 31½ lbs in old money. It was caught on 10 April, 1988 in a lake near Villefort

197

in the east of Lozère. Its captor was F. Magdinier, the modest and charming fisherman who was just coming back from the bar.

The next day we went north. Glance at a fishing map of Lozère and you can see where the pink cake begins. On the limestone of the south the rivers run in gorges though the dry expanses of the Causses. To the north the hills are a tracery of rivulets, dozens of small streams branching through the woods and open moors. Precious little soaks into the land up there. We worked north, stopping to fish the little streams swollen from a night of rain, catching small, dark, boisterous trout that shot up from the depths between boulders of granite to grab a dry fly. You can do that sort of thing in Lozère. A single payment of 125 FF buys you a Cartes Vacances which is licence, tax and permit for a fortnight on virtually every river and stream in Lozère. There are private clubs but they are few and small: there are sections of most rivers where fishing is prohibited to allow the fish to breed undisturbed. You will be left with something over 700 kilometres of water and all of them are first category trout waters. Think about that.

Towards Nasbinals the country opens. This is the top of the Massif Central and it feels it. We stopped to watch a couple of anglers working their way along a moorland stream. They were fishing *au toc*, fishing a worm slung beneath a prodigious length of rod, swimming the bait around each boulder and run and feeling for the "toc" - the tap of a brown trout - through the line. One of them wore a headscarf, a charming grandmother of sixty-something. Below the old couple the river had scoured down to the bedrock, exposing a black polished floor of perfectly regular hexagonal floor tiles, the gigantic crystals of ancient basalt. We had arrived in the volcanic country of the Aubrac.

The Aubrac is hard, high country with more than a whiff of Dartmoor about the place. It is my sort of country. I knew it was my sort of country when I discovered that the dish that the

198

Aubrac region has given to the gastronomic world is mashed potato. *Aligot* is fancy mashed potato, to be sure, but it is still mashed potato. It is wonderful. A mixture of mashed potato, garlic and so much butter and local cheese that the stuff can be poured onto your plate. I can still taste it now - but that is mainly because I made a plate of it last night and the garlic stays with you somewhat. We had our first definitive *aligot* in the Relais de l'Aubrac, a lonely hotel, famous for the stuff. This venerable establishment sits on the bank of the River Bès.

The Bès is a fine moorland river built by the same firm that made the River Dart. The bed of the Bès is a chaos of rounded boulders and sparkling shallows and runs. The water ran clear but it can be peaty, spatey and downright dirty in the weather of the Aubrac and the Aubrac can have a fair amount of weather even in summer: hence, of course, the need for all that *aligot*.

But the Aubrac has another way to keep you warm. The waters that run through the northern Lozère have never quite forgotten their origins in those volcanic rocks. Hot springs are a feature of the region. One of these emerges on the banks of the Bès at La Chaldette where a brand-spanking-new health spa has been constructed within a short cast of the river. Even one of my casts. A low stylish construction of pine and glass and stainless steel houses whispering-quiet salons where everything that can be done to a person with hot water is performed by sublime creatures in crisp white coats. I am not kidding. There are saunas and jacuzzis and whirlpools and masseuses and Turkish steam rooms and things that sound a lot more anatomical in French. There are tiled rooms with straps and straining bars and very large nozzles.

Well, all this pampering is meat and drink to the N-F wife and D of S.A. They can't get enough of warm water squirted at them, so they went off happy as lambkins while Michel and François and I walked round the corner of the building, down the bank and into a different world of granite boulders and trout. Perhaps they are thrown by that warm water: on that day in mid-August the trout of the Bès didn't seem to realise that it wasn't May or June. They rose to a dry fly trundled down the sparkling runs between the boulders and they fought like small terriers. These were not the pale *zebrée* trout of the limestone: nor were they the black trout of the mountain streams. They were tough little nuggets, all sass and bright spots. They looked like they might try to flog you a dodgy wristwatch. They were fun.

It is a bizarre spot. There I was, absorbed in stalking the trout of the Bès, at one with my hunting ancestors and so forth, when my name was called. I looked up. Four yards away, the fluffier members of the family, wrapped in dazzling white towelling and all pink from steaming, squirting and pummelling, were lounging on sunbeds. Michel, François and I had caught enough trout. Also, we had been inside neoprene waders for long enough. We tromped out of the Bès and went to get ourselves a slice of the steaming, squirting and pummelling. Absolute, complete and utter heaven.

There is everything you could want to know about fishing in Lozère at www.lozerepeche.com . The cost of a Carte Vacances covering most of the fishing in the departement for one week is now €30. You can buy it online at the website.

Relais de l'Aubrac, 48260 Nasbinals (tel: 0033 466 32 52 06) is a comfortable, old-fashioned family hotel on the river Bès. It specialised in wonderful regional food with, of course, an awful lot of aligot. Take a look at www.relais-aubrac.com

La Chaldette (therme) spa (www.lachaldette.com) also sits alongside the River Bes. You can cast from the decking into the river.

27

Bridge on the River Wye

*I*t was always going to be difficult taking Philip to the River Wye.

The valley of the Derbyshire Wye is about as beautiful as is good for a river valley to get. Just a fraction more and it would cross the line into utter ootsiness. The Dove valley, a few miles to the south, makes that mistake: the Dove is so ootsy that folk are bussed in by the charabanc-load in order that they can totter down from the coach and gaze about them and point out the beauty of the Dove Valley to each other - only what you notice mostly is the throng of transport and people that have come to look at all that beauty.

The Wye is a little less showy, a little more discreet - but not a whole lot. It is a river of the limestone: it rains a fair bit in the Peak District and throughout the millennia the water that has fallen on the high moors and percolated through the thin soils has etched deep, steep-sided gorges into the porous limestone. The Wye twists extravagantly, fidgeting and flexing against the tight constraint of the towering valley sides. It is not a long river, just fifteen miles from Buxton to Rowsley where it joins the Derwent and for most of those fifteen miles it shares its tight, twisting course with the A6.

I was never a biker. My father has these knees, the result of a motor-bike encounter with the tailgate of a lorry in the dark in 1948, so motor-bikes were never encouraged round our way. But Philip was a biker. And once you have been a biker, it seems, there is always a part of you that hankers for 500ccs throbbing between your legs, dirt under your fingernails and a cemetery of squashed flies on your forehead. Also, it turns out, there are certain roads in Britain that bend and twist with just the right sort of swoop to get a biker's juices going. The A87 is one of them. I discovered this one evening as we were driving back from a fishing trip to Skye. As we bowled along from Kyle of Lochalsh and the road swung around the contours of a hill, Philip's eyes misted over and his hand began to weave from side to side, leaning into the curves, as he tried to describe to a non-biker the perfection of swoopiness of this fabled bit of bikers' road. And the A6 from Buxton to Rowsley, it seems, is another.

It explained a lot. From time to time I get to fish on the Derbyshire Wye as a guest on the Buxton Flyfishers' water high up the valley above Topley Pike where the road and river share every bend and twist. Up here the quickest way to move from pool to pool is often to scramble up onto the road but, as sure as you do, half-a-dozen bikers will come blitzing down the road like a swarm of avenging wasps, leaving you pressed back against the low wall and checking your rod tip. I had often wondered why and now I know.

A biker does not stop being a biker just because has not ridden a bike for years, wears Hush-puppies and plays the dame in the village pantomime every Christmas. Getting Philip to concentrate on fishing with that much hot metal thrashing up and down the road was always going to be a problem. But there was a chance if I could get him out of earshot of the A6. Between Ashford-in-the-Water and Topley Pike the dale becomes too tight and tortuous even for the A6 which carves up and over Taddington Moor whilst the River Wye doubles back through Upperdale and

Monsal Dale.

This is another world. From Little Longstone on the rim of the gorge you tumble down into Upperdale like a tired man sinking into a feather bed. Down at river level a small lane to nowhere turns down between two ancient stone houses to the bridge on the River Wye.

The river through Upperdale, Monsal Dale and on down to Ashford belongs to the Chatsworth Estate. This is pretty classy water and to fish it you really need to be the Duke of Devonshire or family or a friend or a holder of a season rod. I am none of those things and neither is Philip. But there is one beat of the Duke's water, the top beat of the Wye and the furthest from the big house, where an ex-biker can get a day ticket. These tickets must be booked beforehand and are limited to a precious four each day. We had two of them.

We parked by the bridge and leant over the downstream rail. Nothing was rising at nine o'clock on a cool morning on the first day in July but in the clear, shallow water at one side of the stream a large brown trout, a comfortable pounder, was hanging in the side current and swooping like a biker on the A87 out of Kyle of Lochalsh, intercepting goodies that drifted by in the current. Such fish, of course, belong to a separate subspecies that live only below bridges to impress the tourists - but it gives a chap hope.

Above the bridge a low stone cottage nestled comfortably in a flower-decked cottage garden like a broody hen beside the waters of the Wye. A line of white washing hung across the path and waved in the breeze that blew down the dale from the north-east. The scene could hardly be more perfect if you stuck it on a chocolate box and called it "Cosy Cottage". The name of the house is, in fact, "Cosy Cottage". The door opened and a stocky figure with hair the colour of a grizzle cape came down the path towards us. Tom Richardson has been the river keeper on the River Wye for well over quarter of a century. Tom's wife,

Margaret, has lived in Upperdale all her life, in that same Cosy Cottage where her parents and grandparents lived. I dare say there are better places to spend a lifetime but I can't think of one offhand.

River keepers are not a laughing, happy-go-lucky breed of men on the whole. They have seen too much of the darker side of human nature. They explain the rules of the water and look at you with eyes that see the sin that lurks within your soul. And you nod back with the open countenance of a man who would no more think of using a hook larger than a size 12 than he would of grinding up his own mother in the mincer. Also we were not to wade: we understood this and put on wellington boots to make the point.

And so we set off to fish. The top beat of the Chatsworth water runs upstream from the bridge at Upperdale for a little over half a mile. Nothing was rising so we decided to explore the water up to the limit at Cressbrook Mill before we started to fish. It is the sensible thing to do and I don't know why I have never done it. I try to do it each time I visit a new water but this bend or that run looks so tasty that I find myself walking down to the water - just to take a closer look, you understand - but I am pulling the line from my reel as I go. This time we got about halfway, which isn't bad. Of course, it was a rising fish that did it.

It was a strange rise, messy rather than splashy, with a lot of turbulence and bubbles, like a fat man turning round in a small bath. My first thought was of the stewpond.

The River Wye has one very special claim to fame amongst British rivers: it has a population of breeding rainbows. This is a mixed blessing. Rainbows are easier - and cheaper - to breed than the indigenous brown trout but river fisheries are often reluctant to stock them in rivers where they will jar the sensibilities of sensitive fishermen and compete unfairly with the browns who are doing what comes naturally. But in the Wye, so it goes, the rainbows are jolly nearly indigenous and stocking them is only "supplementing a natural head". Hmmm - perhaps. In all events, there are stewponds at Chatsworth where you can buy a bag of pellets and feed the fish and each fat little rainbow, if it wishes to become fatter, must dash and grab the pellet before someone else does. It is not a delicate rise. Sooner or later these feisty little fish find themselves released into the river and anything they find floating on the surface will get much the same treatment - hence the froth and commotion.

It was an elegant piece of deduction and I was proud of it. It had but one flaw: everything I floated over that fish was studiously ignored. I put a fair number of patterns past that supposedly naïve little fish and others that were doing much the same but I never discovered what it was they were grabbing from the surface. Philip was the first to go deep. While I was demonstrating the range of dry flies I carry to the first fish, Philip had returned to a deep pool on a corner we had passed earlier. In the absence of anything obvious on top he had gone searching with a weighted Black and Peacock Spider and the result was bouncing around the pool and flashing silver in the first sunshine of the day. It was a fine fat fifteen-inch rainbow.

A spring in my reel had broken so I wandered back down to the car by the bridge. Monsal Dale is an Area Of Outstanding Beauty as well as being outstandingly beautiful and the first of the day's walkers was striding down the track and over the bridge. In the shallow margin of the upstream side, a shape was gliding over the bright gravel and dimpling the surface in a more orthodox fashion. I put on a small dry fly, a Royal Coachman with a CDC wing, and drifted it over the spot beside the bright weed. The fish ignored it. I was beginning to get fed up with all this neglect. I changed the fly for a tiny Hare's Ear nymph and the first time this touched the water the fish swept across and inhaled it: a splendid golden brown trout flashed across the stream and there is a now a

205

group of middle-aged hikers who believe that fly fishing is really rather easy. I did myself at the time. I will tell you now: that fly did not catch another trout all day.

I do not say it wouldn't have caught a fish eventually but I did not manage to hang onto that particular fly for very much longer - or any fly I used that day for that matter. For some reason I lost more flies, and lost them in more varied and interesting ways, on this first day of July than on any other day I can recall. So did Philip and he took it harder than I did: he was raised on stillwaters where a good fly is reckoned to last you a lifetime and is then handed on to your eldest son. It was the long seed-heads of July that undid us, that and the steep slopes of the dale that rise up behind a man who is not allowed to wade and cast up and down the stream beneath the trees as the Good Lord intended but must remain on the bank in his wellingtons and cast between the trees. And leaded flies don't help. A well-hackled dry fly cast carelessly into a bush stands a good chance of bouncing out but a leaded nymph or goldhead flings itself round every twig like a gaucho's *bolas*.

The goldheads did not solve the mystery of those infuriating rising fish but they solved the mystery of how to catch them. A hefty goldhead nymph cast up into the head of each deep run brought a twitch on the leader and a firm strike brought the solid surge of a fish against the bend of the rod - or it brought a small gold bullet whistling out of the water to lodge firmly in an adjacent bush. My last goldhead had taken that route by mid-afternoon. It was time to try a little experiment.

I had been meaning to try this for years. I hate tying bead-headed nymphs. Either the holes are too small to go round the bend or they are so big they slip straight off over the eye. I had a packet of small copper beads in my fishing bag. I slipped one of these beads onto the line and then tied on an ordinary unweighted nymph, a Hare's Ear. The small bead slides down to the eye of the hook - *et voila!* - a copperhead Hare's Ear. I could turn any fly into a weighted bead-head: if I carried a supply of beads I could even vary the weight and colour of the beaded fly at a whim. And, by golly, the thing worked. Three casts later I had my first trout on a pick-and-mix nymph. I was delighted. I was back in business. Two more runs and two more trout and I knew I was onto something. I was up there with Leonardo da Vinci and Dick Walker. I was onto something, all right: I was onto a new way to lose flies. Suddenly the fly wasn't there. I had not felt it go: it had just fallen off. I slipped on another bead and fastened another fly. That lasted for another couple of fish and then it too disappeared. I looked a little more closely at the end of the leader. It was rough and frayed: a sharp edge of the bead must have scratched the tippet at each cast and the whip of the heavy fly had done the rest.

Back to the drawing-board - I bet Leonardo didn't get the smile quite right first time. I could try a heavier tippet. I could try a smoother bead. But not that day. It was getting late. I did not want to risk breaking off in a fish so I tied on an unweighted nymph and Philip and I fished our way back to the bridge on the River Wye. We had caught a lot of fish on a beautiful river and yet it had been a strange, puzzling, successful, frustrating, triumphant, disappointing sort of a day. I suppose Leonardo must have had days like this.

Perhaps even Dick Walker.

Tom Richardson has long retired. The fishing in Monsal Dale is now controlled by the Cressbrook and Litton Club but day tickets for the Monsal Dale beat are still available at £48. Tickets must be booked in advance from the keeper, Stephen Moores, tel: 01298 871 676 or 07811 991 540 and leave a message. Fly only, using a single fly (maximum size 12). And no wading.

28

Lost Luggage

You know those big paper sacks that barbecue charcoal comes in? And bulk dog food and potatoes and chicken feed. They are fastened at the top by a length of hairy string and a row of cotton stitches. Sometimes you end up having to open the thing stitch by stitch. And other times you pull one end of the hairy string and the whole caboodle unravels of an instant. No-one knows why this is.

Fishing plans can be a bit like that. It was a good plan, too. Look: some of the finest fishing for wild brown trout in the world can be found in the remote and uninhabited bits of the British Isles. The problem with fishing these beautiful bits is that they are remote and uninhabited: it is the devil's own job to get there and when you do there's no-one to give you tea and turn down your bed. Also, no bed.

I had always wanted to fish the Outer Hebrides. It is not hard to see why: take a look at a map of North and South Uist strung out along Skye's western horizon. These islands are about 50% moor and mountain and 50% loch. Which leaves very little room for towns, so there aren't any. They are also a very long way by car and ferry from Banbury. But there, on the map, between South Uist and North Uist, lies the island of Benbecula and in the corner of Benbecula there is an airport. And, what's more, the airport on

Benbecula is within a few yards of a loch and that loch is just a few yards from another - and so on. Everywhere on Benbecula is within a short walk of a loch.

So here was the plan. We had just a few days in early summer: Philip and I would fly to Benbecula, step from the plane with our rucksacks, tent and rods and fish our way across the island. It was a peach of a plan. It had light and shade, it had yin and yang, a happy combination of the ancient and modern. It had the ease and comfort of jet travel and all the rugged manliness of bare legs and life under canvas.

In Birmingham Airport the rucksacks with their straps were deemed "awkward baggage": they had to go through a separate channel. The man on the X-ray saw a small metal box. It was the camping stove. I got it out and showed it to him. It still had some petrol in it. He wanted it emptied so I took it outside the terminal and drained it. I hurried back. He said that it still smelt of petrol. Well, it would. He said we would have to flush it out. So we ran off in search of the washroom. As always, it was at the end of a long corridor in an obscure corner of the terminal. I flushed out the tank in a sink and rushed back to the airport bloke. He sniffed the stove. He said it still smelt of petrol: by this time everything smelt of petrol. He took it off to show it to someone higher up. He came back and said we could take it. He said it reluctantly: you could see he did not like saying it. All this had taken some time time. It was now five minutes after the scheduled time for take-off. We ran for the departure gate.

We made it onto the plane. We got to Glasgow. The rucksack, alas, did not.

The man in the British Airways office was trying to be helpful. He sat down, there and then, and typed me a letter of apology. This did not help. He assured me that the rucksack would be on the next flight to Glasgow, in an hour or so. But the daily Benbecula flight was leaving in fifteen minutes. All right then:

they would deliver the rucksack to us in Benbecula the following day. He asked where we had planned to stay on the island. I said we had planned to stay in a tent. No problem: they would hire a taxi to deliver the rucksack to our tent. Where was our tent? The tent was in a rucksack in Birmingham. Someone had pulled the hairy string and the whole thing had just unravelled.

Plan B was cobbled together at Benbecula airport. It consisted of phoning the Lochboisdale Hotel. This, as it turned out, was one of the better plans.

Lochboisdale Hotel is a fisherman's fishing hotel run by Sharon and Michael O'Callaghan. Our troubles were over. Sharon had a room free: she would organise rods to get us fishing until the luggage caught up with us. "Come on down".

Lochboisdale is at the southern end of South Uist, thirty miles and the best part of two islands away from Benbecula airport. In Banbury I would not attempt such a journey by bus: it would be quicker to walk. In the Western Isles there are buses to everywhere. They are very cheap and very friendly: a gaggle of leggy schoolgirls sang songs and giggled at us for many of the rolling, treeless miles down the length of the islands. We were dropped at the door of the hotel: it was still only lunchtime.

Waiting for us, with a couple of rods, was John Kennedy. Anyone who has fished these islands will recognise the name: anyone who plans to fish here had best note it down. John is the fishery manager of the South Uist Estate which has the fishing on most of the waters of Benbecula and South Uist. John is also is the author of "70 Lochs - a Guide to Trout Fishing in South Uist". This modest little book is quite simply the best where-to-fish guide I have ever seen. We were to learn a lot more of the islands and their trout from John later. But now we had got here, we wanted to be about some fish so I gratefully grabbed a rod and we set off on foot through the scattered houses and up into the hills above Lochboisdale.

It was three o'clock. We were climbing a trackless and windswept hill on a small island below Scotland's western horizon. Despite disasters we were barely more than six hours from Birmingham. And still a good eight hours from nightfall.

On the map there is a track across the shoulder of that hill. It is not there. If it ever was, it is now lost beneath the dense bracken and heather of the hill. We struggled, waist-high, up through the stuff, flushing a grouse which waited until we were one either side before exploding from her nest, frightening us spitless. We were running short of spit as it was: the hills and mountains of Uist are not particularly high - there's nothing above 2000 feet - but they all start from scratch and get there quickly so you feel every foot. We climbed on. Behind us, sheets of water started as bright lines in the moor and expanded into a pattern of lochs as we climbed above them. We had decided to start our Uist fishing on a small, unnamed loch tucked behind the shoulder we were climbing. I forget why. We struggled, panting, onto the low col.

We were met by an unforgettable scene: a stiff breeze was blowing from a cloudless sky; far below us a small saucer of loch nestled in a green hollow; through a notch in the mountainside we could sketch the distant mountains of Skye floating above the horizon of a blue sea. Magical - but one can only take so much magic so after a minute to catch breath we loped off, zig-zagging down through rocks and heather to commence fishing.

Nature did not fashion me for a fisherman. If it had it would have provided more faith. Deep down I regard all waters, particularly small unnamed lochs, as sterile until proved other-wise: it's a hedge against disappointment. I *hope* there will be fish: I just don't quite believe it. So the first tug is always something of a delightful shock. All the more so because the first fish grabbed the garish blue and yellow item that is the Golden Olive Bumble, a fly which seems irresistible to loch trout for some reason I cannot fathom.

211

It was not a big fish. Ten inches would be generous. I didn't care. It would have been nice to have something put a bend in the rod but there was little enough danger of that. John Kennedy had loaned me one of the rods he uses on the other side of the island. There are no hills over there on the west coast of Uist, no hard rocks and highland peat. The lochs of west coast sit on a foundation of sand and crushed shells. These are the renowned "Machair" lochs where the trout grow to prodigious size in those rich alkaline waters. Such fish can bend an 11-foot, #8 rod more than somewhat, but a rod like that, up here amongst the hard rocks and heather, makes you feel a bit of a bully.

Philip had moved around the shore and was steadily taking the same fish or similar from the edge of a weed bed. Those fish will talk about that day till the end of their lives: I doubt they had ever seen a fly or a fisherman before or will ever see another. It was a good place to be on a day that had started in the overcast, overcrowded Midlands. We were ready for more.

We followed a small burn down a narrow gully that led down to a tiny, sandy bay at the eastern end of Loch Stulaval. Philip caught seven fine little trout from this spot while I caught none so I had ample opportunity to look around me as he fished.

Heather is the dominant feature of these hidden lochs. This is not alpine-beds-and-granite-chippings sort of heather. It is woody, knee-high and higher. It takes some getting through. With luck you can clamber around a rocky shore between the heather and the water but in the bays the shore may be a peat cliff with over-hanging heather. Now you must search for a sheep path through the heather or forge your own with an ungainly, high-stepping canter that does terrible things to your knees after a while. I was doing a bit of this when I looked round and saw Philip's rod bending into something more serious. He has never really forgiven me for taking five minutes to get to him and a big fish for a photograph last year in Argyll: he lost that fish. So this time I risked life and limb, recklessly bounding to his side through the heather to record the great fish. It was not a great fish. He had just taken to hooking them two at a time in order to speed things up.

Heather and wind. It blows a bit in the Western Isles and the wind will usually determine where you fish. There is not much scope for casting lustily into the wind when there is a steep hillside of heather behind you and your back-cast. The easiest cast is with the wind behind your non-casting shoulder, carrying the leader and its flies away from your ears. The loch shores are so convoluted that you can always find suitable spots and rocky headlands.

We fished our way around the coast of Loch Stulaval through that late afternoon in early summer. It would take a week to fish it thoroughly and Stulaval is just one loch amongst scores lost in the hills of South Uist. Most of these are not mentioned in John Kennedy's admirable book - there are just too many bigger, better lochs on the machair - but John walks these hills and fishes these smaller waters and can tell you what you will find and where you will find it.

Suddenly, it seemed, it was nine o'clock. It did not look nine o'clock this far north but it was time to head back, chucking a fly into Loch Coragrimsaig as we passed and finding the small, dark trout that John had predicted.

There hardly seems room for much anatomy between the skin and the shin bone but what little there is was aching something fierce as we staggered into the plush lounge bar after a day in the heather. We felt decidedly seedy. The machair lochs are famous and fishing folk come from around the world to stay at the Lochboisdale hotel. This is civilised fishing in boats, between civilised hours. Our fellow guests had bathed and changed into regimental ties, muted tweed breeches, long socks with garters and those little polished slippers beloved of the leisured country classes. We had not planned to move in such circles. We padded through the cultured throng in matted, bog-stained socks that we would be wearing until such time as the rucksack arrived.

The Ties-and-Tweeds were not happy. It had been a bad machair day. The sun had shone from a cloudless sky and the lordly trout of the crystal machair waters had not deigned to take their flies. Hardly a fish had been hooked on half a dozen rods. We were happy. Up in the hills that afternoon the two of us had hooked twenty.

It was blister bright again the next morning. We sat in the elegant dining room overlooking the harbour. I do not say we looked dishevelled but we were a long, long way from the sleek, shevelled look of our breakfast companions. Cars and gillies were gathering outside the hotel to whisk the fishermen off to the lochs on the machair. We waited until the last one had departed and clambered into the back of John's four-wheel-drive with the rods and the dog. He would drop us on the road that runs up the island and we would fish our way back to the hotel and, perhaps, our lost luggage.

There is no need to flog for miles into the hills to find waters that may not see a fisherman from one season to the next. Hereabouts they just have more fishing than they know what to do with. John dropped us beside the main road, a modest three miles from the Lochboisdale. I am looking at a map of the place as I write this, trying to reconstruct our route through a maze of five main lochs, dignified with names by the Ordnance Survey, and over thirty smaller lochans, the end of one within a few paces of the next. The larger lochs are twisted into a dozen arms and bays so that sometimes we found ourselves fishing a spot we had fished hours before from the opposite shore. In that profusion of rocky bays and islands, peat, heather and glinting waters, there are no fixed points in time and space: the day stretches endlessly into a reverie of clambering through heather and casting along a rocky shore beneath the blue sky. From time to time the pattern is punctuated by a trout so overweeningly self-confident that, for a moment, both fish and fisherman are convinced it weighs pounds rather than ounces and act accordingly - until reason returns and a very cross half-pounder is brought, punching, kicking and protesting, to the bank.

Odd images remain. A lamb, bleating with fright, had become mired in shallow water beneath a peat cliff: Philip grappled it up onto dry land and the sheep, perhaps misreading his intentions, bleated ever more piteously. A long snooze taken in the comfort of warm heather and waking to see a posse of red deer peering at me over a nearby ridge. And a tiddler taken triumphantly on a fly dapped from John's enormous rod.

But mostly it is rock and heather and sun and water and small trout.

And that night there was something waiting for us back at the hotel.

*   *   *

"And bring hither the fatted calf and kill it, and let us eat and be merry: for this my rucksack was lost and is found".

The parable of the prodigal rucksack is spot on: there is more rejoicing over one rucksack that is lost and returned by British Airways than over the ninety and nine that make it from Birmingham to Glasgow without a glitch. It was almost worth losing the rucksack, tent, clothes, food, sleeping bag and fishing rods for the joy of getting them back a day or so later. Almost. But not quite.

Plan A had been to step from the plane in Benbecula and fish our way from loch to loch across the island. The rucksack caught up with us in Lochboisdale, one-and-a-half islands away from plan A. So the next morning we got on the bus and headed back to Benbecula.

The buses of the Western Isles are friendly affairs, bustling about the small roads like Postman Pat. We were chatting to Duncan the driver and enjoying the view when, after a mile of so, the bus stopped for a third passenger. The man, it seems, had travelled down the islands on the bus a couple of days earlier and taken the ferry over to Barra. He'd mislaid his camera on the journey. He asked Duncan if anyone had handed it in. Duncan shook his head: they hadn't. The man thought he might have left it on the bus, with a newspaper on the parcel shelf. He looked above his seat: the camera and newspaper were still there. It seemed to be a day for returning prodigals.

At high tide, South Uist and Benbecula are separated by half a mile of the Atlantic but the road is carried on a causeway across the sands. Across the strait, the bus turns to run along the west coast where most of the tiny population is to be found. We were headed to the north and east where there is nothing but peat and heather, rock and water - in more or less equal proportions. We climbed down from the bus and watched as it pootered off into the distance. We shouldered the packs for the first time, stared down the long road to the north, and set off.

But not far. A short distance down the road we came to a garage: we needed petrol. My small Swedish stove burns petrol. It holds seven tablespoons of the stuff in a small brass tank. In Birmingham airport I had been asked to empty the tank and flush it out, so now I needed a fill-up. It is not easy to get seven tablespoons of petrol from a forecourt pump, not through a tiny filler in a little brass tank. The garage did not have a funnel small enough so we fashioned a cone from a sheet of paper and we waited. A petrol pump won't deliver seven tablespoons of petrol: we had to wait until a car pulled in and we could fill the stove from the dribble that stays in the pipe when the pump has stopped.

We marched north. Benbecula is mostly lochs. Along that three mile walk from the south of the island we passed a dozen lochs, large and small, within a cast of the road. We were making for Market Stance, nothing more than a crossroad in the middle of the island from where a track heads east, past the unlovely site of the island's rubbish dump, and on into the maze of heather and lochs. The peat track winds around the only hill on the island of Benbecula. The cone of Ruabhal rises like a great pimple from the wilderness of loch and heather. We were looking for somewhere to plonk the tent. Finding somewhere reasonably flat and reasonably firm is harder than it seems in such a wilderness. Happily, the folks who built this peat road were looking for much the same – somewhere to store their peat - and before long we found a little sward big enough for the tent between the track and Loch Bà Una. The tent was up in a few minutes, all the gear bundled inside and we were setting up the rods to make something of the fag end of that day.

It is not hard to catch the trout of a Hebridean loch. They are not fussy. A team of the traditional wet flies in sensible sizes from 12 to 16 is pulled past a Benbeculan trout and, lo! there is a fish on the end. Easy-peasy. The only really difficult bit is finding the fish to pull flies past. It may, of course, be the other way about: the trout are everywhere but just damned picky. I have never quite decided which it is. Either way, we saw no rises on that grey evening in early June, nothing to say where - or if - fish were to be found. We worked our way around the shore beneath the tent until Philip hooked the small trout that allowed us to retreat for supper with a vestige of honour.

I image you can make a nourishing stew of a small brown trout and the rich pickings of natural ingredients to be found on a highland hillside. In the rucksack, however, I had three of those

217

large and splendid tins to be found in French supermarkets: we could chose between *Saucisse de Toulouse aux Lentilles, Cassoulet de Carcassonne au Mouton* and *Gratin Champêtre au Champignons et Lardons*, all of which tastes much better than any bit of a highland hillside.

It was then I discovered something else inside the rucksack - or, rather, I didn't. The business end of my cunning petrol stove has to be preheated by burning a small sausage of inflammable paste. A little tube of this stuff had been packed along with the stove. But in the kerfuffle over the stove at Birmingham Airport the little tube had been confiscated by the airport bloke. I was tempted to walk back up the peat track and throw the Swedish stove on that serendipitous rubbish dump – but *Gratin Champêtre au Champignons et Lardons* is not good cold. We improvised the paste with a mâché of petrol and toilet tissue - spectacularly dangerous but surprisingly effective. We ate, we slept and the next morning we set out to fish the lochs of Benbecula.

Over a hundred lochs and lochans lie in the four miles of highland wilderness between Ruabhal and the sea to the south. Fifteen are named on the Ordnance Survey and the fishing on most of these is described in John Kennedy's essential guide book, "70 Lochs". Loch Bà Una where we camped isn't. A loch or so south of Bà Una lies Loch nan Clachan: *"This loch is full of fish and the angler can hardly miss here . . . A good loch for the novice, or indeed the experienced angler, to fish to boost his confidence."*

It sounded perfect. It lay just half a mile across the bog and heather.

Let us talk of trousers. I look to Philip in the matter of outdoor trousers. Many years ago, it seems, Philip climbed mountains, proper job, with ropes and pitons and so forth. He has that sort of look about him even now, mainly because he is inclined, on the slightest outdoor excuse, to don a disreputable pair of moleskin breeks, much altered about the waistline these days, and to extol the practical advantages of such garments. He bangs on about the ability to adjust the ventilation by raising or lowering the socks and so on. To listen to Philip, it is a wonder that any trousers are continued below the knee. So I had bought a pair of moleskin breeks for this trip. I had not, though, had the courage to wear them on the businessmen's shuttle flight from Birmingham to Glasgow so they had been packed in my rucksack which had then gone AWOL. And so, for the first two days of fishing among the hill lochs of South Uist, I had been forced to wear the light trousers I'd travelled in. Now I thought I might try my new breeks. I looked at Philip's legs and thought again. It was the heather that had done the damage.

I had imagined strolling through the heather, light fronds brushing my calves in a soft caress, carrying the fragrance of the fresh shoots into the air. Hebridean heather is not like that. It is tall and woody and knotted and gnarled. It does terrible things to the bit between the knees and ankles. If the socks are worn up it catches the threads, teasing them into a thick fuzz like a swarm of tiny bees around the lower limbs. If the socks are worn down, much the same happens to the skin. Philip's calves and shins were a mass of tiny cuts, scabs and scratches: not a pleasant sight. So I climbed back into the trousers I had been wearing since Birmingham and we set off through the heather and mosses.

Loch nan Clachan is one kilometre long and has a shoreline of six times that. Whoever designed Benbecula had evidently been carrying a box labelled "LOCH FEATURES", got fed up humping the thing all that way across the moor and decided to dump the lot into Loch nan Clachan. It has islands and isthmuses, rock basins, weedy straits, shallows and deeps. We started to fish.

We were fishing adjacent rocky points. Philip was soon into a fish. I wasn't. He had another. I didn't. Fishing is funny: if we had been flipping coins and Philip had won the first two or three flips I would not begin to doubt my style of flipping or the coin I was using. Fishing is different. I began to ask him what flies he was using, what depth they were fishing, how fast he was retrieving. Then I began to suspect that his rocky point was besieged by with fish whilst mine was barren. So I change my flies or I move to a new position and, sooner or later, I catch a fish and it feels, for all the world, as if I have cracked the problem. Such is the illusion of fly fishing.

I will tell you what I know, sitting here in the cold light of Banbury, some time after the event. To fish these hill lochs in summer:- a floating or neutral line tapering to a 3lb. tippet, throwing a team of three flies. The flies are to be:- Golden Olive Bumble (top dropper), Cinnamon and Gold (middle dropper), Black and Peacock Spider (point), all size 14. This lot should be fished everywhere they can be cast and retrieved so that the top dropper does not make a wake. Do all this in the sure and certain hope that you will catch as many trout as are allotted to you. I do not expect you to follow this excellent and sober advice: I certainly won't. I will be changing flies and sizes and racing ahead to fish from any long, low rocky point because had I caught my best nan Clachan trout from a similar sort of place that afternoon. This fish was all of 13 inches, about as many ounces, and I was a pleased as punch. There are bigger fish in these lochs, some are a lot bigger, but most are smaller.

We had fished through the long day, sampling a few of the lesser lochs to the south. It would be easy to get very lost in this labyrinth of waters but as long as it stayed clear we had the comforting pointy presence of Ruabhal looming to the north and we could always find our way back to the peat track and the tent beneath it. These peat tracks that meander into the heart of the moor are still used to carry out the peat blocks from the long, neat stacks where they have been cut and dried. On our route back across the sun-dried bog we came across an ancient peat cutting with a tumbled heap of crumbling peat bricks, tinged green with moss. It had been a dry spring and the old bricks were bone dry. We prised some from the heap and carried them to the small bay beneath the camp on Loch Bà Una.

I had never tried cooking over peat before. It took some time to get the hang of lighting the stuff but before long we had a *Cassoulet de Carcassonne au Mouton* bubbling nicely over the embers. The peat did not burn so much as glow. By placing two new bricks on edge, either side of the glowing ashes, the inner surfaces caught and began to glow like an open-ended electric toaster. I realised I had been looking for something like this for years.

I cut a long, green twig from a low bush and sharpened the thinner end. This was carefully threaded through the mouth of a cleaned trout, down the length of the body cavity and pushed into the firm flesh above the anal fin. It looked like a macabre lollipop. This trout-on-a-stick was then threaded between the walls of glowing peat, dorsal-fin-down, and suspended there above the embers by trapping the thick end of the stick beneath a rock. The thick flesh on the trout's back was grilled by the glowing embers and the burning peat blocks on either side: higher up the blocks the heat was less intense, lightly grilling the thinner flesh on the flanks and belly. As sunset soaked into the still waters of Loch Bà Una, the trout came out evenly cooked and peat-smoked to perfection.

The nights are short in June. I was awake early and, lying there with not much to do, I wondered whether Philip was awake as well. I though I would ask him. Pretty soon he was. We got up and made tea by the alarming petrol method and, having nothing else to do, we set off to fish. Then he asked me the time. It was 4.30 am. We were walking to the east, along the peat track that winds between the lochs towards the coast. The wind was freshening from the northeast so we passed Loch Hermidale and made for the windward side of Loch na Déighe fo Dheas. It started to rain.

We'd expected rain when we came to the Western Isles but the days had been warm and dry and we'd got used to that. This cold, wet stuff was a bit of an affront. We worked our way down the coast telling each other that this was simply grand and a change is as good as a rest. We were fooling no-one. We caught fish in the driving rain but, frankly, it was not much fun. By nine o'clock, when decent folk were thinking of a cup of tea and toast, we had been fishing for half a working day. We decided to retreat and wait for it to blow over.

As we reached the tent I spotted that I'd left the back window open. The sleeping bags and everything else sat in a large puddle in the middle of the groundsheet. It was ten minutes past ten.

We had had some great days on these magical islands of the west - but the islands would still be here another time. We looked at each other. The airport is on the other side of the island, four miles as the fisherman squelches: the daily plane to the mainland leaves at 12.30.

We made it – just.

The tickets for the plane had been sitting in the puddle in the tent. We squeezed them out as best we could but in the walk to the airport across the island they had disintegrated into a featureless pulp. We dashed to the airport desk and presented our two shapeless lumps of papier maché. The lady behind the desk smiled and waved us towards the waiting plane, wise in the ways of fishermen. And Hebridean rain.

"70 Lochs - A guide to Trout Fishing in South Uist" by John Kennedy. This is absolutely indispensable. Copies are available from Borrodale Hotel, Daliburgh (tel: 01878 700444) at £10 (including postage)

All the waters we fished (and most of the hundreds of lochs on Benbecula and South Uist) are controlled by South Uist Angling club and available on day or week tickets (DT£6) from MacGillivray's Shop, Balivanich, Benbecula; Daliburgh Post Office, Daliburgh, South Uist; South Uist Estate Office (Stòras Uibhist) by phone (01878 708002), or email (fishing@storasuibhist.com). Go to www.southuistfishing.com for details of all fishing on the islands.

Buses on South Uist and Benbecula are simply splendid. Timetables and other useful information from the tourist information office, Lochboisdale, Tel: 01878 700 286 (Easter-October)

29

Ladybird, Ladybird, Fly Back Home.

The Man From the Council came round on Tuesday: we've had this problem with ladybirds. I didn't know we had a problem with ladybirds. When I phoned the council I thought we had a problem with wasps.

There is a willow tree at the bottom of the garden. From halfway across the lawn you could hear an ominous buzz. Then you saw movement. Then you saw wasps. They were on every leaf. They were crawling on the trunk and branches. Not hundreds but thousands and tens of thousands. They crawled on the ivy that covers the exposed roots and on a pile of old bricks on the ground beneath the tree. Most of all they were on a wooden platform in the tree, the remains of an old treehouse.

They were not swarming and there was no nest. Each wasp was just mooching across any surface it could find. The wasp man from the council said he had never seen anything like it.

The willow tree stands beside the River Cherwell and there were wasps tumbling onto the surface and flailing around like miniature jet-skis. There was something else falling onto the water, making a pattern of tiny rings on the surface like the lightest of showers. We looked up into the branches for the source of this rain. I was looking on the leaves and green branches but, when we found them, they were on the older, darker wood. They looked like scars of damaged bark. They were aphids. Huge, brown aphids were clustered together in tightly packed herds, blotching the bark on every branch. This was the source of that rain.

Aphids are sap-suckers. Most species puncture the softer, green parts of plants to suck the sap: these huge beasts were drilling straight through the tough older wood.

Sap is the Coca-Cola of insect food. It is high in sugars but very low in the protein a growing aphid needs. So an aphid has to suck an awful lot of sap and simply excretes the vast excess of sugars through its anus as "honeydew". Honeydew is - at the very best - aphid wee. We could feel it gently raining down on our faces as we looked up into the tree. To the tens of thousands of wasps, that willow and everything under it was a gigantic toffee apple.

So what we had, it seemed, was a problem with aphids.

It has been a great year for aphids. It is always a great year when the things that eat you fail to turn up.

The things that eat aphids are ladybirds. It suddenly struck me that I had not seen a ladybird all summer. Civilisations had toppled on such trivial events. Was I the first to spot the extinction of the ladybird, harbinger of the Great Aphid Plagues that would devastate the third millennium? I thought I ought to tell someone - or at least ask if they had seen a ladybird. When the man from the council had gone I phoned BBONT, the Berkshire, Buckinghamshire and Oxfordshire Naturalists' Trust. Their insect man said that, come to think of it, he hadn't seen any ladybirds either. I thought this a rather casual reaction to the end of civilisation. He suggested I phone the Institute of Terrestrial Ecology near Huntingdon and asked for a ladybird man. They passed me on to a lecturer in evolution in the Department of Genetics at Cambridge University.

Mike Magerus is not just a ladybird man: he is *the* Ladybird

Man. 1998 has been, Mike said, a terrible year for ladybirds, the worst since records of such things began. It was not the end of civilisation: it was the rubbish summer we've just had. Ladybird populations are very responsive to the weather. Nobody feels much like mating when it is cold and damp but ladybirds find it impossible. During the critical period of late spring and early summer this year it was nothing but cool and damp and the ladybirds simply could not get down to business. It had been very different in the hot, dry summer of 1976 when the ladybird population exploded. Long before the summer was over the ladybirds had run out of aphids. A story on the 6 o'clock news showed bathers being driven from Brighton beach by clouds of ravenous ladybirds biting humans for want of any aphids to eat. The 9 o'clock news, after the watershed, ran the same story, illustrated with footage from a nudist beach at Newhaven.

Chewing on a nudist may tide a ladybird over for a while but there is no danger of them turning man-eaters: to breed success-fully they must eat aphids. A lot of aphids. A single seven-spot ladybird will munch its way through 5000 aphids in its adult lifetime, having already scoffed another 500 as a larva, enough to make a dent in any aphid population. But during this dull, damp summer we've had this problem with ladybirds: there aren't any. So I am stuck with a million or so surplus aphids on the willow tree at the bottom of my garden. Also several thousand wasps.

The man from the council says I do not have a wasp problem: within a month and a few frosts all the wasps under my willow will be dead.

They are not, of course, in *his* garden.

30

If It's Broke, Fix It.

There's a hoary old riddle, I'm sure you've heard it, about a hunter who leaves his camp and walks two miles due south, then turns to walk two miles due east. Here he shoots a bear. He then trudges two miles due north - back to his camp. The question is: what colour was the bear?

Well, I've got another for you.

Two men are driving along a road through a forest. Around a bend there is a large deer standing in the middle of the road. The deer slowly takes off down the middle of the road. Each time it veers towards the forest, it catches sight of the car over its shoulder and shies away towards the middle of the road again before doing the same thing over the other shoulder. We could do this for miles: this is one daft deer. The car slows to a crawl and eventually the creature lopes off into the forest shadows.

A few minutes later the car pulls off the road. The two men get waders and tackle and fly rods out of the car. They walk due east for one mile through the forest. The sea is glinting though the trees and shortly they arrive at a sandy beach. One of the men is feeling rather silly standing at the seaside with an 8-ft fly rod. But the other man looks as if he knows what he is doing: he puts on a small black fly, a beetle imitation, and commences to cast into the gentle waves that lap the shore. Nothing happens. And then there is a head-and-tail rise, a confident fish taking food from the surface. The line straightens, the rod lifts and bends. And from then on it is just like catching any other grayling.

So, the question is . . . what was the name of the deer?

*   *   *

There is a type of Englishman with a feeling for the desert. They love it, can't get enough of it. Wiry sorts, mostly, with chiselled profiles that look good staring at the far horizon from the top of a camel. Then there are others who yearn for the African savannah. They are beefier types in khaki shorts and shirts with lots of pockets and one of those little beards like Roger Whitaker's.

But give me a forest.

I don't mean something Amazonian with creepers and beetles the size of rodents and rodents the size of domestic cattle, all of which sting or bite. Not that sort of forest.

I love the forests of the far north. We don't have them in Britain: perhaps we did once. Now we have afforestation - which isn't the same thing at all. There is light in a northern forest, filtering through pine, spruce and birch. The forest floor is a low springy bed of ground-hugging berries, pine needles and the startling greens of mosses. Once there was ice - and the old grey rocks that poke up between the mosses and berries have been ground smooth by its passage. They are blotched with the subtle shades of lichens now.

A northern forest looks like nothing much from the road: it looks like a lot of trees. But as soon as you step into it you are in a different world. It is a world that stretches right round the chillier bits of the globe but the bit I stepped into is in Lapland. Lapland is mostly forest and the bits that aren't forest are water - which were the bits I had come to see.

I had come to see a man about a river. Greger Jonsson restores rivers. Greger is the fisheries consultant for the Lycksele kommun, a vast region of forest, rivers and lakes in northern Sweden and the traditional capital of Lapland.

Now, you might have thought that Lapland, with its endless pristine forests of pine and birch, threaded with a thousand bright streams and not a lot else, was the last place to need its rivers restoring. Well, ironically, it's those endless forests that have been the undoing of Lapland's splendid rivers.

For generations the rivers had been regarded as little more than natural conveyor belts to transport the timber from the inaccessible forests to the coast. But natural rivers are far from ideal conveyor belts: they have lumps and bends, narrows, pools and falls where logs can eddy and jam. For centuries almost every river and sizeable stream in Lapland had been blasted and bulldozed into neat, smooth-sided culverts. Bends were straightened, pools were filled and falls were flattened. Rocks from the riverbed were dragged out and built into retaining walls. Lapland became a land of log flumes.

And then, well into the second half of the twentieth century, came the railways and the roads and better ways of getting the timber out of the forest and down to the markets of the south. But some of the finest fishing in Europe had already been ruined, with rivers of all sizes left barrelling through the forests between sterile stone walls. It was Paul Simon, I fancy, who sang "everything put together, sooner or later, falls apart". True - but it's Greger's job to see that it happens sooner rather than later, by tearing down the walls and putting back all those lumps and bends, narrows, pools and falls. In the past decade Greger and his fellows have developed some pretty fancy brushstrokes with hydraulic diggers.

I went to see how it was done. The machine crawls down the middle of the river, dismantling the massive stonework on the banks, scooping and pushing the huge boulders to create depth and variety of current. It is a staggering transformation: downstream the thing looks like Lincolnshire's South Forty Foot Drain: upstream it looks like the River Dart. And they do all this at the rate of one kilometre each week. After such major surgery the patient is rested for three years before fishing is allowed.

Here's one they'd done earlier . . .

The Olsbäcken flows through the forests of Sorsele kommun, another swathe of Lapland forest between Lycksele and the mountains of Norway. We were a few miles south of Arctic Circle. Just how many miles depends on whether you are using Swedish miles or British miles: 1 Swedish mile is 10 kilometres – or 6-and-a-bit British miles. I didn't know that.

Tommy caught the first fish, a fine well-spotted 13-inch trout from a deep run between two lichen-dappled rocks on the Olsbäcken. This is now lovely water: a swift, clear stream that tumbles through the forest, pausing to swell into a broad pool dotted with ancient boulders, then slipping down another fast run and on and on and on, deeper into the forest. The Olsbäcken is a forest river. The waters of Lapland are categorised by their origins: the rivers that flow from the mountains are cold and relatively poor in nutrients. The rivers that begin in the forest are richer, the fly life more abundant and the fish fatter.

In August, the caddis is king on the rivers of the forest. The fishing may be at its best for a couple of weeks in June when the ice has left the lakes and the water warms. Then the hatches of ephemerid flies make their brief appearance and, for a few days, the fishermen of Lapland search through their fly boxes for the dainty upwing imitations that fill most of a Brit's box. Our grandfathers' obsession with chalkstream ephemerids has a lot to answer for: John Goddard's "Waterside Guide" devotes three times as many pages to ephemerid flies as it does to caddis flies. But come high summer, the average Brit is armed only with a Cinnamon Sedge and G&H Caddis to see him through the rest of the year. Meanwhile, the nations without our obsession for olives and suchlike have developed and adopted any number of wonderful patterns which imitate the whacking great juicy larvae and pupae of the caddis that infest all trout streams. Open a Belgian's box and there are ranks of the things, lying plump with promise. They may look just a little too much like a box of maggots for some tastes but, by golly, they work. Tommy handed me something that looked alarmingly like a rather unsuccessful bird-dropping. It would have been more alarming for the bird: it was bright green and floated like a cork. It tumbled through the currents like the little green free-swimming sand-fly larva it represented.

Greger caught the next fish, swinging a long-shank streamer across a fast run in a very unentomological manner. The trout didn't seem to appreciate the difference and grabbed it anyway. We moved down the river, deeper into the forest, taking trout to about a pound from the pools and pockets of the bright little Olsbäcken.

It was lunchtime. Tommy asked if we fancied coffee and settled to lighting a fire. To light a fire in any forest round our way you'll need planning permission and a special dispensation from the pope. But in Sweden they have *allemansrätten*.

Listen to this. Allemansrätten is unique. It is the ancient law that gives everyone access to open country, forest and private land without asking the owner's permission. There is more: you have the right to camp for a day or so and to light a fire. You even have the right to take a boat onto private water.

This is powerful permission. It carries with it some obvious duties and obligations. They can be summed up as "do not destroy: do not disturb". You can't tramp across someone's lawn: they have a right to privacy and you shouldn't pass with 100 metres or so of a private house. Also you can't camp in their garden or on any land used for agriculture - obviously. In short, if anyone realises that you're there then you're probably too close.

And no-one should know you have been there. All rubbish must be taken with you. Camp-fires should be carefully sited, never on a rock surface as this leaves ugly scars, and carefully extinguished. All fires are banned in times of drought. You shouldn't damage any living tree or anything else - so allemansrätten does not allow any motor vehicles, 4-wheel-drive or otherwise, to go looping about the countryside. Heaven preserve us - are you mad? In fact, if a fragile habitat would be damaged even by walking on it, don't walk on it.

I was stunned by the prospect of this allemansrätten. I wanted to dash of a letter to the Ramblers Association, telling them to forget Kinder Scout and peaceful trespass and so forth: just come and ramble in Sweden. Perhaps they already do. All this opportunity makes the Swedes, particularly those of the north, enthusiastic and responsible campers. They cook at the drop of a hat. Tommy had a little fire going and set about boiling some coffee while Greger and I held suspiciously large sausages on sticks over the flames. As we sat and ate lunch beside the Olsbäcken, Greger and Tommy talked of the fish and fishing to be had hereabouts. They talked of trout and char and of the prodigious grayling to be caught in the rivers and lakes. And the sea. The sea? You can catch grayling in the sea? Of course, said Greger: he would show me. And next day, on my way to the airport at Umeå, he did.

Greger stopped the car by a magnificent waterfall on the Rickleån, one of Sweden's finest sea trout rivers. We crossed over a rickety footbridge and threaded our way off into the forest, winding between the trees with the sound of the waterfall fading behind us. We walked on. We could see a grey expanse of water through the thinning trees and before long we were standing on sand, It was a beach. We were at the seaside. We walked across the smooth rocks of a low headland and stood with the Baltic Sea lapping our boots. Greger started to cast a small black fly, a beetle, out into the gentle sea swell. So I did the same. It felt ridiculous. But then a grayling serenely broke the surface to take Greger's fly.

And so to that conundrum. As far as I know, the northern Baltic is the only sea where grayling are to be caught and you can only walk *east* to the Baltic from Sweden. The only deer daft enough to run down the middle of the road in Sweden are the semi-domesticated reindeer of Lapland.

And everyone knows that a reindeer's name is "Rudolph".

31

A River Runs Under It

*I*t is not textbook procedure to build an airport over a river - but London's Heathrow Airport is built over two of the things. The Longford River and the Duke of Northumberland's River are not mighty rivers but they're plenty big enough for canoeists to visit every year. And they were here before the airport arrived - although not by much, in geological time. Both rivers are man-made, taking their waters from the River Colne, a mile or so north of the airport. The Duke of Northumberland's River was cut in the 16th Century to provide power for a water mill and to feed the lake at the Duke's home at Syon Park. The Longford River was ordered by Charles I to feed the fountains and ponds of Bushy Park and Hampton Court Palace, which it does to this day.

Three hundred years later Heathrow Airport arrived in the fields to the east of the two rivers. As the airport grew in the years after the war, the runways were extended across the two rivers which were simply led through large pipes beneath the concrete. It was an ignominious fate for any river but no different to that of a thousand other streams that have disappeared into culverts beneath London's sprawl. Between the runways, the rivers emerged briefly as two dead-straight, featureless channels leading, side-by-side, past the airport's sewage works. It might be expected that even these sections would eventually disappear beneath the expansion of the world's busiest international airport. In fact, it is this very expansion which is bringing about the resurrection and resuscitation of these two rivers. The duke and the king had cut their rivers right where the British Airport Authority wanted to build Terminal 5.

In another age that might have ended what life the rivers had, channelled through pipes buried deep beneath concrete and steel. But we live in greener, more enlightened times – or, at any rate, we live in troubled times when no-one wants a couple of hidden tunnels leading underneath a major airport terminal. Either way, it was decided that the twin rivers would be shifted to run around the perimeter of the airport.

Thus the Twin Rivers Diversion was born. Its midwife is David Palmer, the man whose task it is to construct two rivers from scratch. But why not just make one bigger river? The Duke of Northumberland and Charles I were individualists: they cut their rivers with a difference of two feet in water height. And so, if both rivers are to go their separate ways beyond the airport, they must be kept separate.

The plan called for the creation of two new, thriving rivers in the narrow gap between the airport and its perimeter road. A river is much more than water running through a channel. That may eventually become a river but only after a century or so and only if it is allowed to create its own meanders, pools and riffles with their variations of flow, to grow its own flora of bank-side vegetation and water weed in its own silt and gravels. This in turn supports a healthy population of insects and organisms, fish and other aquatic beasties. There wasn't going to be time or space for all this. The alternative was to construct, within a confined channel, an artificial river with all these features built in.

It began with a concrete channel. The walls have been precisely textured to encourage the growth of micro-organisms at the base of the food chain. Meanders, runs and eddies are provided by huge gabions filled with stones and gravel on alternating sides of the channel. The gravel is dug locally to match the chemistry of the water. Submerged tree trunks and branches, pegged in the channel, provide cover and refuges for fish and other creatures. These artificial rivers come complete with plants: 80,000 native river plants from 37 native species have been grown on coir pallets. These are installed on the riverbed and on the gabion banks. The plants species have been carefully chosen: none of them will produce berries which might attract birds to the river. Birds and planes don't mix.

Other colonists can be transferred from the old rivers within the airport. A precious colony of water voles has already been rescued and taken to safe keeping. The fish followed: the chub, roach, pike and perch were netted before the old channels were drained. Insects and other invertebrates vital for a healthy ecosystem have been transferred in the sludge sucked into vacuum tankers and pumped into the new rivers but not before the duck- and swan-mussels had been picked out by hand and moved to their new home.

These freshwater mussels will not be troubled by ducks or swans. The whole river channel, banks, islands and all, will be covered by a lightweight net to discourage herons and cormorants and other water birds. The Twin River Diversion is remarkable for its attention to detail. The mesh size of the protective netting will be 75mm after tests showed that this was the smallest mesh to allow the free passage of the *Anax imperator*, the largest species of dragonfly found on British rivers.

You will have spotted by now that you and I will not be able to fish these pristine sections of the Longford River and the Duke of Northumberland's River. Nor will we get to see them, unless we catch a glimpse as we come in to land. But for millions of the smaller, wetter residents of the London Borough of Hillingdon, the coming of Terminal 5 has brought a better, brighter future.

32

Something Good on the Box

*T*here's going to be a fair amount of nostalgia coming shortly. The Box Brook is that sort of place. It is not a grand water. It is not the sort of water one aspires to, if only one had the time and money: it is not a Rolls Royce. It is a Morris Minor Traveller of a water. It is cosy.

Box Brook nestles in a lush dairy valley to the north-east of Bath, sharing the tight space between the rounded, wooded hills with the old A4, now little more than a country lane, and the old Great Western Railway which crosses the river and road a couple of times before disappearing into the hillside at the village of Box. I doubt that one in a thousand of the travellers by road and rail know it is there: you could miss it standing a yard or so back from the bank. The banks are steep and deep and shaded by old trees and bushes so that down in the water you are standing in an intimate green tunnel that twists through the rich pastures. I went there this time in late April. The grass was still bright green and the first of the hawthorn flies hovered beneath the trees. The water was clearing, sweeping over banks of bright gravel and into darker pools scoured deep beneath the tree roots. If you could make the Box Brook into an ointment it would cure all known diseases. For a short but unpleasant period of my life it saved my sanity.

For some years I had been a lecturer in psychology in a small college in Lincolnshire. Teaching psychology to a small group of eighteen-year-old girls is pleasant work but not something you would want to spend the rest of your life doing. I rather fancied pushing back the frontiers of science. In my own college days, one text book had impressed me above all others. Its author was now the Professor heading the Brain and Perception Laboratory at Bristol University. I wrote to him with the results of some experiments I had been doing in Lincolnshire and he invited me down to meet him at the laboratory. The result was that I was taken on as his research assistant. A month later we moved from the huge, haunting skies of the fenland to the middle of a city.

Sometimes I meet people who have lived in Bristol. Their eyes mist over and they wax on about the village atmosphere, the pavement pubs and cafés, the leafy Georgian terraces with the Downs beyond. And I realise they are talking about Clifton. We didn't live in Clifton. In the fens we had been used to more space than we knew what to do with and now we were cooped up in the bleak wastes of a city. I hated it. The job didn't help. On the first night the professor and I had gone for a drink in the pub and had a violent row about some obscure philosophical point of science and discovered that we cordially loathed each other. I had moved to Bristol in December: by March I was going stir crazy. And then, in that distant April, just a few miles from the city centre, I had discovered the Box Brook. Every few days throughout that season the city and the professor would get to me. I would get into the car and plunge into the middle of Bristol to Veals Tackle shop to get my day ticket for the brook. It cost 25p. Then the drive east from Bristol, out through the featureless suburbs and small towns that the city had absorbed in its inexorable expansion, out into the countryside to the north of Bath. The change from city driving, lurching between traffic lights, to poling along a country road, started the healing process, easing the tension between the shoulders. At Marshfield I would turn off into the maze of wooded lanes that wind south down the rolling slopes of the Avon valley, crossing the Fosse Way and the border into Wiltshire to arrive on the banks of the brook below Box village, hidden behind the wooded railway embankment. The city and the professor were forgotten.

Before I came back to Box this April I rootled about amongst my old fishing papers and found the last ticket I had for the brook. It was the last day of the '79 season. Looking closely at this ticket I realised I should have handed it in after my day's fishing *"with the return completed. This is most important in order that the fishery may be improved"*. I did not like the sound of this lovely wild fishery being "improved". I had loved it the way it was and I dreaded the thought that I might find it pruned and trimmed and tucked into shape, and stocked with shiny bright new fish fresh from the fish farm. I need not have worried. There was no sign of any improvements. Perhaps they were still waiting for my completed return.

The Box Brook is where I really learnt to fish for trout. Here you either learn or give up. It is no chalkstream: there is no strolling the bank looking for a rise and then casting to the fish. The banks are too steep and overgrown, the rises are often hidden beneath a trailing bramble or hawthorn, and if you can see a fish through the foliage then you are all too visible up on the bank against the sky. The trick is to get down into the water. The bottom is clean gravel on a clay bed in the faster sections, suddenly dipping down to deep green depths on the outside of the tight meanders. Wading is essential. I am tempted to recommend chest waders because too often you are teetering on the brink of thigh waders when you should be thinking of other things. But I am not sure you wouldn't lose your amateur status using chesties on such an intimate English stream. Every cast must be steered over, under and through the foliage with a flick here and a miniature roll cast there, always improvising. An impeccable casting technique is more of a hindrance than help: you may be lulled into thinking you can use it. You can't. It is wrist rather than arm and a rod of more than eight feet is a serious disadvantage. There are compensations for all this toil. The trout are very free rising. The wealth of food tumbling out of the overhanging branches keeps them looking up so a dry fly will often bring a trout up when there are no obvious rises. And with such variety on the menu, almost any small fly will serve well. They are also supremely confident. Most of the fish are found in the deep shady pools where a trout feels safe and secure and they will rise happily just a few feet from a waving rod tip, oblivious of the fisherman lost against the foliage. This is a joy. Once you have worked your way up to a small pool it is quite possible to take several fine fat little fish without moving an inch. And there is just such a pool on every bend. When the wind blows up on the meadows you can always find sheltered spots down between the banks. And when the sun beats down on the open meadows there is always a rising fish to be found beneath the shaded banks.

Not a big fish, mind. The trout of the Box Brook are wild fish with brilliant vermilion spots on a grey background and almost certainly the indigenous stock of the brook. The biggest, years back, was just over four pounds and was taken up to the Northey Arms by the top beat to be photographed and marvelled over and they talk about it still. My biggest was 1lb 6oz and you have to be there for the mayfly to tempt up monsters like that. A sizeable fish (as defined on my old 1979 ticket) is 12 inches and you might fish all day and not see such a one. But you would see a lot of fine fish of nine or ten inches, which is the average fish of the early season. And you might hook a score or so of those in a day. Some folk have hooked over one hundred fishing both beats on a long day: it is entirely possible but smacks of working far too hard.

Bathampton Angling Association has two beats of the brook

below the village of Box. Each beat is about a mile or so long and feels several times that when you have struggled and inched your way through a hot afternoon. A mile or so is plenty. Joining Bathampton AA will cost you £15 and for that you will get any amount of coarse fishing in the waters around Bath and Bathampton. The Box Brook is their only trout water and an additional day ticket must be bought for either beat before each trip. They cost £1. Fifteen years ago it was a major pain to flog into the centre of Bristol (or to Crudgingtons in Bath) to get this ticket and now there is an easier way. For £25 club members can have a season ticket to fish both beats of the brook any time they want.

A confession. Do not look for the Box Brook on your map: you won't find it. It is there, just where I said it was, but on the maps it is called the By Brook. It is called the Box Brook around the village of Box and on the Bathampton AA membership card and so I have always known it as that. Also I was intending to work in a joke about photographing a "Box Brownie" but my nerve has failed at the last moment. This attack of good taste is rather surprising: I once fished a tiny stream called the Quinn in County Clare just so I could write about "The Mighty Quinn". For years I have been scouring the world for a lake named after some explorer called Emerson (there must be one somewhere). When I find this place I will fish it loch-style with a palmered fly on the top dropper: all this just so I can call the story "Emerson Lake and Palmer".

Upstream of Box the brook becomes the By Brook and is inaccessible to the average fisherman as it winds down through small, fortunate syndicates and the narrow wooded valley around Ford where it is preserved by a conservation-minded owner as a wild-life refuge for the trout and the otters. But higher still there is just one other opportunity for the visitor to fish the By Brook.

The village of Castle Combe is often called the prettiest village in England. I have no idea how one might set about such an evaluation but on any scale Castle Combe must be in with a shout.

241

The cottages of Cotswold limestone cluster around the church and the pub and straggle down to a stone bridge over a babbling Cotswold brook. The By Brook. Or Bybrook, or Bye Brook: this is a stream with an alarming identity crisis. Below this bridge the stream flows in a deep run along an ageless stone wall and the occasional large trout dimples the surface in the way that large trout are obliged to do in the prettiest village in England. Above this bridge the stream has been broadened to flow serenely through the well-tended parkland of an English Country House. The ancient Manor House is a now sumptuous hotel in an idyllic setting, backed by terraced Italian gardens with manicured lawns running down to the stream. It is hard to believe this is the same stream that fusses beneath the bridge in the village or twists and turns its way past Box. It seems above all that sort of thing. In the parkland of the Manor House it is on its best behaviour and flows slowly without a murmur. There are trout here too, bigger than the small fish around Box but then they are not working so hard. But you will have to work for these fish. In the slow, unruffled water they glide away at the slightest incautious movement.

All this serenity is the result of a series of ancient sluices and weirs that constrain the brook, ageing it before its time. In places, away from the croquet lawns and gardens, the impetuous nature of a young brook bursts out like a giggle as a swirling pool beneath a sluice or a fast run or shallow riffle over bright gravel between the pools. And here the trout are as small and dashing as one might expect. The Manor House is by no stretch of the imagination a splendid fishing hotel. But it is certainly a splendid hotel with fishing. And if wading between the deep, tangled banks of the Box Brook in pursuit of ten-inch wild brownies is not your idea of heaven, then perhaps you would settle for a stroll across a dew-damp croquet lawn after a sumptuous meal in a 17th century English manor and casting over lazy trout rising in the quiet water above the weir.

I'd settle for that.

For anyone interested in these things, the row in the pub was with the late Professor Richard Gregory. It was over the use of the word "function" in relation to parts of the brain. Is the function of a particular organ what it does or what it is meant to do? There are problems either way. If it is the first, do we accept that it is the function of an organ to get cancer or fall apart in some other way – that is, after all, what they do sometimes. So perhaps it's the second meaning – what the organ is meant to do, what it's designed to do. But designed by whom, meant by whom? And how do you decide what was meant? Tricky stuff.

Bathampton Angling Association has an excellent website with details of its beats on the Box Brook and the arcane, but eminently sensible, rules for fishing it. Visit www.bathampton.org for details

The Manor House, Castle Combe, Wiltshire SN14 7HR, Tel: 01249 782 206, has about 1 mile, double bank of the By Brook above Castle Combe, Fishing is free to residents. It also has its own superb 18-hole golf course, tennis courts, croquet lawn and all the trimmings - including a small stocked trout lake. Visit www.manorhouse.co.uk

33

Characters on the Cover

So, you've read the stories. Did you spot who was who on the cover? From the left, the blokes in the top row are:-

Luc Bodis crouching beside a stove at Tjuonajokk on the River Kaitum. He was cooking a couple of grayling in an ingenious hot smoker that infuses the fish with flavour from an evergreen shrub – myrtle? *(Graying for the Gourmand)*

Digby Lewis beside a very different stove in Memurubu, Norway. The stone oven was built by Lees and Clutterbuck when they camped here in 1880. Digby was determined to recreate the scene. His false moustache is improvised from local lichen. *(Three More in Norway)*

Bill Gibson and Jeff Carroll on Coniston Water. Jeff is at the oars: Bill is watching the poles and listening for the tell-tale tinkling from the bells at the end. *(Boys from the Deep Stuff)*

Michel Genolhac on the River Bès in Lozère. You'll get a better idea of this lovely upland river from the photo in the middle of the book. *(Chalk and Cheese)*

Marcus Brown on the River Allen, Dorset. Marcus left the National Trust and emigrated to New Zealand – where, I believe, all fly-fishermen go if they've lived a pure and blameless life. (*Two Cheers for the National Trust*)

John Young on the River Earn, near Crieff. He's baiting the hook before giving a masterclass in the gentle art of worming for a salmon. (*Laird of the Rings*)

2nd row

Mr Collins on the River Wylye. Obviously he comes from the era before we learnt that one must wear fishing clothes to catch fish. What a delight to meet this gentleman on the river. (*First Chuck on the Chalk*)

Vojko Bizjan on the Sava Bohinjka, near Bled, Slovenia. Vojko is a delicate, size 22 dry-fly man. He was mortified at the success of a rubber-tailed monster on his beloved river. (*Alpine Events*)

Vaughan Lewis beside the Afon Claerwen. He is looking in his fly box and deciding whether to fish with a Coch-y-bonddhu or 100 volts. (*Current Affairs*)

Gordon Williamson on the road to Twatt, Shetland. Sandy Leventon once used a photo of me standing by the same sign - with the caption: "But surely the sign is pointing the wrong way" (*Man's Dog Ate My Trousers*)

Lipo čru. Or the grub of the Greater Wax Moth, *Galleria mellonella*. If you find it in your bait box, use it for char or grayling or chub. If you find it in your beehive, kill it. (*Alpine Events*)

Teal, the dog-who-ate-my-trousers, standing in the Loch of Houss, East Burra, Shetland. *(Man's Dog Ate My Trousers)*

3rd *row*

Tommy Stenlund making coffee over a fire beside the Olsbäcken in Lapland. Tommy has restored the Olsbäcken from a sterile stone-clad culvert to a vibrant, rock-strewn wild river. He dearly loves to light camp fires. *(If it's Broke, Fix It)*

Brandon, our guide on Lake Willachuck, somewhere lost in Tweedsmuir Provicial Park, BC. He has just borrowed my whiskey fly and is suffering the consequences. *(Somewhere, overrun with Rainbow)*

Richard Beer, my father, on the River Laver near Ripon. The fish started to rise just after the cows (in the background) crossed the river. Coincidence? *(Ripon Yarns)*

Tom Richardson, one-time keeper on the Monsal Dale beat of the Derbyshire Wye, in front of his "Cosy Cottage" beside the river. And me. In wellingtons – so I wouldn't be tempted to wade. *(Bridge on the River Wye)*

Philip Bezencenet and Captain John Kennedy somewhat daunted, it appears, by the prospect of limitless fishing on the lochs of South Uist. *(Lost Luggage)*

4th *row*

Odd Erik Aukrust with his otterboard, about to fish the Otta river at Lom, Norway. This otterboard, bought at the local supermarket, is foldable: it hinges in the middle. The line, with its row of flies, is wound on the orange plastic frame to the right. *(Unnatural Practices)*

The Duns Tew Snooker Club filling their faces at a picnic beside Lake Vyrnwy in Wales. They are, from the left, Philip Bezencenet, Terry Miall and (guest member) Nick Hancock. *(Snooker Break)*

Tim Vinnicombe aboard his oyster boat, *Boy Willie*, on the Truro oyster fishery, Falmouth. The boat in the background is, I think, *Dolly*. *(Fishing on Sail)*

Bottom right corner

François Magdinier on the August-thin headwaters of the River Tarn, Lozère. Another of those fanatical French fly-fishers and one-time holder of the European brown trout record. *(Chalk and Cheese)*